D1522460

LATIN IN THE SERVICE OF ENGLISH

Lawrence Giangrande
University of Ottawa

UNIVERSITY
PRESS OF
AMERICA

Lanham • New York • London

Copyright © 1987 by

University Press of America,® Inc.

4720 Boston Way
Lanham, MD 20706

3 Henrietta Street
London WC2E 8LU England

Printed in the United States of America

British Cataloging in Publication Information Available

Library of Congress Cataloging-in-Publication Data

Giangrande, Lawrence.
Latin in the service of English.

English and Latin.
Bibliography: p.
1. English language—Foreign elements—Latin—
Problems, exercises, etc. 2. Latin language—
Influence on English—Problems, exercises, etc.
3. English language—Word formation—Problems, exercises,
etc. 4. English language—Roots—Problems, exercises,
etc. 5. Vocabulary—Problems, exercises, etc.
PE1582.L3G53   1988   422'.471   87–20921
ISBN 0–8191–6641–3 (alk. paper)
ISBN 0–8191–6642–1 (pbk. : alk. paper)

All University Press of America books are produced on acid-free
paper which exceeds the minimum standards set by the National
Historical Publication and Records Commission.

PREFACE

If you wish to improve your vocabulary systematically you study the Latin and Greek elements in your language.

You can complete the twenty-one lessons and twenty-seven exercises in five months. Do not attempt to complete all the questions in the exercises in class. You will have ample opportunity for independent work, if your professor assigns you special exercises according to your requirements.

Even if you are not formally enrolled in a course at University, you may use this book to teach yourself the introductory material which will help you to understand how Latin plays its role in the formation of English vocabulary. Increase your stock of words accordingly. Scientific vocabulary is included in the Greek companion text for those of you in technical fields.

Some of my predecessors are D.M. Ayers, L. Casson, W.C. Grummel and J.D. Sadler. Their enthusiastic commitment to improving our aesthetic appreciation of English as a linguistic and literary phenomenon inspired this project.

Johane S. Lalonde provided her typing skills. I am grateful for the suggestions and criticism of Professor Daniel J. Taylor of Lawrence University, Dr. P.W. Sage, St. John Fisher College and the help of S. Giangrande and P.A. Grygier.

Both author and publisher are grateful to The Classical Journal for permission to reproduce "Sexism in Language" (p. 66). It is in volume 80/N°3, Febr., 1985, p. 257-258.

Gisèle Lalonde and Solange Grimard prepared this book on a word processor for Sigma, 338 Somerset West, Ottawa, Ontario, CANADA K2P 0J8.

To quote Winston Churchill:

> "I'd let the clever ones learn Latin as an
> honor and Greek as a treat."

To cite Shelley:

> "We are all Greeks. Our laws, our
> literature, our religion, our art, have their
> root in Greece."

Languages and their interrelationships are similar to growing bodies. They change and are changeable, are always colorful
and exciting, and enable us to understand and appreciate our own
language.

ABBREVIATIONS

AF	Anglo-French
AL	Anglo-Latin
AS	Anglo-Saxon (= Old English)
Cdn E	Canadian English
Cdn F	Canadian French
D	Dutch
E	English
F	French
G	German
G or Gk	Greek
IE	Indo-European
It	Italian
L	Latin
LG	Late Greek
LL	Late Latin
ME	Middle English
MF	Middle French
ML	Medieval Latin
NB	Nota bene (= note well)
OE	Old English (= Anglo-Saxon)
OF	Old French
OHG	Old High German
OL	Old Latin
OP	Old Provençal
P	Portuguese
Skt	Sanscrit
Sp	Spanish
VL	Vulgar Latin

TABLE OF CONTENTS

INTRODUCTION

Greek and Latin belong to the Indo-European family of languages, along with Indo-Iranic, Albanic, Armenic, Celtic, Germanic and Balto-Slavic. Members respectively of Hellenic and Italic, the former includes Modern Greek, the latter, the Romance languages. We have no documents of Indo-European. The language family has to be reconstructed by linguists on the basis of evidence drawn from all the cognate languages which have developed out of that common source, the "mother tongue."

Most living IE. languages show a remarkable kinship to Greek, Latin, Sanskrit (an Indo-Iranic tongue whose geographical location lay in the Punjab originally), Balto-Slavic, Armenian and Albanian, Celtic or Germanic. The oldest recorded IE. Language is Hittite; its records go back to the 19c B.C. Recent discovery has added 'Tocharian,' preserved in Buddhist manuscripts dating from the 6c A.D. Indo-European developed in Central Asia in the Oxus valley; from there Indians and Iranians set out to colonize their respective regions.

LATIN IN THE SERVICE OF ENGLISH

LATIN IN ENGLISH

Latin's first contact with the inhabitants of Britain brought few of its words into common use. During the Roman occupation (43-410 A.D.) the island's native Celtic speakers picked up a few place names (e.g., those ending in -chester; London; York) and some words connected with Roman military life (e.g., mile, street).

The Germanic or Anglo-Saxon invasion of Britain, which largely paralleled the Roman occupation in time, brought more popular words -- especially military terms, to enrich the native Celtic of the Britons. Chalk, pitch, post, wall and wine are some words of Latin origin borrowed in Britain in this period.

When Christianity was introduced to Britain in 597, the use of Latin, the language of the western Church, spread. Latinized Greek words were added to the stock of Old English: alms, angel, bishop, deacon, litany, minster, monk, pope, priest, and school. From Latin itself came altar, candle, creed, mass, pall, master and temple. The educated minority was now familiar with the Latin language: the Venerable Bede (673-735) wrote an ecclesiastical history of England in Latin. King Alfred "translated" it into English, ca. 900. The hierarchy, the nuns, monks, and priests of the churches and monasteries read and spoke Latin as a second language. When their own Anglo-Saxon failed them, they took recourse to Latin words and introduced them into their speech and writings. Christian Latin learning spread in the seventh and eighth centuries.

The coming of the Norman French under William, Duke of Normandy, brought French culture and vocabulary into Anglo-Saxon England (1066 A.D. to ca. 1200). Norman-French, a slightly modified form of Latin, was spoken and written by courtiers and other cultured people. Still, Norman-French and Anglo-Saxon, existing side by side, underwent little interfusion. Some Norman-French words adopted were canker, castle, cattle, cauldron, reward, warden. Indeed, since 1066, English has borrowed most from French.

During the Old French Period (ca. 1200-1500 A.D.) Latin and French vocabulary extensively modified the native language, especially in the vocabularies of art and intellectual activity. This was a period of bilingualism in which French words were introduced into English contexts. Chaucer, familiar with both Latin and French literary traditions, represented these in the late 14c (Middle English period) Canterbury Tales. French culture and language would continue to play a role in extending the English cultural language in the succeeding 16th century. Attributable to this period are words from every walk of life: bounty, challenge, chattel, custom, dainty, guardian, joy,

2

language, law, miserable, order, poignant, regard.

The influence of classical learning, especially Latin literature, spurred on by the invention of printing (Caxton, 1476), further stimulated the infusion of Greek and Latin words into English. Words from the classical languages were taken over or Anglicized. Some writers, e.g., More, wrote in Latin. Others were content to enrich their works with Greek and Latin words. Among these are Marlowe, Shakespeare, Sidney and Udall. Greek and Roman literature became the staple of the university curriculum, partially displacing the pre-eminent role of philosophy and theology.

Although the largest number of words was borrowed from Latin at this time, Greek was not neglected. Tyndale translated the NT from Greek into English. Scientists turned largely to Greek to create or supplement necessary technical terms. Meanwhile, Howard translated part of the Aeneid, Robinson translated More's Utopia from Latin into English, and Heywood translated Seneca's tragedies.

The last of the six periods discussed above is most important in terms of the enrichment of English through classical sources. We are now ready to turn to Latin, which has exerted such an impact on English as to become an important ingredient of the modern language.

LATIN NOUNS ARE DECLINED

Latin nouns are declined*; there are five declensions. The cases of a Latin noun (or adjective) are six, whereas English has only three: nominative, possessive and objective case. Memorize the nominative (subject) case and the genitive (possessive) case for each noun you encounter. This helps you in word-formation and word-derivation. Take a noun of the first declension which appears in late Latin: camera-ae. When so written, the word means 'room, of the room,' and reveals the nominative and genitive cases respectively. The word's base is obtained by dropping the -ae ending, so that we have camer-. Almost all Latin nouns ending in -a are feminine, e.g., arena, area, causa, corona, cura, fabula, forma, fortuna, justitia, lacuna, nota, opera, rota, scintilla, tabula, vita. Certain nouns which refer to masculine occupations are masculine, e.g., agricola, nauta, poeta.

2nd declension nouns are usually masculine or neuter. Masculine nouns in -us (-er and -ir) predominate. Animus-i means 'mind, of the mind,' puer-i means 'boy, of the boy,' vir-i means 'man, of the man.' Nouns ending in -um are neuter. Filum-i 'thread, of the thread,' like cerebrum, pretium, spatium, verbum, vitium, is a 2nd declension neuter noun.

---

* to decline a noun is to change its form, and correspondingly, its meaning, e.g.,

fāma	'reputation, fame,'	nominative case
fāmae	'of reputation'	genitive case
fāmae	'to reputation'	dative case
fāmam	'reputation'	accusative case
fāmā	'by, in, because of reputation'	ablative case
fāma	'O reputation'	vocative case

The nominative case is the subject case. The genitive case corresponds to the English possessive case. The dative indicates the indirect object. The accusative case shows the direct object, e.g., You know our reputation. The ablative case may usually be translated with 'from, by, with, in, or at.' The vocative is the case of direct address, e.g., 'O fame.'

Less common than the -us masculine ending is -er as in
ager-ri,* field,' minister-ri 'servant,' magister-ri 'teacher,'
and puer-i. In the first three cases illustrated here, the e
preceding the r is dropped in the genitive case so that we get
agri, ministri, magistri. In pueri it is retained.

3rd declension nouns may be either feminine, masculine or
neuter. Unlike 1st and 2nd declension nouns, their nominative
endings exhibit variety.   In the genitive, an -is ending is
consistently added to the base. Pax, pacis, 'peace,' ars, artis
'skill,' sermo, sermonis 'conversation,' genus, generis 'race,
type, kind,' corpus, corporis 'body,' origo, originis
'beginning,' dens, dentis 'tooth,' gens, gentis 'people,' pars,
partis 'share, portion,' finis-is 'end,' vestis-is 'garment,'
illustrate some 3rd declension endings; you memorize the bases of
such nouns.

Take margo, marginis 'edge, border.' Drop the -is ending to
obtain the base margin-. Thus, the bases of the above words are
pac-, art-, sermon-, gener-, corpor-, origin-, dent-, gent-,
part-, fin-, and vest-. Another third declension word, opus,
operis (base: oper-) 'work' is not to be confused with ops, opis
(base: op-) 'influence, wealth, ability.'

Latin words may pass into English unchanged, e.g., area,
arena, corona, genus, lacuna, opus, rota, stimulus, Virgo. Or,
the Latin word's base is adopted, e.g., art, herb, form, norm,
verb. A silent -e may be added to the Latin noun's base, e.g.,
ire, fate, palate. A final -o in the Latin word may become -e,
e.g., image, turpitude, or be retained: libido, ego, farrago,
ratio. Final -ia, -ius, -ium preceded by -c-, -g- or -t- become
final -ce, -cy, or -ge in the E. derivative, e.g., fallacy,
Horace, vestige, respectively from fallacia, Horatius,
vestigium. Unpredictable spellings may develop from linguistic
influences, e.g. L. scutarius >** squire, poena > pain,
peregrinus > pilgrim.

Five declensions were mentioned.   The 4th and 5th are
rarer. The 4th ends in -us or -u as in hiatus-us 'gap' and
cornu-us 'horn'; the 5th ends in -es, e.g., species, facies,
dies; you drop both these endings to obtain the base. Some words
of the 4th and 5th declensions are borrowed without change, e.g.,
impetus, sinus, congeries, rabies, series.

---

* Latin dictionaries and word-lists commonly give the forms:
  ager, agri; minister, ministri; magister, magistri.

** means 'giving rise to.'

6

LATIN PRONUNCIATION

All consonants and vowels are pronounced. The vowels a, e, i, o, and u are either long or short, and the y, borrowed from the Greek, has a pronunciation between that of Latin u and i, hence something like the French u. All consonants are hard-sounds, but j is pronounced like English y, and v like w. Diphthongs are pronounced as follows: ae as in ie (cf. lie); au as in ou in mouse; ei as in eight; eu = short e plus double o (oo), hence it forms a sound strange to English speakers; and oe as in toy. The Latin alphabet lacks k, w, and z (but the equivalent of Greek kappa is the hard c, and the v in Latin is pronounced like a w). It is only in the rare imported loan word that Latin will have a z, e.g., gaza, 'wealth, treasure' from the Persian. The Latin accent normally falls on the next to the last syllable, but occasionally, the third syllable from the last, the antepenult, is accented, e.g., genius, taedium, opera.

EXERCISE 1

I. Form an English derivative, as illustrated, from the Latin
    nouns of the first and second declension listed in Column
    one. Retain or modify the base, as required.

Latin Word	Significance	English Derivative
spatium	room, distance	space
animus	disposition, mind, soul	
bulla	bubble, amulet, seal	
contumelia	insult, abuse	

Do likewise for digitus 'finger, toe;' figura 'shape;'
granum 'grain, kernel, seed;' norma 'measure, pattern,
standard;' pretium 'worth, value;' verbum 'word;' and
vitium 'blemish, fault, imperfection.'

II. Briefly define the underlined word, as illustrated.

Borrowed Latin Word	Etymological* Meaning	Current Meaning
the play's focus	hearth	central point, theme
an activities area	threshing floor	
Corpus of Latin Inscriptions	body	
persona non grata	mask, character	
the stimulus of reward	goad, whip	
Onassis was not to the villa born	farmhouse, country estate	

III. Determine the declension of the following Latin nouns:

alumna-ae 'foster-daughter, pupil'   memoria-ae 'memory'
alumnus, alumni 'foster-son, pupil'   mus, muris 'mouse'
arbiter, arbitri 'judge'   nebula-ae 'fog, mist,
                                                vapor'

---

*   The etymological meaning is the derivative word's meaning
    in Latin, whence it derives. These words, derived from
    Latin, have undergone significant changes in meaning, so
    that no one of them is likely to retain its original
    meaning in current use. Often the literal meaning of a
    Latin word used in English dies out and only the
    figurative meaning is retained; e.g., arena, campus, crux,
    humor, lacuna, miser, radius.

cerebrum, cerebri 'brain'   piscina-ae 'fish-pond'
dominus, domini 'lord, master'   pons, pontis 'bridge'
fulcrum, fulcri 'prop, bedpost'   puer, pueri 'boy'
lacrima-ae 'tear'   pupa-ae 'girl'
leo, leonis 'lion'   sermo, sermonis
                                     'conversation'
locus, loci 'place'   usura-ae 'loan, payment'
matrona-ae 'matron'   via-ae 'lane, road,
                                     street'

IV.   Define etymologically, as exemplified.

      ratio ‹* ratio reason, reckoning,   sinus ‹ sinus inlet,
                      account, calculation   bosom,
                                                          curve

      antenna, corona, crux, domino, lacuna, matrona, omen,
      opus, radius, tedium.

      * is a symbol which means 'derived from.'

V.   What is the base of each of the following words: ars,
      artis 'skill,' focus, foci 'hearth,' margo, marginis
      'edge,' and opus, operis 'work'?

VI.   Where specific questions are not asked, fill in the
      blanks:

      a) What is the etymology of nerve? of pulpit?
      b) What are Jung's animus and anima? (Clue: Word notes,
          Lesson III)
      c) A germ carrying a disease is called a _____.
      d) "For who would bear the whips and scorns of time,
          The oppressor's wrong, the proud man's _____?
          Hamlet, 3.1.71
      e) "You that look pale and tremble at this chance,
          That are but _____ or audience to this act..."
          Hamlet, 5.2.323
      f) Define the underlined words in
          The poisoner comes in with mutae personae who take no
          part in the action.
      g) "Roman fingers": pollex, _____, medius, anularis,
          and minimus (sc. digitus). (Clue: the one you point
          with)
      h) Cura = concern, care. What is a sinecure? (Clue:
          sine 'without')
      i) In Felis leo, Felis represents the _____, and leo
          the species.
      j) A manuscript book, e.g., Scriptures, the Classics, is
          an interesting _____. (Select one: album,
          codex, memoir)

9

k) An enraged politician gives vent to his _____, a spirit or feeling of hostility. (Clue: the word is in question I)

l) "Helen, bride of spears and conflicts' _____, ... Proved a hell to ships and men ..." (L. MacNeice, Agam., 687) (Clue: a word in question V)

m) Les si, les car, les pourquoi sont la porte
Par où la _____ entre dans l'univers. (LaFontaine)
(Select one: fortune, noise, passion)

n) What is the semantic* development of nausea > noise? Or, is noise from L. noxia 'injury, hurt?'

o) What is the doublet of bill; crown; dominie; master; person; plain? Doublets are pairs of words which derive from one and the same, in this case Latin, word.

p) The sun's atmosphere of gases is called the solar _____.

q) L. crux becomes F. croix (cf. croix gammée). Draw this.

r) What does Carleton University's Sock and Buskin refer to? (Clue: soccus 'light shoe' worn in comedy)

s) An examination made after one's death is a _____ - _____. (Clue: L. post = 'after.')

t) The stiffening of the muscles several hours after death is called _____ _____.

VII. Explain the use of underlined words:

1) A party of General Parson's troops found out the residence of a number of Tories, alias cow and horse thieves. Québec Gaz.

2) The sugar maple, elm, ash, and the arbor vitae, termed by the Canadian voyagers cedar, grows on various parts of the Saskatchewan. Franklin

3) The Philosopher's stone, potable gold, or any of those Arcana Sir T. Browne (Clue: neuter plural of arcanus, adj. 'shut in, hidden')

4) Hurons and Algonquins had to explain to the Iroquois that the supply of Castor was "disproportionné." Wildlife Rev.

5) The Jamaican immigrant's corpus of folklore should enrich the culture of the British Isles. V. Newall

6) To each visitor the porter immediately cries "Deo gratias." E.S. Duckett

7) Chawcer, who had geneyus, was so unedicated. He's the wuss speller I know of. A. Ward

---

* relating to the meaning

8) "You have unmade your bed, now lie about it."
   Quickly now, which of you will keep the <u>Lares</u>,
   Which the <u>Penates</u>? J. Hollander

9) If any satisfaction attaches to posthumous glory, we
   may hope that the <u>manes</u> of the ... philosopher were
   then finally appeased. T.H. Huxley

10) L. <u>Palatium</u> (a hill on which Augustus lived) gives
    F. <u>palais</u>, It. <u>palazzo</u>, E. palace. L. <u>palatum</u> gives
    F. <u>palais</u>, E. palate. Give two meanings for palatine.
11) Mann was, with seven children, very much of a
    <u>paterfamilias</u>. H. Levin SR
12) We spent two nights at Pile o'Bones, later to be
    renamed <u>Regina</u>. Tyre
13) A muffin is simply a lady who sits beside the male
    occupant of the sleigh -- <u>sola cum solo</u>. Russell
14) One identifies the <u>species by the</u> second element in
    these formulae: Felis catus, Felis leo and Felis
    tigris; Equus caballus and Equus zebra. Specific
    names are nouns in apposition to generic names.
15) It seems ungracious to refuse to be a <u>terrae filius</u>,
    when so many excellent people are. Arnold

VIII. By referring to the list of nouns and adjectives in the
       vocabulary, determine the pronunciation of arena, camera,
       digitus, forma, linea, locus, matrona, medius, miser,
       nota, opera, pretium, sanus, scintilla, solus, terminus,
       usura, vipera*, virago, viscera. (Macrons, short,
       straight, horizontal marks placed over a vowel to denote
       length, have been omitted).

IX.   Norma, Regina, Clara, Sabina, Stella, Ursula are Latin.
       By consulting a list of Common English Given Names, you
       could add at least half a dozen, all female.
       Caesar, Dominic, Marcus, Pius, Felix, Rex are Latin names
       for men. Add six others that come directly from Latin.

X.   Pair off the synonymous words in Lists A and B:

       List A: atrium, aura, corona, cumulus, lacuna, odium,
                onus, rostrum.
       List B: burden, speaker's platform, gap, hatred, rounded
                cloud, Roman living room, visible emanation
                (= halo around a person or thing), sun's aura
                (= halo around the sun).

NB: vīpera 'viper, snake' and <u>viscera</u> 'internal organs' (see
     p. 29) bear the accent on the antepenult, i.e., the third
     from the last syllable.

11

LATIN ADJECTIVES

Latin adjectives are of two types: first- and second-declension adjectives, and third-declension adjectives. The former use endings of the two declensions: e.g., grātus grāta grātum, 'acceptable, pleasing,' where grātus is masculine, grāta is feminine and grātum is neuter. An example of its use as a feminine adjective in the first declension is ars grāta, 'pleasing skill.' Grāta, adj. is to be distinguished from grātia,* noun 'favor, loveliness, courtesy, thankfulness, grace.' Second declension masculine and neuter are respectively amor grātus, 'pleasing love,' dōnum grātum, 'pleasing gift.'

The L. adj. agrees with its noun in gender; it also agrees in number. Plurals of the examples above are respectively: artes grātae, amores grātī and dōna grāta. Cf. pater noster 'our father,' masculine sg., mare nostrum, 'our sea,' neuter sg., māter nostra, 'our mother,' fem. sg., and the plurals: patres nostrī, maria nostra, mātres nostrae.

Second-declension adjectives have three endings: masculine, feminine, and neuter. Third-declension adjectives have only two, e.g., gravis, grave, 'heavy.' Gravis is both masculine and feminine, grave is neuter, e.g., nāvis gravis - 'heavy ship,' feminine; mīles gravis - 'heavy-armed soldier,' masculine; grave tempus - 'severe weather,' neuter. The Latin adjective's position varies with the emphasis placed on it. When the adjective precedes the noun, it bears greater emphasis.

Numerous flocks, oppressive labors and heavy bodies are, respectively, graves greges (fem. pl.), graves labōres (masc. pl.), and gravia corpora (n.pl.). What is being stressed here are numerousness, oppressiveness, and heaviness, respectively.

Many third-declension adjectives end in -is; e.g., grandis, 'great, lofty,' inānis, 'empty,' juvenis, 'young,' levis, 'light (in weight), light-minded,' quālis, 'of what sort?' similis, 'like,' tenuis, 'slender,' vīlis, 'cheap.' One obtains the base by dropping this -is ending.

Simple derivatives are sometimes obtainable directly from the Latin adjective; e.g., bonus, album, miser, pauper, simile, vile; Alma, Bella, Pia.

---

* Gratiā in the ablative case expresses the idea of 'on account of, for the sake of,' ars grātiā artis. E.g. abbreviates exemplī gratiā; Latin verbī gratiā meant 'for instance.'

From the comparative forms of <u>juvenis</u> and <u>senex</u> we have junior, senior. Most Latin adjectives (see below) are compared regularly, as in our fine, finer, finest. Some of them are compared irregularly; good, better, best exemplifies this in the Latin version.

POSITIVE	COMPARATIVE	SUPERLATIVE
bonus-a-um 'good'	melior, -ius 'better'	optimus-a-um 'best'
magnus-a-um 'large'	major, majus	maximus-a-um
malus-a-um 'bad'	pejor, pejus	pessimus-a-um
multus-a-um 'many'	plūs, plūr- (gen.)*	plūrimus-a-um
parvus-a-um 'small'	minor, minus	minimus-a-um
posterus-a-um 'following'	posterior, posterius 'later'	postumus 'last'

Regular comparison of adjectives:

grātus-a-um 'pleasing'	grātior, grātius	grātissimus-a-um
fortis-e 'brave'	fortior, fortius	fortissimus-a-um
plēnus-a-um 'full'	plēnior, plēnius	plēnissimus-a-um

ADVERBS

Many Latin adverbs appear in English where, however, they may function as nouns or adjectives. Alias, alibi, interim, and item are examples of noun-uses. Gratis, infra, supra and ultra retain their adverbial function. Quondam and tandem function as adjectives, the latter also as a noun.

The meanings of the Latin adverbs most often met in English are originally <u>aliās</u> 'at another time,' <u>alibī</u> 'in another place,' <u>extrā</u> 'on the <u>outsīde</u>,' <u>grātīs</u> 'out of kindness; for nothing,' <u>infrā</u> 'below,' interim 'meanwhile,' <u>item</u> 'likewise,' <u>quondam</u> 'formerly,' <u>tandem</u> 'at length; finally,' and <u>ultrā</u> 'on the other side; beyond.'

Since Roman times, <u>litterātim</u>, ML. <u>seriātim</u> and <u>verbātim</u> have also been adopted.

_____

* genitive case; it provides the adjective's base.

A Latin adjective's neuter may be used as a Latin noun. Latin words in this form often become nouns in English; e.g., optimum, maximum. The Latin neuter refers to a thing, e.g., bonum - 'the good thing;' surprisingly, we adopted the masculine form bonus in the sense of 'gift,' possibly from Stock Exchange slang. Most neuter adjectival forms are borrowed intact, e.g., album, decorum, magnum, medium, minimum, nostrum, quantum. Boon companion and our noun boon both go back to French bon. A French nursemaid is a bonne.

A writer who begins a story in medias rēs (= into the middle of things) achieves the effect of immediacy. The adjective in the neuter, medium, is the spiritualist who communicates with departed spirits. A medium (pl. media) is also a source of public information. Medius combined with locus (F. lieu) gives milieu. Medius diēs gives F. Midi and midi (i.e. Southern France and noon); and F. midi plus dinette, 'light lunch,' gives midinette, a Parisian shopgirl. We have lately been forming compounds with midi-, mini- and maxi-. The bases of medius + -ālis (a suffix) yield medial. The bases of medius + aevum +-ālis yield medieval. Those of medius + diēs and -ānus yield meridian.

L. pāgus, 'country, canton, province' yielded pāgānus, 'country dweller.' This led to F. païen, its virtual doublet paysan (cf. F. pays, from LL. pāgensis), and pagan. Pāgānus developed its religious sense in the 4c when Christianity was characteristically the faith of townspeople. A pāgānus was a civilian as opposed to a miles, soldier of Christ. In Christian Latin, pāgānus connoted heathen as opposed to Christian or Jewish. Pāgānus then pejoratively connoted 'one of a community which does not worship the true God.' Later, by transference, a pagan was one of heathenish character or habits. To this type, we may compare our comparatively uneducated or uncouth peasant, < LL. pāgensis. It. paesano, one of the same district as oneself, is not pejorative. The symbol < means 'deriving from,' as already stated.

'Grease' comes from OF. gresse, graisse, 'fat,' from LL. grassus, L. crassus, 'fat, thick,' whence crass ignorance. A stag is said to be 'in prime (pride) of grease' when it is in proper condition for hunting and killing. We are all familiar with Mardi Gras and foie gras.

L. brūtus, 'dull, stupid,' was also a family name in early Rome. Brutus feigned stupidity in order to rid Rome of its tyrannical king. Lucius Junius Brutus became the cognomen of the patrician gens, Junia. Cicero, as a cognomen, is said to have developed because of a facial blemish (cf. cicer-is 'chick-pea').

15

L. varius 'varied' gave F. vair, 'a kind of parti-colored fur," as noun in 1138.   Cinderella wore 'souliers de vair' and not 'de verre.'   Balzac pointed out Charles Perrault's mistake, published in Cendrillon in 1697.   F. menu vair 'little vair' gives E. minever, miniver, any fine white fur, especially of the ermine.

Youngsters in Rome wore bullae around their necks. L. bulla 'bubble, boss, amulet' came to have the special ML. meaning 'document, seal, papal edict.'   The last was a papal letter sealed with a bulla, or a red-ink imprint of the device on the bulla, because of the importance of its contents.   An imperial edict, as of the Holy Roman Empire, was called a bull. The seal was of gold, silver or lead, attached to the edict.   Most famous was the Medieval Golden Bull of Charles IV; it established rules for election during his rule as emperor of Germany.   AF. bille and AL. billa are probably responsible for our bill, an itemized account of indebtedness for goods sold, services rendered, etc. Bill and bull come from one and the same Latin bulla (see Doublets, p. 18).

SEMANTIC CHANGE

> Is Brutus sick and is it physical
> To walk unbraced and suck up the humours
> Of the dank morning?

> (Julius Caesar)

L. humor 'liquid' is used here in its etymological sense. There were thought to be four humors in the body: yellow and black bile, blood, phlegm.

The predominance of one of them over the others was believed to determine a person's temperament. By the 18c, one subject to humors came to be called humorous, ludicrous, comical. None of these meanings appears in the Latin. A humorous person was capricious, whimsical, odd or fantastic; it was a small step from 'odd person' to 'facetious, comical or droll person.' We still retain the special 15c meaning of mental disposition, e.g., good-humored, but our use of 'humor' no longer connotes moisture or fluid. Humorous took on the meaning of eccentric, while humorist became one skilled in the literary or artistic expression of humor.   In Shakespeare, Portia's question is serious: "Is it good for a person to walk in the damp humidity?" Humorous exemplifies a restricted usage.

Generalization of meaning

Generalization of meaning occurs when a word's area of significance is extended or enlarged; e.g., L. injuria 'injustice'

16

now means any kind of harm or damage, especially physical hurt. L. poena 'fine, punishment' is now pain, any physical or mental suffering, whether inflicted by way of punishment or fine or not. L. virtūs 'manliness, courage' has become both generalized and specialized. Its extended meaning, virtue, includes any excellent quality, mental, moral or physical. When restricted in meaning or specialized, it is limited to chastity.

Specialization of Meaning

Specialization is illustrated in L. officium 'duty, service, kindness, courtesy, employment, magistrate's court, office.' Office may now refer to church service, official position, or place of business. The last meaning is predominant. A word formerly used to represent several objects or ideas now expresses a smaller group or only one of those objects or ideas. L. sānus meant physically and mentally healthy, but sane refers only to mental health.

Pejoration or Degeneration of Meaning

We saw earlier how pejor was the comparative degree of the adjective malus 'bad.' Pejor means 'worse.'

When a word loses prestige or respectability, one may speak of its degeneration to a pejorative meaning. We can trace the meaning of L. vīllānus 'farm-laborer' to E. villain, a term of disparagement applied by the gentry to a low fellow whose conduct or language was reprehensible.

Melioration or Elevation of Meaning

As for the adjective bonus 'good,' we noted that the comparative degree was melior. Melior means 'better.'

When a word loses its less respectable denotation and becomes more elevated in meaning, it undergoes melioration. It gains prestige. L. minister 'servant, attendant' today refers to a high officer in the church or to one of the highest officials in government. Other words of improved status: ancillary, codex, constable, marshal, nice.

****

Cognates

Words in different languages which can be traced back to the same original or primitive word or root are cognates. For instance, Greek oktō 'eight' is cognate with L. octō, F. huit, Sp. ocho, Skt. astāu, Russian vosem, Polish osem, G. acht, and

17

E. eight. Linguists trace words or roots back to IE. to show that a modern English word is cognate with a word in one or several of the IE. languages. E. mother is cognate with L. māter, Greek mētēr, Skt. mātar, Dutch moeder, G. Mutter, Norwegian and Danish mor, Icelandic modir, Polish matko, Russian mati, It. and Sp. madre, F. mère, and P. mãe. Cognates are different from doublets. Linguists speak of cognate languages.

Doublets

Doublets are pairs of loan words which originate in one and the same word in the original language; for our purposes, let us say momentarily, in one Latin word. Each member, however, develops separately.

Gk. nausia, 'sea-sickness,' whence L. nausea, comes to us via OF. noise as nausea and noise. Victims of sea-sickness would utter moans and groans, all very noisy, to express their distress.

L. dīgnītas gives rise to popular OF. deintié, 'a delicious morsel' and the learned F. derivative dignité, whence E. dignity. 11c OF. daintier 'morceau d'honneur' from VL. dīgnītas came to mean 'testicules de cerf' in the 12c, the choicest morsel. Dainty earlier meant choice, refined. It still signifies what is elegant. Like nausea and noise, dainty and dignity are therefore doublets. Doublets are rarely synonymous.

From slightly different forms of Anglo-Saxon are bake, batch, dike, ditch, drink, drench, skirt, shirt, and wake, watch. Latin-derived doublets, however, are belladonna and beldam. Belladonna is a plant from whose leaves and roots atropine is obtained. Italian ladies used the drug to dilate the pupils of their eyes. From LL. bella domina French formed beldam which meant grandmother, aged woman, and eventually hag, witch. Cape (promontory, headland) comes from MF. < OProv. cap. The base of caput, capitis was altered into F. chief and chef, the former a military, the latter, a culinary head. Kerchief is OF. couvrechief and cuevrechief (AF. courchief). Corpse and corps are from L. corpus 'body.' Cf. esprit de corps, corps de ballet. A learned word, corpus, derived directly, unchanged from Latin, forms a triplet. Core is not related to these.

Other doublets are custom, costume, example, sample (L. exemplum, taken directly into English, is a triplet), firm, farm (land acquired by a fixed sum for cultivation), vote, vow.

From L. scintilla, 'a spark,' we have the triplets stencil, tinsel and scintilla. From VL. stincilla, metathesis* of scintilla, French gets étincelle < OF. estincelle. Tinsel meant spangles, ornamental strips or threads. Partially retaining this meaning, it now may refer to gaudy or tawdry ornamentation. De La Vigne's La Toilette de Constance retains the original meaning of 'spark.' Près du foyer, Constance s'admirait. / Dieu! sur sa robe il vole une étincelle! Cf. Régnier's verbal use: La flamme de ton coeur par tes yeux étincelle.

---

* transposition of letters or sounds in a word

FILL-IN QUIZ

I. Latin belongs to the (1) _____ group of languages.
    This group itself is one member of a larger (2) _____
    family of languages, all of which are related or
    (3) _____, to use the technical term. Other
    members of this larger family are (4) _____,
    (5) _____, (6) _____, and (7) _____.
    From Latin are derived (8) _____, (9) _____,
    (10) _____, and (11) _____. These are
    known as the (12) _____ languages. English
    borrowed Latin vocabulary at (13) _____ (number)
    definite periods. The last of these periods,
    (14) _____, was when the (15) _____ amount
    of borrowing took place directly from the pages of
    (16) _____. To the cultivated Sir Thomas
    More, (17) _____ was a second language or, indeed,
    a (18) _____ language when he wrote Utopia. Latin
    adjectives agree with the nouns they modify in gender and
    (19) _____ .

II. Ray is a (20) _____ of L. radius. Māter (L.) and
     mātar- (Skt.) are (21) _____. The given name
     Grace is from L. (22) _____, 'beauty, charm,
     favor.'

III. Choose the correct answer:

      (23) The pronunciation of L. ae rhymes with E. hay lie
           bee.
      (24) The pronunciation of L. i rhymes with E. ray me pie.

IV. Fill out the columns below as demonstrated by the example:

LATIN WD.	LATIN BASE	ENGL. MEANING	ENGL. DERIVATIVE
Ex.: causa	caus-	reason	cause
(25) persona	_____	_____	_____

     Do the same for (26) antenna, (27) lacūna, (28) locus,
     (29) scintilla, (30) grātia, (31) pretium, (32) racēmus,
     (33) socius.

Additional questions:

V. Which are specialized, and which generalized in meaning:
    alibi, animus, ego, focus, libido, minister, piano,
    prince, salary, sane, sermon, tempo?

20

VI.   a) Define passim; b) What does semper fidēlis mean?
        c) Define the Latin expression as it is used in English:
        (the) nē plūs ultrā (of); d) Use five of the Latin adverbs
        listed above (p. 14) in English sentences.

EXERCISE II

1.   Derive simple* English derivatives, as illustrated.

Latin adjective	Engl. derivative	Morphological change
acerbus, -a, -um "bitter"	acerb	drop adjectival ending
albus, -a, -um "white"	album	retain neuter adj. ending
strenuus, -a, -um "vigorous"	strenuous	final -us > -ous
duplex "two-fold, double"	_____	_____
integer, -ra, -rum "whole"	_____	_____

        Do likewise for: noster, -ra, -rum "our," optimus, -a,
        -um "best," spurius, -a, -um "false," vacuus, -a, -um'
        "empty."

        * Simple derivates come from L. words without any prefixes
        or suffixes attached.

II.   a) What semantic change have album, bonus, integer, miser,
           nostrum, pauper, simile and sinister undergone?
        b) What forms provide our nouns plus and forte?
        c) In what language was the Magna Carta written?

III.   Define the Latin word from which the underlined words
        derive. Give current meanings.

	Latin wd.	Etym. meaning	Current
the prude's excessive decorum	_____	_____	_____

        Do likewise for: the gods' intestine war, the
        Mediterranean's lingua franca, the pristine simplicity of
        Anglo-Saxon, a quondam friend, an ulterior purpose.

IV.   Define alma māter, bellum jūstum, campus Martius, equus
        Troiānus, fidēs Pūnica, magnum opus, prīmā faciē, sui
        generis, terra firma.

V.   Etymologize inferior, jejune, limbus, modicum, noxious,
        rabies, robust, supine.

21

VI. Analyze the underlined words; determine their contextual meanings:

1. Beati pauperes begins the Beatitudes (Matt. 5, 3-12).

2. The pyx cloth is also known as the Corpus Christi cloth.

3. The University of Ottawa's motto is Deus Scientiarum Dominus Est.

4. Aurelian (Roman emperor, 270-75) had himself called Dominus et Deus.

5. A typical Roman prayer, under the Empire, would address Jupiter Optimus Maximus.

6. Magna Graecia was Eastern Sicily and Southern Italy.

7. The Roman name for the Mediterranean was mare nostrum.

8. The words of Solomon (Eccles. 1.10) are, in Latin translation, Nil novi sub sole.

9. Typing is now a per ardua ad astra task to me. O'Casey (Clue: per, a preposition, means 'through.')

10. Italian and Spanish terremoto derive from L. terrae motus (motus = movement).

11. There seems no good reason not to let Dennis Brutus remain (rather than be deported to South Africa). Et tu, Mr. Attorney General? N. Y. Times, July 19, 1983.

12. When uttering a blessing or an encyclical, the Pope makes it known Urbi et Orbi.

13. Varium et mutabile semper femina. Vergil

14. Verbum sat sapienti. (Clue: sapienti is a dative)

15. Via crucis, via lucis.

16. A famous essay by R.L. Stevenson is entitled Virginibus Puerisque. (Clue: both words are datives; -que = 'and')

17. Vita brevis, ars longa.

18. Vita sine litteris mors est.

22

19. Vox populi, vox Dei.

20. Vultus est index animi. (Clue: est = 'is')

VII.   Analyze underlined words; give etymological and current meanings where appropriate.

1. Linnaeus made up categories to subdivide the genus of butterflies, honoring them with mythological names.

2. Some Caribbean governments are in extremis.

3. Lab technicians recreate biological processes in vitro.

4. Milton's magnum opus was 'Paradise Lost.'

5. There are numerous narratives of movement without contact on the part of material objects, in the presence of certain mediums.

6. The urban ghetto's nature, nurture and noxia
   What rhetorical device do you notice in this phrase?

7. When we know a person's ordo amoris we truly know that person. G. Allport

8. Every Italian house with a large door is a palazzo.

9. To his followers, ... Hitler gave panem et circenses.
   M. Josephson

10. To parliament man the law of economic rent is a pons asinorum. Shaw (altered)

11. In short supply are cuprum, argentum, aurum, stannum and plumbum. Identify them.

12. Under the rubric of "Politics of the Box Populi," most children aged 4-6 when asked whether they preferred TV or Daddy said TV.

13. Port has one etymology, two meanings: 'haven' and 'a kind of wine.' Find the original Latin word.

14. Prior in tempore, fortior in jure. Goldoni

15. After six rostra were captured from pirate ships, a rostrum was set up in the Roman forum as a kind of pulpit for public speakers.

23

16. Chronos, devouring Time, eroded one Archilochian poem to a single letter: ... n. <u>Sic semper poetis</u>.

17. Doctor's report: the heart valve of <u>Sūs scrōfa</u>, common domestic pig, is the best substitute for a human heart.
(Clue: <u>scrōfa</u> is a breeding-sow)

18. A battle royal was in medieval days one in which <u>   </u> on both sides took command. Now, a <u>battle royal</u> is a fight between two teams of gamecocks. (Fill in)

19. Comme un chapelet de chars celestes,
que ma bicyclette devienne un grand <u>tandem</u>,*
que tous ensemble nous enfourcherons pour le meilleur.
Roch Carrier

20. The motto of the University of British Columbia is: <u>Tuum est</u>.

VIII. List B has the doublets of individual entries in List A. Match the pairs.

List A: a) chief, b) corpse, c) decor, d) farm, e) noise, f) parson, g) radius, h) ratio, i) spirit, j) stencil, k) term, l) foil, m) genie, n) limbo, o) price.

List B: 1) decorum, 2) ray, 3) esprit, 4) person, 5) nausea, 6) reason, 7) chef, 8) firm, 9) tinsel, 10) corps, 11) limb (=edge, hem), 12) folio, 13) prize, 14) terminus, 15) genius.

---

* An adverb's adventure:

Tandem is a freak formation, seemingly the result of a wisecrack by a University student in medieval England. He humorously applied <u>tandem</u>, 'at length,' to a pair of horses harnessed one behind the other. We now have tandem bicycles, tandem nursing -- two infants are nursed simultaneously or consecutively -- and tandem hitch in Canada, a method of harnessing sled-dogs in single file, e.g., in unobstructed country, the bush. It is an arrangement in contradistinction to "the fan." But, even in Montréal, traineaux were drawn by French ponies, and toboggans, loaded with furs, by dogs <u>in tandem</u>.

IX.   Give the doublets of bull, camera, crass, duenna, lagoon, Madonna,* potion,** raceme, rotund.

X.   Determine the meanings of the underlined words, or fill in:

1. Colōnus 'settler, husbandman' gave rise to colōnia, whence colonial, colonize. Distinguish between colonial, and colonel (< It. colonnello).

2. Take cum granō salis the legend that the Spartans burnt Archilochus' poems to protect their children from his slanderous tongue.

3. The first ministers adjourned their plenary session and withdrew to the building's attic for an in camerā meeting.

4. Which term is closer to Latin: terra alba, terra cotta?

5. You are issued a legal document, a _____, when required to appear in court.

6. Age counts for nothing among those who have learned to know life sub speciē aeternitatis. E.K. Rand

7. Specie payment was originally payment in specie, the preposition now being omitted.

8. Under French influence L. nouns ending in -ia, e.g., calumnia appear in English with this ending replaced by -___, and nouns ending in -tia have this ending replaced by -___, e.g., grātiā, 'favor,' avāritia 'greediness.'

---

*   What would mea domina 'my Lady' give in English besides Madonna which comes via Latin?
** What would L. potio 'potion, drink' give when the meaning of the word stresses the pejorative element?

25

WORD NOTES

Latin exerts a subtle influence on our language. Unless we are attuned to its intricacies certain observations escape us. For example, the ending -a is not congenial to English, but Latin sometimes prevails. Vocalic endings in English are commonly -e unvoiced, -y, and occasionally -o. It is primarily when English adopts Latin-derived words that we do see the final -a: alumna, arena, aura, camera, candelabra, circa, fauna & flora, genera, incunabula, inertia, lacuna, marginalia, media, memorabilia, militia, nebula, opera, prima donna, scintilla, stamina, terra alba, terra cotta, terra firma, via, Victoria, villa, viscera. Some of these are not fem. sgs, but rather n. pls. More often than not a Latin word ending in -ia will be converted to an English ending in -y; e.g., colōnia became F. colonie, E. colony. West Germany's Cologne was formerly Colonia Agrippina, capital of Germānia Inferior. Cōpia 'plenty' became F. copie, our copy. But copula, a linking, retains its Latin form. Lingua franca, a dialect formed of elements of Provençal, Italian, Spanish, Greek, Arabic, spoken during the 19c in the Levant, also remains. It now means a mixture of languages used in communication, such as pidgin English.

*** *** *** *** *** ***

Henceforth, we deal with compounds or compound derivatives. These contain prefixes, suffixes or both, so that the words formed are compound nouns and adjectives. We shall study compound derivations from verbs later.

In the section on adjective-forming suffixes, we find -i-; this combining or connecting vowel (see item 9, pestilentus) is, in Latin, the most prevalent. Some modern word coinages follow the precedent set in late Latin where the -o- combining vowel sound often appears. There is no unvarying pattern in the use of combining vowels. No single criterion for correctness can be established in their use in modern coinages from Latin (or Greek) elements on the basis of classical linguistic precedent.

26

LESSON III: PART I

ADJECTIVAL AND NOUN-FORMING SUFFIXES

Ancient speakers of Latin formed compound words, composed of more than one element, by adding suffixes. In English, we may, for example, add -dom to official (= officialdom), -ship to director (= directorship), -ish to girl (= girlish) or to wasp (= waspish), and -like to lady (= ladylike). We now look at how Latin-speakers produced their compound words.

ADJECTIVE-FORMING SUFFIXES. To a noun- or ajective-base, Latin added:

1. the suffix -ālis (>* E. -al); industri- + -ālis, means etymologically 'pertaining to, connected with, or having the character of diligence;' cf. equal, social, marginal, brutal, original, focal, natal, manual. Bases containing l, e.g., popul-, simil-, mīlit-, līne- in either of their last two syllables usually attract the -āris ending.

2. -īlis (> E. -ile, -il); vir- + -īlis means etymologically 'belonging or appropriate to, concerned with, pertaining to a man;' cf. anile, civil, febrile, gentile, hostile, juvenile, servile. Note the uses of the neuter pl. ending of (1) -ālis: marginalia, regalia, paraphernalia and of (2) -īlis: juvenilia, memorabilia.

3. -āris (> E. -ar, -ary); jocul-** + -āris means 'pertaining to, concerned with, having the character of a joke;' cf. granular, insular, ocular, peculiar, military, ancillary.

4. -ārius (> E. -ary, -arious); auxili- + -ārius means 'having the characteristic of aid;' cf. bestiary, coronary, honorary, lapidary, momentary, gregarious.

5. -ānus (> E. -ane, -an); urb- + -ānus means 'belonging to, characteristic of a city;' urbane and urban develop different meanings; cf. german and germane; median, mundane, veteran. N. pl. nouns formed on this base are Canadiana, Shakespeariana, Moreana, Americana, Victoriana.

6. -īnus (> E. -ine; -in: Chemical terms); fer- + -īnus means etymologically 'pertaining to, characteristic of a wild beast;' cf. bovine, leonine, ovine, porcine, sanguine, vaccine, melanin, insulin.

---

*   means 'giving rise to'
**   The j in jocul- is a consonantal i. It is pronounced like a y.

27

7. -eus (> E. -eous); oss- + -eus means etymologically 'pertaining to, characteristic of bone;' cf. aqueous, luteous.

8. -ōsus (> E. -ose); ōti- +-ōsus means etymologically 'full of, given to leisure;' and (> E. -ous); e.g., avāriti- + -ōsus means etymologically 'full of, given to greed;' cf. calumnious, cellulose, copious, curious, emulous, fabulous, generous, grandiose.

9. -lentus (> E. -lent); N.B. a connecting vowel, -u-, -o-, or -ī-, is usually inserted betwen the base which ends with, and the suffix beginning with a consonant. pest- + -i- -lentus 'pertaining to or characterized by plague;' cf. sanguinolent, turbulent, violent.

10-
11. Of Greek origin are the endings -icus* (> E. -ic); generic, histrionic, and -ticus (> E. -tic); aquatic, operatic, rustic. Cf. L. silvāticus and VL. salvāticus > F. sauvage > E. savage. VL. formāticum yields 13c F. fromage. F. assemblage and atterrissage are formed on this ending. 16c F. langage, from L. lingua and ME. langage yields E. language.

12. The ending -nus forms adjectives relating to family relationships (e.g., māternus, paternus, frāternus), place relationships (e.g., infernus, externus), time units (hodiernus, diurnus, nocturnus, hesternus, aeternus). To form an English derivative, add -ālis: diurnus +-ālis gives journal, through F., and diurnal.

13. The ending -ter (-tris), -ester (-estris) means in a general way 'belonging to,' especially of place and time, as in bimestrial (every two months), equestrian, pedestrian, semestrial, (every six, or during six months), terrestrial. N.B. -ester is formed by adding -tri to stems in t- or d-.

14. The English ending -ad, confined to medical terms, does not come from a Latin suffix but from the Latin preposition and prefix ad, meaning 'in the direction of,' 'toward.' In this modern development -ad may be added to a noun, an adjective or an adverb to form an adverb; examples are aborad, apicad, caudad, cephalad, dextrad, dorsoventrad, ectad, retrad and viscerad. To understand these words, avail yourself of the following definitions: ōs, ōris, 'mouth,' apex, apicis

---

* -cus and -icus are native L. endings in cīvicus > E. civic, and classicus > classic. They indicate a sense of belonging as in corona cīvica and classica bella (naval wars).

'top, summit, extreme end of a thing;' G. kephalē means 'head' and ect- is from Greek ektos 'outside.' All the others contain Latin bases. Viscera, neuter plural of viscus, means 'internal organs, bowels.'

N.B.: Somewhat rare is -ensis 'belonging to' as in amanuensis, and forensis which, when suffixed by -icus gives forensic. In Modern Latin it is found in certain species names, e.g., the Canada jay is Perisoreus canadensis, and in University titles: Universitas Ottaviensis, Universitas Neo Eboracensis.

Hybrids

L. hybrida (hibrida)* is the cross-breed offspring of a tame sow and a wild boar. A hybrid in zoology or botany is the offspring of the union of a male of one race, variety, species, genus, etc. with the female of another, e.g., a mule which is the result of the mating of a horse and an ass. The term hybrid is also used in language to refer to a word composed by elements from more than one language, e.g., grateful is half Latin (grātus 'pleasing') and half English (-ful). Other examples are automobile, charming, joyous, lake-side, painful, price-wise, talkative, television. A special type of hybrid is the centaur word, one with a Latin head and a Greek tail: quadraphony or quadraphonics, bicycle.

Many words ending in -ous are hybrids. Starting out from their Old English base, they attract the -ous ending to themselves, e.g., boisterous, flirtatious, gorgeous, heinous, murderous, uproarious. Humorous formations develop, e.g., gossipaceous, rambunctious and scrumptious. Hellacious persons are more than just mischievous. OF. meschief, from meschever 'to be unfortunate,' is composed of F. mes- (< L. minus 'less') + chief 'end, head'.

---

* Gk. hybris 'insolence, outrage' is the source.

29

The suffix -eus does not, as in aqueous, always come out as -eous. Take LL. mellaceus, 'honeylike,' from mel, mellis 'honey.' LL. mellaceum 'must' yields P. melaço, whence E. molasses. Sp. melaza was adopted, meantime, as 17c F. mélasse (till then, meslache). Gk. melimelon, L. melimelum, 'honey-apple,' gives P. marmelada,** 17c F. marmellade, whence marmalade. F. -ade gives E. -ad as in salad, ballad. While Sp. yields armada and bravado, It. contributes brigade through F., cantata and innamorata. Armada, ballad, brigade and cantata are formed on the base of denominative verbs. These are taken up later.

** Note the dissimilation in the first syllable of -el-, in P., F., and E., to -ar-. Cf. dond- › gond- in the Word Notes following, at gondolier.

WORD NOTES

L. classis, 'Roman citizen body called out, army, navy, class, rank, division,' gives classicus 'pertaining to the classes of the Roman people, relating to the highest rank, superior.' Classical works, the classics, refers, since the 17c, to those of Greece and Rome. L. gens, gent-is, 'race, nation,' appears in Gentile. When -īlis is added to the base, we have gentle, genteel, even jaunty. Gens forms the basis of gendarme. A 14c F. gent d'armes was a soldier on horseback; a 16c one is a policeman. L. magister, 'helmsman,' comes to mean 'master, teacher.' It gives rise to magistrālis, whence magistral and its doublet mistral, a cold, dry N. wind blowing over France's Mediterranean coast. Maestro, mister, maître (d') and master are quadruplets. Nominal, 'pertaining to a name,' may mean 'existing in name only' as distinct from real or actual, whence 'nominal fee.'

L. persōna, 'mask, role, character,' combining with -ālis, gave personālis 'of, or belonging to a person' whence personal and its doublet through F. personnel. Acceptable or welcome is a persona grata; dramatis personae are characters in a play or novel.

Some Latin words are used to identify new concepts. For example, C.G. Jung's persona is one's role in society, determined by early training. One with a strong ego has a flexible persona. His puer aeternus and puella aeterna refer to adolescent mentalities with strong conscious attachments to the parent of the opposite sex. A man's unconscious feminine side is his anima 'soul' and a woman's unconscious male side is her animus 'spirit.' A man projects his anima onto a real woman when he falls in love. A woman projects her animus onto a man when she falls in love.

The F. suffixal ending -age refers to an action or collective state, as in courage, Chanson de Roland, 1080, which meant 'disposition' of the heart. Cf. lavage in 'lavage de cerveau.' In medicine, lavage is the washing out of an organ. Garage is a place for keeping, storing or preserving, ‹ F. garer, 'to protect.' It is the L. suffix -āticum which yields F. -age; E. -age: L. viāticum › voyage, missāticum › message. Whereas -aticus produces both adjectives and nouns (cf. savage and lunatic), -āticum yields only nouns through F. -age* as in

---

* Formed on this ending are bondage and other familiar words: camouflage, damage, forage, garbage, homage, language, marriage, sausage, vassalage, village. Garbage is from OF. garber 'to make fine,' (cf. OF. garbe 'sheaf'). ME. garbage meant 'the entrails of fowl.'

brigandage, chantage, espionage. Do not confuse this suffix with the origin of age, < L. aetas, aetātis, to which aeternus, eternus, adj. 'eternal' is related).

Still another suffixal ending is -tic. This -tic is an ending of Greek origin (cf. -ic). It tends, in Latin-derived words, to have a pejorative denotation.** L. lūnāticus, 'living on the moon, moonstruck, crazy,' developed in Church Latin, e.g., the Vulgate. Lunatic illustrates the use of a concrete term for an abstract conception 'affected by the moon, temporarily insane.' Even in Rome, Horace's fānāticus, one who stood before a fanum 'temple' and worshipped, deteriorated into its present meaning of frantic, mad. Cicero called philosophers who opposed him superstitious and practically fanatic.

The suffix -ārius (m.), when added to a noun or adjective base, yields nouns meaning 'a person connected with.' It often comes through OF. (-ier) as -er, -ier, or -eer. LL. caballārius 'horseman' < LL. caballus 'horse' (which replaced equus in popular speech) produces OF. chevalier and cavalier, It. cavalliere. We adopt Sp. caballero. On the other hand, a cavalier belongs to the horsey set and is scornful, though he started out brave and generous.

'Chivalrous' leads us to think of a moral quality rather than a horse. In pre-Norman England, the feudal gentleman possessed a 'destrier' or warhorse. Chivalry originates from F. chevalier, whence chevalerie 'the status of a knight.'

F. canonnier yields cannonier and cannoneer. Cashier is from L. capsārius. He filled a capsa 'box.' F. caissier gives us our noun cashier. Our noun, cashier, is not to be confused with the verb meaning 'to dismiss, to break with disgrace,' inasmuch as OF. casser 'to discharge' derives from LL. quassāre or cassāre 'to bring to naught, destroy.'

A Gaulish two-wheeled vehicle, carpentum, gives rise to carpentārius, whence carpenter. LL. coquinārius gives F. cuisinier, a cook. L. cupa 'tub, vat, cask, barrel' yielded cupārius, a cooper. L. consuetudinārius develops into ML. custumārius and AF. custumer, whence our customer. Its chief current sense goes back to the 15c.

** Rustic once meant 'artless, simple.' Later it connoted the uncouth.

From L. dēnī, 'by tens,' the distributive numeral (cf. decem), we have L. dēnārius* (cf. It. denaro, Sp. dinero, and Yugoslavian, Iranian, and Israeli dinar). A denier is a measure of weight for hosiery and dresses. In this case, the noun produced from -ārius is a thing, not 'a person connected with' a thing.

Gondolier, however, and gondola** come from Italian. The Romance base, by dissimilation,*** may be dond- 'to rock.' In Canada, gondola is restricted in meaning to an observation booth occupied by sports announcers, e.g., of hockey games, and to a funicular used by skiers.

L. mare 'sea' gives L. marīnus 'pertaining to the sea.' L. marīnārius 'one concerned with the sea' becomes OF. marinier; it then refers to anyone employed on a ship. It. marinara is a sauce. Its origin is marinare 'to pickle.'

L. mōnētarius 'minter' gives OF. mon(n)ier, mon(n)oier, whence moneyer. L. mons, montis 'mountain' gives VL. montania (sc. regiō, terra) whence OF. montaigne 'mountain region' whence mountain. -eer is added for 'a native dweller among mountains' or 'a mountain-climber.'

L. ōstiārius 'doorkeeper' produces our doublets ostiary and usher. The former is the doorkeeper, usually of a church. OF. ussier produced huissier in 1138 meaning porter, but in the 16c the huissier became a bailiff; huis, door, developed out of L. ostium. Porter comes from F. portier. LL. portārius 'gate-keeper, doorkeeper' is the source.

L. scutārius 'a knight's shield-bearer,' became VL. escūtārius, OF. escuier (Chanson de Roland, 1080), whence F. écuyer, specialized later to mean 'a groom for horses.' From this, we get squire and esquire; both have undergone elevation in meaning. L. terrārius is the origin of our terrier who pursued animals into their holes in the earth. L. voluntārius has virtually given doublets in French, an adverb and a noun. We get an adjective, a verb, and two nouns. Volunteer is a voluntary from F. volontaire. F. volontiers is technically an adverb of voluntārius.

Besides gendarme, cavalier and squire, others have gained their titles from equally modest linguistic sources. Among these are captain, chancellor, corporal and courtier. Constable was

---

* a coin used in Roman times, it contained ten parts of a more valuable coin.
** the etymology of this word is obscure.
*** the process of making sounds unlike; dond- > gond-.

once LL. <u>comes stabuli</u> 'count of the royal stable, marshal.' F. <u>connétable</u> was once a high-ranking officer in charge of the whole <u>gendarmery</u>.   General, commander of the whole army, is from L. <u>generālis</u>, 'pertaining to the class, kind, or race,' < L. <u>genus</u> 'kind.'   The supreme commander of a combined naval and military force, or of several armies in the field is a generalissimo.

Marshal, a high position in officialdom, is from the Germanic roots <u>mar-</u> 'horse' and <u>scal-</u> 'servant.'   Formerly a groom in charge of the stable -- cf. F. <u>maréchal ferrant</u>, 'blacksmith' -- he enjoys the highest military rank in France.

EXERCISE III: PART I

I.   Analyze aqueous, esquire, guttural, infirmary,
        lapidary, larder, notary, plumber, privateer, rotary,
        somnolent, tiller.

II.   Analyze the underlined words and determine their
        contextual meaning: gregarious person, histrionic
        pretence, jocose remarks, magnanimous generosity, onerous
        task, specious reasoning, spectral analysis, spectral
        Christmas tale, vicarious pleasure, vitreous china.

III.   Distinguish between these often confused pairs: aquatic,
        aqueous; judicial, judicious; official, officious;
        sensuous, sensual; torturous, tortuous.

IV.   1. Why were the months January and February so called?
        2. Give an example of fastidious taste; of nice
           distinction.
        3. Find the blunder: A $5,000 prize goes to the
           institution or person deemed to have achieved
           effective results in fighting literacy.
        4. What made the boxer edentulous in both jaws?
        5. ... Fagus, Ilex, Almus, Scirpus,
              Such names rang out in Roman fora,
              Before Linnaeus had his hora.   J. Dwyer
           Forum is cognate with forensic. What is forensic
           medicine?
        6. What would be kept in a funerary urn?
        7. Like awful, nice and awful nice*, what can we say
           about stupendous, terrific, colossal, fabulous,
           horrible?
        8. What is objectionable about a farinaceous diet?
        9. What is the doublet of digital?
        10. Which two months have men's names?

V.   What suffix went into the composition of amanuensis,
        aquarium, estuary, granary, itinerary, lapidary, library,
        notary, premier, salary?

---

* L. nescius 'ignorant' gave nice. In 1560 it meant stupid; it
  also meant hard to please. Shakespeare uses it (J.C. 4, sc.3),
  'nice offence,' to mean trivial. In 1713 nice refers to
  appetizing food. By 1769 the agreeable sense is recorded. By
  the way, Sp. necio still means 'foolish,' as does F. niais.
  But niais, from pop. L. nidax, nidacis 'a bird that cannot
  fly,' is ultimately from L. nidus 'nest.'

VI.   Define: (a) Ovid's aurea aetas, (b) Augustine's patria communis, (c) Spinoza's ipsissima verba, (d) Hobbes' summum bonum, (e) Santayana's ignis fatuus.

VII.   Milton and Shakespeare frequently use words in a sense much nearer their original meanings. Determine the meanings of the following Latinisms.

1.   Needs must the Serpent now his capital bruise
     Expect with mortal pain. Milton, PL 12.383
2.   ... letters sadly penned in blood,
     ... and sealed to curious secrecy. Lover's Compl. 49
3.   I am so fraught with curious business
     That I leave out ceremony. Winter's Tale 4.4.524
4.   Hor.: It is a nipping and an eager air. Haml. 1.4
5.   What boots it, Sire, / To ... / Hold me travailling
     through fineless years? Hardy, Dynasts 1.1.2
6.   As hardy as the Nemean lion's nerve   Haml. 1.4.83
7.   Call country ants to harvest offices. Donne, The Sun
     Rising 8
8.   Buy terms divine in selling hours of dross. Sonnet
     146.11 (Clues: careful, painstaking; chores, duties;
     deadly; end, limit; pertaining to the head; sharp;
     sinew; without end).   All words in the exercise,
     obsolete in their Latinate sense, are still used in
     present meanings except fineless (5).

VIII.   Sometimes Latin phrases have been borrowed directly from the Latin, whether classical or modern.

        Define the following expressions (Use the Latin vocabulary at the end, or a dictionary):

        (a) amīcus cūriae, (b) magister lūdī, (c) socius crīminis, (d) in locō parentis, (e) corpus dēlictī, (f) bacillus amātōrius, (g) in camerā, (h) rara avis, (i) sub rosā, (j) taedium vītae.

        Clues: the 2nd word in a,b,c,e,j and the 3rd word in d
                are genitives.   The 2nd word in d,g,i is
                ablative. in + abl. case indicates location. in
                is figurative in d, as is sub 'under' in i.
                a,c,d,e, & g are legal terms.

        Translation hints: cūria 'court,' crīmen, -inis 'crime,'
                            parens, -entis 'parent,' LL. bacillus
                            'small staff, wand;' here: 'bug,'
                            amātōrius 'pertaining to love;' here:
                            'love-.'

36

NOUN-FORMING SUFFIXES

The following suffixes were added to adjective or noun bases to form new nouns:

1. -itās (> E. -ity) e.g., clar- + -itās > clarity; cf. acerbity, dignity, purity.
    -etās (>* E. -ety) e.g., pi- + -etās > piety; cf. sobriety, variety, satiety.
    -tās (> E. -ty) e.g., pauper- + -tās > poverty; cf. liberty, puberty.
    * Instead of -itās, -etās is added to the base of adjs. ending in -ius.

2. -itūdō (> E. -itude) e.g., turp- + -itūdō > turpitude; cf. altitude, aptitude.

3. -itia (> E. -ice) e.g., jūst- + -itia > justice; LL. caritia > F. caresse > E. caress; LL. ricītia > F. richesse > E. riches, but note: militia.

4. -ia (> E. -y) e.g., modest- + -ia > modesty; custody, memory, but note: concord, vigil; insomnia.

5. -mōnium and -mōnia (> E. -mony) (these suffixes are added to adjective or noun bases) e.g., mātri- + -mōnium; and acri- + -mōnia > acrimony;* cf. ceremony, patrimony, testimony.
    * Cato uses acrimonia to mean 'pungency, irritation, smart.' It later appears with the meaning 'sharpness of speech, sharp talk.'

NOUNS FORMED BY ADDING SUFFIXES TO NOUN BASES ONLY:

1. -ium (> E. -y) e.g., augur 'soothsayer, priest' + -ium > augury, but note: hospes, hospit- 'host, guest' + -ium > hospice, servit- + -ium > service.

2. -ātus (> E. -ate) 'holder of office of, the office of' magister, magistr- + -atus > magistrate; cf. pontificate.

3. -ismus* > -ism 'practice of, concern for,' ego + -ismus > egoism; cf. separatism, socialism.

4. -ista* > -ist 'one who is concerned with, one who advocates strongly,' human- + -ista > humanist; cf. altruist, fabulist.
    *   an adjective base is sometimes also used with these suffixes which are, properly speaking, Greek.

Many English words derive from Latin diminutives whose suffixes and development are:

-ellus, -ella, -ellum > -el, -le, or unchanged, e.g., libellus, > libel, particella > parcel.
-illus, -illa, -illum > -il, e.g., codicillus > codicil, pūpilla > pupil of the eye.
-olus, -ola, -olum > -ole, or unchanged, e.g., vacuolus > vacuole.
-ulus, -ula, -ulum > -le, -ule, or unchanged, e.g., scrūpulus > scruple; molecula > molecule, granulum > granule.
-culus, -cula, -culum > -cle, -cule, or unchanged, e.g., musculus > muscle, vesicula > vesicle, particula > particle.
-leus, -lea -leum > unchanged in nucleus.

Some diminutives have come directly into English as loan words, e.g., cerebellum, calculus, and the triplets reticulum, reticule, reticle.

ABSTRACT NOUNS

The five endings at the beginning of Part II form abstract nouns which express three types of ideas: a) quality, e.g., the tone-purity of music; b) condition or state, e.g., sobriety; and c) the naming of an act, e.g., ceremony, vigil. Abstract nouns derived from verbal bases also name an act, e.g., habitation is from the base of the past participle of L. habitāre, habitāt-us 'to dwell (in), dwelt (in)' + the base of -iō, -iōnis 'act of.' In Lesson IX you will study this type.

Concrete nouns name a thing, or a class of things, e.g., alarm clock, canoe, furniture, house, table. A noun which was originally abstract, e.g., riches, formerly a condition of wealth, may assume a concrete meaning. Hence, riches now signifies wealth itself. Other examples are caress, charity, city, divinity, and justice. Caress originally meant the quality of being dear. It is a particular or specific show of endearment, a kiss, a loving embrace or an affectionate gesture. Charity first meant 'dearness,' but we may use it as a concrete noun in "to give to a favorite charity." Divinity, from L. dīvīnus 'godly' + -itās (> -ity), abstract in "the divinity (= godliness of God)" becomes concrete when we refer to God or a pagan god. In the American Pledge of Allegiance's "justice for all" we have the abstract use of the noun, but in "married by a 'justice' of the peace" justice is used in its concrete meaning. L. cīvitās was originally "the condition of being a cīvis 'citizen,'" but came to mean 'city.'

38

WHERE SOME DIMINUTIVES END UP

Diminutives denote any small, young or endearing person or thing (cf. statuette, pupil, puppet, darling). L. angulus 'corner' gives F. and E. angle. Bugle is from OF. bugle 'a young bull,' L. buculus, diminutive of bos 'ox.' 13c OF. bugle also meant 'hunting horn,' for it was made of the horn of a wild ox. L. cancellus 'a cross-bar' gives E. chancel, and the verb cancel. Cf. G. Kanzel = 'a pulpit.' L. capra 'she-goat' yields It. capriola 'fawn,' E. capriole, which is shortened to caper. L. cavea 'cage' gives F. and E. cage. VL. caveola gives F. geôle and E. jail. LL. cappa 'cloak' gives E. cap, cape, cope; from LL. cappella 'cloak' we derive chapel. Capellānus, 'cloak man,' produces chaplain. Other derivatives are chaplet, chaperon (originally 'large hat'). L. costa 'rib' gives F. côtelette, whence cutlet. L. fūr 'thief' gives the diminutives F. ferret and E. ferret. L. furunculus yields felon, i.e., 'a bump or swelling.' L. joculus 'little toy, plaything' gives jewel. Juggler is from L. joculātor 'jester, trickster.' From L. monachus F. gets moine (by metathesis)* and then moineau 'sparrow.' LL. rotulus 'cylinder roll' yields F. rouleau, and rôle 'text learned by an actor.' One notes that the diminutive denotation of the original Latin has often been lost on the way.

A 'measly child' is not necessarily pejorative. The child may be infected with measles. It has been suggested, perhaps by popular etymology, that the origin of this disease is the word misellus 'little wretched one.' The ME is meseles. From Middle Dutch maseren 'little spots' we get D. mazelen. English made it an adjective. ML. misellus meant 'leprous' as did measle, a 13c word.

L. scamnum 'bench' gives L. scamellum, whence shamble (cf. G. Schemel 'stool'), 'a butcher's bench.' Shambles are 'butchers' stalls for meat-display' and figuratively, 'a scene of destruction or disorder.'

Tabernacle is at bottom the same word as tavern (L. taberna 'shop'; L. tabernāculum 'tent'), though the words are differently associated. Uncle comes from the diminutive of avus 'grandfather,' avunculus. When we flex a muscle, it is 'a little mouse,' mūsculus. Oriole is from aureolus dimin. of the adj. aureus 'golden, beautiful.' Particula, dimin. of pars, partis 'share, portion' gives particle and parcel, but a parcel is no longer thought of as something small. A novel (L. novella, n.pl. of novellus, whence It. novella, F. nouvelle 'short story') need not be short either. Neither clientele nor decibel is a diminutive; the first is French; the second, a hybrid, conceals

---

* transposition of letters or sounds in a word

39

the name Bell.   L. viria 'bracelet, armlet' yields LL. virola
'ring, bracelet;' OF. virole 'iron ring put around the end of a
staff' gives ferrule. Erasmus tells us the Latin teacher of his
day "beat the little wretches with ferrules."   To discipline
children and slaves, the Roman used a ferula 'small branch.'
Italians now bear the ferula, a staff, in church processions.
Morsel was sired by OF. morsel, morcel, F. morceau, derivatives
of L. mordēre, morsus 'to bite,' morsum 'bite,' and dimin. LL.
morsellum 'piece.'

     Cadet, caddie and capitellum are triplets.   The Latin
diminutive of caput is capitulum. Borrowed by Carolingian French
(1119) as chapitle, it becomes chapitre.   In Christian Latin,
capitulum meant a passage from the Scriptures, a short lesson
read in some Church services or at the beginning of assemblies.
By extension, it came to mean a meeting of members of any
religious order; cf. ME. chapitre. It also meant a division of a
book.   The notion of assembly permits us to understand how a
chapter may be a local branch of a society or fraternity.

     Also formed from the noun capitulum is the ML. denominative
verb capitulāre. This yields capitulate, to surrender.   To
recapitulate is to restate briefly, as it were, by heads or by
divisions. Cadet < F. dial. capdel 'chief' and caddie derive
from L. capitellum.   The capitellum (1872) is the rounded
eminence on the outer surface of the lower end of the humerus (at
the elbow-joint).

     L. domina 'mistress, lady,' the source of dame, Donna,
duenna and It. donna (cf. prima donna), gives dimin. VL.
domicella, 10c F. domnizelle, 12c dameiselle, 13c damoiselle.
14c demoiselle's doublet, damsel, is from ME. dameisele, borrowed
from OF. Mademoiselle, now popularly abbreviated mam'zelle, was
crystallized in 16c F. as a term of politeness applied to an
unmarried French-woman. Specialized, it came to mean a French
governess in the 17c.

     Omelet derives from an OF. alumelle 'sword (or knife) blade'
whose suffix changes from -elle to -ette.   -ette, a feminine
ending, is found in fillette, noisette, tablette, Lisette,
Odette.   It corresponds to m. -et: jouet, valet, blondinet,
rondelet. L. lamella 'a thin plate' is the etymon* represented
by well-attested F. forms: lumelle, lamelle, lemelle. Because
there is agglutination to the noun of the article's vowel sound
in la, MF. forms alumelle, alamelle and alemelle respectively.
14c alumelle changes to alumette, and by metathesis of the l, 15c
has amelette, since the intervocalic u weakens to e in a
proparoxytone word, i.e., one accented on the third from the last

---

* an original root or primitive word

syllable. Late 16c omelette appears concurrently with dialectal doublets: aumelette, oemelette, etc.

A curious oeufmolette results from a contamination under the influence of oeuf (also found in oeuf-mollet, another product of folk-etymology). Omelet, therefore, results from a comparison with a blade or a thin plate because of its own thinness.

L. calumellus 'a small reed' gives chalumeau (the lowest register of the clarinet) and, through its parallel form chalumet in Norman F., calumet, a tobacco-pipe used by certain Indian tribes on the sacred occasion of peace-making and adopted by the white traders in their dealings with them. Time Cdn. ed., February 4, 1957, 63/1: "the calumet used at the powwow is supposed to have been sucked by Sitting Bull himself." LL. calamellus 'small reed' may have given Sp. caramelo (in P. it means 'icicle').

L. mortārium was the trough in which pork was crushed with a pestle, producing mortadella,* the Italian version of our bologna, a sausage emanating from Bologna** (< L. Bonōnia), a Gallic town founded around 200 B.C.

WORD NOTES

Let us start with familia. To its base famili- we add āris to get familiar. To the base familiār- we add -itās to form familiarity. Members who belonged to the familia were referred to individually as familiāris. A related word, L. verna, is from a root meaning dwell (cf. was, were, and AS. wesan). L. verna, 'a slave born in his owner's house,' provides the derivative vernāculus 'native.' Our loanword, vernacular, now refers only to the language spoken by a people or country, the native dialect.

The familia constituted all household-members. It had a collective meaning, starting out from famulus 'servant' and including therefore all the household servants and the members of the family, in our sense, which controlled them. It was sometimes then used of the domestics as distinct from those whom we consider to be the family. The head of the household was the paterfamilias (old genitive form), literally 'father of the family.'

---

* L. murtatum < L. myrtus 'myrtle bay' is the preferred etymology.
** by dissimilation, Bonōnia became Bologna. We call its sausage baloney.

All the IE. words for father are cognate. Cognate with Gk. pater is L. pater, used colloquially in Britain. Pater Noster, the Lord's Prayer, produced a vulgarization, patter (glib or rapid speech). Perhaps a childish corruption of Gk. pater was pappas. It ended up as pope, papa, paw and pop. Patrick and Patricia are also from this source. German Vater is cognate with AS, fader, whence father. In Sp. Padre Eterno is God, el Santo Padre is the Pope, and el padrenuestro, the Lord's Prayer. By adding -itas to the adjectival base of paternus we get paternity, and to maternus, maternity. Deriving from mater is materies or materia, whence matter, material. P. madeira first means 'matter,' then 'wood.' An island colonized by Portugal which contained forestland then took the name as did a wine there produced. The base of mater + -i- + -monium produces a familiar derivative. Societies which have unilineal descent may be matrilineal, as the principle of descent and ties of filiation are so determined, or, on the other hand, patrilineal. Two nouns are juxtaposed in Sp. madre patria, the nation as colonizer.

L. deus 'god,' is cognate with Skt. deva 'god.' The Roman Deus Pater is Jupiter (from OL. Jovis, 'Jupiter' + pater). From one of the adjectives of deus, divus, comes It. diva, a prima donna or leading woman singer. Deity is formed by adding -itas to the base de-. Divinity is constructed on the adjectival base. The former comes into English through OF., the latter through Middle English. L. deus's Greek cousin is not Theos (God), but Zeus (cf. Skt. dyaus-pitar). A figure of a Chinese god, a Chinese idol, is a joss (variation on P. deos, < L. deus). It is pidgin English.

Going farther abroad, we may glance at 'literary' and 'financial' matters. We add the noun suffix -atus to the base of littera to get litteratus (also spelled literatus), a man of letters or learning. The French equivalent was developed in 12c lettré, since L. littera became lettre. From illiterārius 16c illettré was formed.

Pecūnia meant money. It derives from L. pecus 'flock.' This is cognate with AS. feoh 'cattle,' whence 'fee.' Both words come from Skt. paçu 'beast'. In antiquity a man's wealth was estimated by his flocks and herds, so that in our use of fee the sense-development has been reversed. From pecus comes pecūlium 'a little part of the flock reserved for the slave's private property' or 'a little garden plot given to a child,' or 'what a father or master gives his son, daughter, or slave.' Out of this develops the adjective peculiar which, when attached to the idea of property or monetary possessions, used to mean 'personal.'*

42

Cab originates with L. capra 'a she-goat.' It. capriola 'little she-goat' leads to F. cabriolet, 'a little cabriole,' a light vehicle taking nimble jumps. Around 1820, cab develops. It is a two- or four-wheeled public carriage drawn by one horse and seating two or four persons. Taxi is the curtailed taximeter-cab which became taxi-cab (1907).

Species and spice are doublets from L. speciēs 'kind.' Because different kinds of aromatic substances came to be referred to as spices, spice developed as a singular noun. OF. developed espice, adopted in ME. We drop the initial e. Obsolete E. spicer, a dealer in spices, was an apothecary or druggist. This was borrowed from OF. espicier, retained by French as épicier 'grocer.' F. épicerie, where spices and imported goods were sold, originated in the 13c.

L. bellus 'fair'** is the origin of beau and belle. LL. bellitās 'fairness' produced MF. beauté adopted by ME. as bealte and beute. MF. beauté > E. beauty illustrates how a noun-ending (-itās) may be partially concealed, because -itās usually gives -ity; cf. equity, parity, quality.

City originates in L. cīvitās 'citizenship,' 'the status of a cīvis 'citizen.' When its meaning was transferred from 'citizenship' to the collectivity of Rome's citizens, it became the equivalent of urbs. Imperial Latin gave cīvitās this meaning of collectivity.

MF. cité meant the ancient part of the city. 16c French and English restored to the word both its political and figurative sense. French differentiates between citizen, citoyen, and city-dweller, citadin.

VL. caveola (popular L. gaviola), diminutive of cavea 'cavity, cage' gives ME. jaiole < 12c OF. jaiole. Developing into F. geôle, it helps to explain why English authors spell the word gaol, a ME. survival. F. enjôler meant 'to imprison;' it now means 'to captivate.' Cognate with jail 'a little cage' is the -coy in decoy. This may come from D. de kooi 'the cage,' a pond into which wild fowl are lured for capture, and by transference, an artificial bird used to attract live birds. By further extension, it means enticement.

---

* cf. ... there's millions now alive
    That nightly lie in those unproper beds
    Which they dare swear peculiar. Othello 4.1.67-69
** i.e., pretty, attractive, handsome; fairness = attractiveness, prettiness, handsomeness.

Not to be confused with -coy in decoy is our adjective coy (cf. F. coi, coite 'tranquil, calm, peaceful'). It derives from L. quiētus and VL. quētus, 'shyly reserved or retiring.' Coy and quiet are doublets. Quite is the triplet.

In the 1550's, Ronsard provides a literal use of a derivative from L. caput: "J'ai la dent noire et le chef blanc" (Odes, 4.13.3). A Mafia leader is a capo. This is a figurative use. L. caput is also the source of our culinary chef.

French has chef d'oeuvre, chef d'orchestre, chef-lieu, chef de file, d'une armée, d'une entreprise. Chef is invariable in French: mère, chef de famille. Involving this base is corporal (non-commissioned enlisted man), from OIt. caporale. F. capot may represent Provençal cap 'head,' which in turn seems to have given rise to G. kaputt 'spoilt, broken, killed.'

Exercise III: Part II

I.   Identify the adjective and noun-forming suffixes in animal,
      corporal, aquiline, osseous, bellicose, verbose, lacrimose,
      fortuitous, virulent, opulent.

II.   Identify the Latin noun from which the following pairs are
      derived:

	Latin noun	Meaning
e.g., civic, civil	cīvis	citizen
a) annals, annual		
b) cattle, chattel.		

      Do likewise for focal, fuel; hostel, hospital; jaunty,
      genteel; lineal, linear; moral, morose; nebular, nebulous;
      sanguine, sanguinary; spacial, spacious; special, specious;
      sine, sinuous. Specify which of these pairs are doublets.

III. Add an adjectival ending to each word's base in Group 1 and
      match the word produced with an appropriate noun from Group
      2 to make a phrase, e.g., copia + -ōsus = copious, as in
      'copious supplier.'

      Group 1:

      1) annus   6) latus   11) radix
      2) augur   7) mos   12) rus
      3) civis   8) nota   13) silva
      4) genus   9) omen   14) urbs
      5) insula   10) peculium   15) vestigium

      Group 2:

      | _____ pass | _____ mentality | _____ goings-on |
      | _____ prophecy | _____ public | _____ blight |
      | _____ forebodings | _____ remains | _____ duties |
      | _____ principle | _____ solution | _____ report |
      | _____ tranquillity | _____ contribution | _____ retreat |

IV.   Analyze the underlined words and define them in the
      context:

      1. The basest of created animalcules, the Spider
          Carlyle
      2. My brother Joe chuckled approvingly at me, adding a
          stentorian spur to my antics. A. Wiseman
      3. Double   jonquils,   hyacinths,   anemones,
          single-wallflowers and auriculas in flower   Gray

45

4. Two squyers blewe ... with ij (=their) grete <u>bugles</u> hornes. W. Caxton
5. <u>Calculus</u> racked him; / ... / Tussis attacked him. <u>Browning</u>
6. The sweetest <u>Canticle</u> is Nunc dimittis.   Bacon
7. ... yet 'twas <u>not a Crowne</u> neyther, 'twas one of these <u>Coronets</u>.   Shakespeare
8. A <u>wine-flushed Syrian damsel</u>, a turban on her hair -- Beat out a husky tempo <u>from</u> reeds in either hand.
9. This <u>fascicle</u> is a new section of the journal.
10. The <u>sporting</u> and crusty <u>gentry</u> may play polo.
11. A dialect of Cdn F. is <u>joual</u>.
12. They all began to ... <u>dance</u> ... a combination of Scotch horn-pipe, Indian fox-trot, syncopated Irish jig, and <u>Siwash</u> hula-hula.   Berton
13. The <u>beaver is a</u> social kind of animal, living in ... families.   De<u>Boilieu</u>
14. ... the abbot Gelasius ... had a <u>codex</u> in parchment worth eighteen <u>solidi</u>.   H. Waddell
15. 'He made a tip <u>of the</u> slung' is a <u>lapsus linguae</u>.

V. a) Aureola and aureole, doublets, come from L. <u>aureola</u> (corona). Show how F. <u>auréole</u> is not the doublet, but rather only the cognate, of oriole.
    b) Rockcliffe Park Public School's motto is <u>Maximus in Minimis</u>. Translate it.

WORD NOTES

Before Molière wrote <u>Les Précieuses Ridicules</u> in 1659, précieux and précieuse were taken in good part. It was a compliment to a woman to call her une précieuse. Segrais, to the duchess of Châtillon:

Obligeante, civile et surtout précieuse,
Quel serait le mortel qui ne l'aimerait pas?

In a 1661 dictionary about précieuses, for instance, the author listed the outstanding women of his century. But once Molière's play took effect, women were, no matter how accomplished, fearful of being called précieuses lest it be associated with the idea of being ridiculous, though Molière himself said he was attacking the false précieuses. LaFontaine subsequently uses préciosité (1668), borrowed from the L. pretiosus (< pretium 'value') to describe anyone affected in language and manners. Fastidiousness and overrefinement become the hallmarks of certain authors and critics; they are then called precious. Here is an obvious degeneration of meaning, for L. pretium originally meant 'worth,' a meaning it still retains, for instance, in 'precious stones.' To Molière's title for his play we owe the sudden degradation first, of précieuse, second, of precious. Colloquially, we now even speak of a precious liar meaning a great one.

L. prōfānum meant that which is unholy, common, not sacred; by extension, wickedness, impiety. Its literal meaning was that which is outside of the temple. Only priests were allowed to enter the temple, all others being prōfānī, i.e., uninitiated. In later Latin, it comes to mean 'the ignorant.' We tend to use it as the counterpart of sacred, e.g., Biblical and profane literature. Here it has a neutral use, but when we speak of profane remarks, the word takes on a pejorative meaning. From 'that which is secular,' it degenerates to 'that which is blasphemous and irreverent.'

The three parts of a church are the nave (< L. nāvis 'ship'), the chancel (< L. cancellus 'gate'), and the sanctuary (< L. sanctuārium, post-Augustan for sacrārium, 'place for keeping sacred things).' Here, even an evil-doer could obtain asylum, or sanctuary.

Some words change their form and meaning, quite concealing their Latin origin, e.g., chancellor, cheers, court, custom, pavilion and travel. Chancellor is from cancelli, (pl. of cancellus), 'lattice, enclosure, the bar in a court of justice, the barrier in public spectacles.'

LL. cancellārius was a porter, doorkeeper or secretary. He could be an usher in a law court stationed at the cancelli, the latticework separating the public from the judges. IIc OF. chancelier meant emperor's bailiff; it then took on the meaning of court clerk. It is now the title of the head or president of some universities. The British call the highest finance minister and member of the Cabinet Chancellor of the Exchequer. From being an officer in charge of records who stood behind the latticework we now have, by elevation of meaning, a distinguished participant in higher education and government.

Cheers is for drinkers, salutations, and farewells. It comes from LL. cara 'face.' Greek has kara 'the head,' related to Skt. ciras. OF. chere, chiere and ME. chere meant the face, look, demeanor, welcome. A shout of joy is "three cheers." "Cheers" is a popular toast since about 1945, a salutation before drinking. By way of Africa and Spain, it came into ME. as chere. Defoe cited it as a shout of encouragement among seamen. This matey word retains a whiff of the public bar and doughty British seamen. Anywhere, it says 'Goodbye.'

OF. cortois, changed in form and eventually narrowed in meaning, survives in 'courteous,' and 'courtesy.' A doublet of this is curtesy, a variety of which is curtsy. Curtesy is the right a husband has in law in the lands of his dead wife; the

47

curtsy is a quondam stylish female salutation, with a knee-bend and slight body-dip. These words originated in LL. cortis, 'courtyard, palace,' < L. cohors, cohortis (or cors, cortis), 'court, enclosure, yard, division of an army, multitude.' 11c F. cour 'farmyard, villa, palace' (Chanson de Roland) became 16c royal domain and court of justice. 13c basse-cour is 'cour des écuries' till the 17c, then poultry-yard, one of the meanings of ancient L. cohors.

Custom comes through OF. costume into ME. Its L. origin is consuētūdo (acc.: consuētūdinem) which meant 'custom, habit.' Habit, itself a Latin word, combines the meanings of both derivatives of consuētūdo. Look at the French spelling to see custom's doublet. Cf. customer (< LL. custumārius 'toll gatherer, < OF. costumier). Pavilion came into English through French papillon. Its F. doublet is pavillon. L. papiliō meant 'butterfly' and tent (from its shape). It may have been the flapping sides of the tent which reminded its occupants of the motion of a butterfly's wings. A modern fair will have buildings (pavilions) for exhibits and entertainment. The word can also mean a decorative shelter or summer house.

Concealed in 'travel' is a Latin numeral tres (tri-) '3.' L. trepālium was an instrument of torture consisting of three stakes or beams (pālus). Trepālium first entered English as travail, 'toil.' Like the French, we still use travail to mean parturition, and in its general meaning, hard work, but English travel is travail's doublet. Pilgrimages and migrations were trials and tribulations. Tribulum is from L. tero 'to rub, bruise, grind.' LL. tribulātio 'distress,' is from L. tribulāre 'to thrash, beat' from tribulum 'a threshing sledge, or wooden platform studded with iron teeth drawn over the grain to remove its husk.'

I.   Show how the following adjectives and nouns are formed.
       Add adjective-forming suffixes to the noun-base: give the
       base of the Latin word, and the suffix; then give
       etymological and current meanings.

E. wd.	Latin origin	Etymol. meaning	Current meaning
e.g., antiquary	antiqu-ārius	'a person connected with ancient things'	'a collector (student) of antiquities'
anile	_____	_____	_____
arbitrary	_____	_____	_____

       Do the same for cordial, coroner, diurnal, magisterial,
       marginalia, popular, truculent, venal.

II.   The following pairs of words derive from a common noun.
       Identify it; give etymological and current meanings of
       each, e.g.,

       a) imperial, b) imperious < imperium - 'rule, empire,'
          'sovereign power.'
       a) pertaining to an empire or emperor;
       b) arrogant, lordly,* urgent.
          carnal, charnel (house) _____ _____ _____
          civil, civic _____ _____ _____

       * Cf. Sinclair Ross, The Outlaw: '[Isabel's] imperious
          head.'
          Do likewise for Gentile, gentle, literal, literary,
          primer, premier, temporal, temporary.

III.   The etymological meaning of the underlined words will help
       you to fill in the blanks, e.g., a bestiary is a medieval
       compilation of animal stories with a moral turn, or a
       place for animals.

       One who heads a column of men (cf. It. colonello) is a
       _____ .
       Things connected with a king are _____ .
       A superficial solution skims over the _____ of a
       problem.
       Silvan scenes are viewed in a _____ .
       A voluptuary is a person devoted to _____ .

49

IV.   Form English words with the following etymological meanings: connected with a step, pertaining to a name, full of signs of future events, pertaining to the best, full of value.

V.   a) Dean Swift disapproved of the words stingy, clever, fun and mob, but they have endured.   Determine mob's etymological meaning.
      b) A novel's linear plot presents all essential details chronologically.   Differentiate the meaning of lineal from linear.
      c) Explain the form and meaning of the suffix in Shakespeariana and Victoriana.
      d) Explain why you would eliminate one word: television, martyrdom, dictaphone, sphinx-like, inimical.   (Clue: think of hybrids).
      e) The media (exploit, exploits) children.
      f) Hydrophobia has given way to the more descriptive
         _____ .
      g) Things connected with the young are _____ .
      h) Vitium passes to vice and illustrates (melioration, pejoration).
      i) "When presently through all thy veins shall run
         A cold and drowsy humour." R&J 4.1
         Define humour in this context.

VI.   True or false:

      a) Palate, palace and Palatium (Augustus' residence) are triplets.
      b) Tips abbreviates "to insure proper service."
      c) News is so called because it emanates from the four corners of the globe (N., E., W., and South).
      d) The four humours of Pythagorean and Empedoclean fame include liquid.
      e) There is greater prestige in being nonsalaried than in being unpaid.
      f) The pejorative non as in nonbook, nonentity, nondescript, non-native, nonstandard is distinctly polemical in tone.   (Clue: see Ex. V, question V)
      g) Pretium and praemium are cognates.
      h) Knowledge of a word's etymology leads to immediate comprehension of its current meaning.

VII. Give the doublets of: butler, esquire, loyal, maestro, menu, royal, spice, volunteer.

VIII. Fill in. Your answers will be in alphabetical order.

      1) A place for keeping birds confined is an _____ .
      2) The triplet of cattle and chattel is _____ .

3) Adroitness, skill and ease in the use of "the right hand" and of the mind is _____.
4) A cardiac stimulant and a diuretic, foxglove is also called _____.
5) The quality or state of being deferential or submissive is _____.
6) A person without principles or a code of conduct is _____.
7) Letitia, Lucretia, Monica, Olivia, Portia, Stella, Sylvia, Ursula, Venus and Victoria are _____ -derived girls' names.
8) A very sensitive person who has impulsive changes of mood is _____.
9) Another name for an indigenous inhabitant is _____.
10) Things pertaining to shepherds or their occupation are _____.
11) Property inherited from one's father is a _____.
12) The totality of an individual's behavioral and emotional tendencies is his _____.
13) The observation of fixed times for the performance of actions is _____. (Clue: L. regula 'ruler, rule, pattern')
14) Animals which live on the bank of a natural watercourse (stream or river) or of a lake or a tidewater are _____.
15) A card game played by one person alone is _____.
16) A club of girls or women especially at a college is a _____.
17) A politician who may be bought and sold is _____; a pardonable sin is _____.
18) A word by word report is one given _____.

IX. Many pairs of words have the same bases but different suffixes. Distinguish the meanings of the pairs:

funeral, funereal; Jovian, jovial; similar, simile; urban, urbane; verbal, verbose.

X. a) Change underlined words to Latin-derived adjectives:

I will talk of things heavenly or things earthly, things moral or things evangelical, things sacred or things profane, things past or things to come,* things foreign or things at home, things more essential or things circumstantial ...

Bunyan, Pilgrim's Progress

---

* Esse, 'to be,' has a future participle futūrus-a-um 'about to be.'

b) What is common to interim, seriatim and verbatim? What part of speech are they? What is common to alias, alibi, item and tandem in Latin? in English? What is common to passim and toto caelo in English? What part of speech is quondam in Latin? in English?

c) Is there a linguistic relationship between liber 'book' and lībertās?

XI. Define the underlined words in the context:

1. The professor had an avuncular conversation with the student.
2. Rise in the morning as bilious as a Bengal general. Disraeli
3. A girl of fourteen is the psychological coeval of a boy of fifteen or sixteen .... John Barth
4. And as natural selection works solely by and for the good of each being, all corporeal and mental environments will tend to progress towards perfection. Darwin
5. An extemporary collation. J. Evelyn
6. The doctrine of public regulation of privately owned resources has its roots in Roman law and the tenet of justum pretium.
7. A Greek comedy was a farrago of licentious nonsense. Chapman
8. Mediocrity has strong claims on the forgetfulness of posterity. G.P. Goold
9. You held him up, replete with his warm formula ... and waited for the postlactic all clear signal. Nabokov
10. He was dressed with a dandyish preciosity which gave no impression of well-being, only of nervousness. R. West

XII a) We distinguish between civil manners and civil war. Which of these meanings is apparent in Romeo and Juliet:

"Where civil blood makes civil hands unclean?"

b) Our use of sacrament is confined to religion, but determine its meaning in Richard II:

"A dozen of them here have ta'en the sacrament,
And interchangeable set down their hands,
To kill the king at Oxford."

c) Determine the commendable quality referred to in: "He did it to please his mother, and to be partly proud; which he is, even to the altitude of his <u>virtue</u>." <u>Coriolanus</u> (The answer is on page 59)

Editorial and etymological notes

Emotional words are associated with our hopes, fears, and interrelationships. Motherhood, patriotism, truth, peace all sound deep chords in our hearts. Father, mother, friend, husband, wife, marriage, love are others. Perhaps, money, too.* Money goes back to a Latin root, <u>mon-</u>, ‹ L. <u>monēre</u> 'to advise, warn.'

Rome had a temple dedicated to Juno Monēta, the goddess who, guarding the state, warned Romans in times of emergency and danger. As state-guardian, Juno also protected its finances, so the logical place to produce coins was in her temple where a mint was located. L. <u>monēta</u> 'mint, coined money' is cognate with AS, <u>mynet</u>, and until <u>the 16c</u> mint kept the meaning 'money.' It was <u>then</u> coined by a <u>mynetere</u>. OF. <u>moneie, monoie</u> became <u>monnaie</u>, 'mint, money.' There <u>is</u> a shift <u>in the</u> Latin meaning <u>from the</u> place to the product made or coined in the place. <u>Monētārius</u> 'coiner of money' yields monetary. From F. <u>monnayer</u>, 15c agent nouns <u>monnayeur</u> and <u>faux-monnayeur</u> arose.

FIGURATIVE LANGUAGE

Roman gladiators fought in an arena (‹ L. <u>harēna</u> 'sand, beach'). Today, we have the literal 'hockey <u>arena</u>' and the figurative 'political arena,' where the issue is how to govern. The Roman male was protected by a god, a <u>Genius</u>: our inventive person is a genius. A Roman whipped an <u>animal</u> with a <u>stimulus</u>, 'goad.' Our figurative meaning is incentive, our <u>literal, an</u> agent for starting a nerve impulse. Literal meanings produce figurative meanings by suggestion. These metaphors enrich the language. 'All the world's a stage,' 'plans nipped in the bud,' 'screaming headlines,' 'storms of protest,' 'threshings out of arguments,' 'a host (‹ L. <u>hostis</u> 'army,) of golden daffodils,' all these are poetic, <u>imaginative</u> and figurative expressions. Troops readied for warfare (not a sheet of daffodils) is literally a host.

---

* On money, see <u>The Classical Journal</u> 80.3 (1985), 259-262.

LEARNED WORDS

Words which require attention and study are 'learned,' for instance, the special vocabulary of scientists and educators. Words we are all familiar with are 'popular.' When a learned word enters into current use, e.g., curriculum vitae, escalation, it too becomes popular. An important consideration in the use of language is appropriateness. Learned words tend to be out of place in everyday conversation; language which is too informal is inappropriate among the highly educated. To improve communication, use 'le mot juste.'

LESSON IV

COMPOUND ADJECTIVES AND COMPOUND NOUNS

In Lesson III, we saw fourteen suffixes that form compound adjectives. Most are attached to noun bases. They turn the noun which supplies the base into an adjective. In some cases, the suffixes are attached to adjective bases, producing adjectives somewhat different in meaning from the one that supplied the base. We also saw how new nouns are formed by adding suffixes to adjective and / or noun bases, and how Latin diminutives are formed. Diminutive endings are almost always added to noun bases. Occasionally, the diminutive suffix -culus, -culum is attached directly to the noun's nominative ending rather than to the base (cf. animalcule, corpuscle, muscle, opuscule, tabernacle). Vehicle,* not a diminutive, is formed on a verb base (vehere, vectus 'to carry'). OF. has given us the diminutive -et,** -ette (cf. burette, coronet, cutlet, puppet, quintet, statuette, turret).***

EXERCISE IV

I. Analyze the following words by dividing them into segments and by defining each segment as in the example provided.

    vestigial < vestīgi-   'trace, footprint' + -al
                                            'connected with'

          < vestīgi/ālis

    augury, codicil, gladioli, linguist, military, and radical.

II. Add a noun-forming suffix to the base of the following Latin adjectives to form English nouns as in the example provided.

---

*   This will be dealt with in Lesson IX.
**   F. chevalet 'easel', lit. 'little horse,' started out as an instrument of torture. D. ezel (cf. G. Esel) 'ass' is from L. asellus and Gothic asīlus. F. chevet 'headboard' dim. of chef 'head' is in the eastern end of the apse, especially in French Gothic churches.
*** Also, L. carrus 'car, wagon' gives OF. chariot, a diminutive of char. The same source is responsible for ME. cart, and Ir. cairt, a diminutive of car.

sōlus, 'alone' base: sōl- + ending: -itude Engl. noun:
solitude; celeber, -bris, -bre 'frequent, thronged,'
clārus, 'clear,' fātālis, 'fateful,' fidēlis, 'faithful'
'loyal,' ferox, feroc- 'fierce,' lātus, 'wide,' multus,
'many' 'much,' pār, pāris, 'equal,' servus, 'slavish,'
ūtilis, 'useful,' varius, 'different' 'varied.'

III. Form nouns by adding the appropriate suffix to the base of
the adjective; give the etymological meaning of the
derivative, as in the example.

corp-u-lentus corp-u-lentia › corpulence, 'state of
excess weight'

Do likewise for fēcundus; fraud-u-lentus; indolens,
indolentis; jocosus; pulcher, pulchr-; regalis;
somn-o-lentus; truc-u-lentus.

IV. By translating each segment of the following words, as in
the example, determine the etymological meaning:
alt-itude = high-ness, ampl-itude, anim-os-ity, asper-ity,
civil-ity, com-ity, duplic-ity, fatu-ity, felic-ity,
long-itude, parsi-mony, partial-ity, scrupul-os-ity.

V. Separate the segments of the following words by drawing
slant lines, as illustrated. Define the words in their
current meanings:

acr/i/moni/ous rancorous or caustic in feeling,
language, or manner.

equity, jocularity, meticulous, nucleolar, palatal,
peninsula, preciosity, succulence, turpitude,
verisimilitude.

VI. Give the Latin-derived words that are synonymous, element
for element, with the following native English words:
dearness, godliness, greediness, healthiness, heaviness,
loneliness, smallmindedness (contemptible timidity),
womanliness, thankfulness, wordiness.

VII. Give the etymological meaning of: article, junior,
master, rostrum, senate.

VIII. Fill in the blanks with Latin-derived words:

a) The annual recurrence of a date marking a notable event
is an _____ . b) One records daily events in a _____ .
c) Some read a _____ daily. Its doublet, diurnal, once
meant _____ . d) A hostile or unfriendly person is _____
(adj.). e) A brief, transitory or short-lived pause is

56

_____ . f) All men are subject to death or _____ . g) Birth, or the process or being born is a _____ . h) That which relates to, or occurs in the night is _____ . i) What continues uninterruptedly year after year is _____ . j) Sir John A. Macdonald was called fox populi on account of his cunning and _____ .

IX. Determine the contextual meaning of underlined words:

1. ... thou art a boil, / A plague sore, an embossed carbuncle, / in my corrupted blood. Lear 2.4.219-21
2. The Universe is not dead and demoniacal, a charnel-house with specters .... Carlyle
3. And let us not be dainty of leave-taking. Shakespeare
4. John Heywood loved debate and intellectual dexterity.
5. 'Vous' evokes titles ..., 'tu' is the egalitarian pronoun. S. de Gramont
6. Excelsior, popular motto, has been appropriated by New York State.
7. But whither is senile garrulity leading me? Jefferson
8. My daughter has a lactose intolerance. D. Taylor (Clue: -ose is not ⟨ -osus 'full of')
9. ... an itching ear, delighting in the libellous defamation of other men Donne
10. Not, of course, that (Swinburne) had achieved a feat of longevity. Beerbohm
11. It seemed as if the millennium were dawning. W. Irving
12. Thy hopes grow timorous, and unfixed they powers, And thy clear aims be cross and shifting made; And then thy glad perennial youth would fade. Arnold
13. Wit is a propriety of thoughts and words .... Dryden
14. Astrology gives us jovial, mercurial and saturnine, terms for people's dispositions according to their 'stars.'
15. And, though her body die, her fame survives, A secular bird, ages of lives. Milton
16. There is society, where none intrudes, By the deep sea.... Byron
17. We have passed the tercentenary year of Bentley's birthday.
18. Vernal flowers, ... beautiful and gay, ... intended as preparatives to autumnal fruits S. Johnson
19. More important than the bizarre and the vestigial is the normal and the general.
20. He awoke in ... darkness with only the visceral time sense of its being 2 or 3 a.m. Pynchon
21. ... he no sooner espied a company of rabbits, but he cried aloud, 'ecce multi cuniculi....' Bacon (in S. Johnson, Dict., 1755)

57

22. Philosophical opinion in America is rooted in the genteel tradition.   Santayana
23. Lingua francas frequently serve as "trade languages."
24. A 1980 addition to our stock of words is palimony.
25. The sol is Peruvian currency. What is a parasol?
26. He was baying on about the scurrilous nature of the inscription ....   J. Metcalfe
27. The gods were local and territorial divinities. Priestley
28. Moses, Aristotle and the Christians forbid usury.
29. We want no bacchanal for this carnaval.   Trinidad Calypso (carnival is pronounced in the song so)
30. A film star obtained her fourth decree nisi. D.L. Sayers

X.   Form diminutives from these Latin nouns and adjectives:

artus 'joint,' auris 'ear,' cerebrum 'brain,' clarus 'clear,' coda 'tail,' gladius 'sword,' granum 'seed, limes 'boundary line,' minutus 'small,' modus 'measure, fashion,' moles 'mass,' nodus 'knot,' novus 'new,' nux 'nut,' pannus 'cloth,' pars 'portion,' rosa 'rose, scalprum 'knife,' tuber 'bump, swelling,' vacuus 'empty.'

XI.   Identify the language of origin of aureole, epaulet, falsetto, frisette, homunculus, lambkin, libretto, pony, punctilio, tarantula.

XII.   Do the same for baronet, briquette, brunette, castellet (castlet), chiquita, flotilla, gauntlet, globule, guerrilla, mantilla, streamlet, vermicelli.

XIII. Analyze the underlined words:

1. A given name in Spanish-speaking countries is Gladiola.
2. After a siesta, the vaquero said adios to the padre, got his palomino horse out of the corral, mounted it, and rode off to the corrida.
3. I have heard / that though the animal is singular, / Two billion particles make up a bird.   D. Hall
4. Adventurous boys dare to walk on railroad trestles.

XIV.   In whose company would you use either of the words in the following pairs: childlike, puerile; devil, Lucifer; funny, ludicrous; lucky, auspicious; mean, truculent; protective, tutelary; related, germane?

SEMANTIC CHANGE

Time has wrought many changes on word-meanings. By (1) narrowing, a word which had a large range of meaning comes to have more specified or "narrowed" uses, indicating a smaller range of things. Deer* once meant any small animal; meat, food of any sort; starve meant 'to die,' but is now used of only one kind of death. Lust meant pleasure. It now refers to intense sexual desire. Silly earlier referred to what was blessed or blissful. It now means foolish. Ninny originated as a shortening of innocent. The lilies of the field in the Bible were flowers of any sort, its fowls of the air, birds of any sort. A chambermaid in a hotel uses linen and silver in specific senses. Huntsmen use hound in a specified sense, as we do when we associate glass with a drinking vessel made of glass. In many of these cases, the broader meaning remains, so that a narrowed meaning or narrowed meanings may exist alongside the broad one(s), e.g., a copper (coin of low value) and copper, the metal. It is also a cooking/washing cauldron.

By contrast, (2) broadening occurs when a word develops a wider range of meaning than formerly. As in the case of narrowing, we again understand something different by the words in question from what those who used them previously understood. A barn originally stored only barley, a bird used to be a young fowl, a bonfire contained bones, a box was formerly made of boxwood, a butcher killed and sold goat-flesh, a larder only held bacon and a pannier, bread (cf. pantry); a steward no longer merely looks after the sties.

Shakespeare's "clamour of the host," i.e., shouting of the army, contrasts with the modern meaning of indiscriminate noise (Coriolanus 1.9.64). His "heart of generosity" (Coriolanus 1.1.212), then heart of the nobly born, now signifies liberality in spirit or act, kindness. His "comfortable" meant strengthening (Coriolanus 1.3.2, Romeo and Juliet, 5.3.148); today it means producing physical ease, restful, cozy. Virtue (Coriolanus 1.1.41) meant valor, not moral rectitude. In all these cases, only the original Latin meaning can render the poet's meaning intelligible, since their use has changed so drastically since Elizabethan times.

Some words undergo a (3) prestige-loss, cf. caitiff, knave, awful, bureaucracy, egregious, patronage, patronize, provincial, sententious. Contrariwise, alderman and penthouse apply respectively to a person and thing more highly esteemed

---

* But mice and rats, and such small deer,
  Have been Tom's food for seven long year.
  (Shakespeare, Lear, 3.4. 129-130)

than their earlier referents. Cavalier, chamberlain, fond, knight, nice, pastor and squire have risen in esteem. Genius meant a man's tutelary god or spirit, assigned to him from birth, and attendant upon him throughout his life (cf. our 'good or evil genius'). It also meant talent, natural bent or disposition, notions it still retains. By (4) elevation, it acquired the sense of inspiration and extraordinary power of invention; hence, our genius is an originator. Genie, (cf. jinn), its doublet, is a supernatural spirit often taking human form to serve his summoner.

Words may undergo either devaluation or amelioration, i.e., become pejorative or meliorative in meaning, respectively. When an adjective is complimentary, it is an epithet that flatters, e.g., comfortable, genial, prestigious, relaxed. If an epithet changes to one that is either mildly derogatory or uncomplimentary, we say it has developed a pejorative meaning. This same phenomenon affects nouns. What was originally artificial was skilfully constructed. Now artificial means fake. Egregious meant of outstanding excellence. Now it means remarkably bad. A fabulist was one who told a story or invented stories. A liar or inventor of deliberate fictions, he was originally an inventor of fictitious stories. Lībertīnus, a Roman freedman, or child of a freedman, gives libertine, a rake who indulges his desires without restraint, a debauchee. A nostrum, n. sg. of noster 'our,' was originally a medicine whose ingredients were kept secret by its manufacturers; now it is a quack medicine. Obsequious once referred to the dutifully obedient; now it identifies the overly submissive. The officious were serviceable, friendly, courteous and obliging; now they are meddlesome, and, in diplomacy, unofficial or informal. A parsimonious person was thrifty; he is now a penny-pincher. A saloon was originally a large room, e.g., the elegant dining saloon on shipboard. Now it is a drinker's haven or tavern. A sententious person was one full of judgment, but now he is pompous or ponderously trite and moralizing. If you were sanctimonious, you were holy; now you are priggish -- you pretend to be holy. Vīllānus in Rome was a 'farm laborer;' now a villain is an unprincipled character. Mister (formerly master) enjoyed much more respect than now; mistress is pejorative.

By degeneration of meaning a word comes to denote or suggest the objectionable, unpleasant, or otherwise uncomplimentary. Consider whether these are sometimes or always indicative of pejoration: amateur, animus, grandiloquent, insane, peasant, profanity, puerile, questionable, rustic, sensual, stupid, sullen, verbose, victuals (vittles), and vulgar. Most of these have been lowered in status. Senile, for instance, would normally mean 'pertaining to old-age,' but now it refers to someone who is weak with age and diminished intellectual acuity, even feeble-minded.

Conversely, by elevation of meaning, a word comes to mean something more pleasing and dignified than it did originally. Consider (Jungian) animus, chancellor, chivalrous, civil, constable, court, fame, maestro, marshal, minister, nice, premier, squire, urbane, and virtue. All tend to refer favorably to situations, events, and people. Regal, doublet of royal, suggests a splendor greater even than that surrounding a king. Majesty derives from the comparative of magis, majus, hence to a root simply meaning greater. Urbane, doublet of urban, has the added quality of suggesting elegance and refinement. Seemingly low-brow words can climb to lofty heights of nobility, if not special interest, importance or elegance.

PREFIXES

Many English words begin with a Latin prefix, placed before words or bases. When the prefix ends in a consonant, e.g., ad-, cum-, (con-, co-, cor-), in- (il-, im-), sub-, this consonant is often changed either (a) to the same consonant with which the word to which it is attached begins (e.g., affluent, connubial, immortal, suffix), or (b) to another consonant more easily pronounced in combination with the first consonant of the attached form or word (e.g., assimilation, corrugation, impression and suspension). Similarly, when the prefix -ex- is attached to words beginning with s, the s is dropped. Cf. expire from ex- + spirāre 'to breathe;' extirpate from ex- + stirpāre 'to root out,' < stirps = 'stock, stem, stalk, root;' and exude from ex + sudāre 'to sweat.' In 'escape,' which derives from a verb formed out of ex- + cappa 'cloak,' the x of ex- changes to s. Scamper is derived from the verb developed out of ex- + campus 'field;' here the x changes to s and the e is dropped. Its earlier meaning was to flee from the battlefield. Ex- may appear also in the form e-, ef-, cf. egregious and effigy. This prefix should not be confused with the adjectival ex- which means 'former,' as in ex-child actor or ex-president. Sometimes, even the base of a noun or adjective is altered slightly when compounded with a prefix; e.g., in + amīcus + -al < -ālis gives inimical, per + annus + -i- + -al gives perennial, and super + faciēs + -al gives superficial.

The most common prefixes and their meanings:

ab-	away from, off	inter-	between, among
ad-	toward, to, for	intrā-	within
ante-	before	ob-	meeting, against, to
com-, con, co-, cor, coll- very (as intensive), with		per-	through, by, to the bad, very (as intensive)
contrā-	against	prae-	previous, before
		prō-	in front of, instead of, forth, for

dē-	down, from, away	re-*	back, backward, again
dis-	separately, not, un-, apart	sē-	apart, without
		sub-	under, secretly
ex-, ē-	out of	super-	over, above, on, on top, upon, more than enough
extrā-	outside of		
il-, im-,	in, on; not	trans-*	across, through, to the other side of, into a different condition or place
īn-,			
		ultrā-	beyond

Prefixes play an important role as constructive elements in the formation of Latin words. Some Latin prefixes are separable, that is, they can be used independently as separate words, e.g., ad, in, super, trans. They appear in expressions such as in camerā, cum grāno salis, prō patriā, sub rosā. Inseparable prefixes cannot be used in this way. They adhere to some following noun, adjective or verb stem, e.g., ambi-, dis-, re-, se- (cf. ambidextrous, discrete, reform, separate). When a prefix is attached at the beginning of an English word it may, but need not, convey meaning. It may convey its literal meaning, e.g., adrenal, 'near the kidney;' peroral, 'through the mouth;' subcostal, 'under the ribs;' transcontinental, 'across the continent.' Or it may convey a metaphorical or figurative meaning, e.g., cohere, 'to stick together;' company, 'group eating bread together;' pervert, 'person turned to the bad;' profane, 'disrespectful, non-religious;' subnormal, 'under the standard, below the normal;' supermundane, 'concerning the ideal or the heavenly.' Or it may indicate an intensifying or perfecting force, e.g., corrugate, 'to wrinkle thoroughly;' inebriety, 'inveterate or habitual drunkenness;' peracid, 'very acid;' recondite, 'little known, obscure,' from the idea contained in the verb condere 'to store away, conceal;' surexcitation, 'increased irritability, arousal to action or excitement,' from excitāre 'to arouse.'

Exercise V

I.   Determine how the prefix is used in each of the following words. Is it literal, figurative, intensive? aboriginal, ante-bellum, circumoral, consort, dementia, discord, egregious, immortal, infracostal, interdentium, irresuscitable, obnoxious, post-bellum, perfidy, prejudice, pronoun, proverb, refrigerant, subacid,

---

* re- (red- before vowels) and trans- (tra-) are used in the formation of compound verbs rather than nouns; retro- 'back(ward); behind' is similarly used.

subfusk, supercilious, supernumerary, suprarenal, transhuman, transmaterial, ultrastellar.

II. English is so versatile that it has adopted certain Latin prefixes for occasional use as nouns; e.g., sub stands for a submarine in a snack-bar or an ocean vessel; pro stands for a professional in sport or the theatre; an ex may be a former spouse or erstwhile friend.

a) Show how 'extra' and 'pros and cons' serve as nouns.
b) When we say an ad, do we use the L. prefix as a noun? What do we mean when we say "the super"?
c) What is a nonpareil performance?
d) Explain a preposterous proposal.
e) Etymologically speaking, what is a consort? a contre-temps?
f) In prison talk, what is a con? This is clipped from _____.
g) What is a quid pro quo? (Clue: quid is an indefinite pronoun: 'what thing,' 'something').
h) In poker, a stake that must be put into the pool before the cards are dealt is an _____.
i) Super is used now as an exclamation of approval. What are some word combinations in which it expresses intense meanings?
j) What does the novel combination de-hire mean?

III. a) Using appropriate prefixes and negator (non), form the negative of favor, flammable, legal, noble, responsible, tasteful, temperate, transigent, union, vocal.

b) Johnson defined "wit" as "a kind of discordia concors, a combination of dissimilar images, or discovery of occult resemblances in things apparently unlike." Comment on the underlined words.

c) In 1866, Leonard Tilley, impressed by Psalm 72.8, provided the motto for Canada 'a mari usque ad mare.' Do you consider this appropriate? Define the phrase.

d) "They are at a loss, and their understanding is perfectly at a nonplus." Locke   Nōn is a negating prefix and plus is an adjective; what part of speech is nonplus?

IV. Pronounce the following homographs which are differentiated by the stress or accent given to a certain part of a word, and which is shifted to indicate an alternative meaning: compact, conduct, contest, contrast, object, perfect, record, subject. Note also that when you

65

unvoice the final consonant sound you get a different meaning for close, house, mouth, and use.

V.   Words compounded with non (non-) may be:

a) pejorative, b) privative, c) euphemistic or prestigious, or d) technically legal in meaning.

Indicate how the following compounds would be categorized: nonadult (contrast: minor), nonappearance, nonart, nonbelligerent, non-book, noncitizen (contrast; alien), nonclaim;   nondescript,   nonevent,   nonfiction, nonintoxicating, nonlaughter, nonmarital, non-military, non-nuclear, nonparent, nonpartisan, nonpublic (contrast: private), nonreader (contrast: illiterate), nonsalaried (contrast: unpaid),   nonsense,   nonsuit,   nontenure, nonverbal, nonviolence.*

SEXISM IN LANGUAGE

Many women have been made to feel like non-persons because of the use of masculine pronouns and words, like chairman and spokesman, to designate a position or job-title irrespective of the gender of the person occupying the post.   In French, a movement is under foot to change this situation so that such words as la professeur, la psychiatre, la directrice may come into full play. English has paid lip service to the feminizing principle, so that we do have words such as aviatrix, benefactress, executrix, huntress, mediatrix, equestrienne, stewardess, actress and waitress.   Thanks to legal consider- ations, administratrix, heiress and testatrix are in good standing, but the very word 'female' which a 19c writer might use for 'woman' is now a largely scientific sex-discriminator when it is not being used in otherwise generic ways.

Incidentally, there is no linguistic relationship between male (from L. masculus) and female (from L. fēmina). L. fēmina gave rise to the diminutive L. femella, which became OF. femelle, then ME. femelle. Meanwhile, L. masculus had moved through OF. to ME. male. People came to believe that the similar words male and femelle were related and, in accordance with the male dominance tendencies of folk-etymology, began to spell femelle so that it would accord with male. F. limits the use of femelle to animals, and femmelette has been overtaken by 'petite femme.'

_____

* Consult J. Algeo's article in American Speech 46 (1971) 87-105: "The voguish uses of non."

L. mātrona 'married woman' conveys the notion of dignity, responsibility and virtue. Lucretia, Brutus' Portia and Octavia come to mind. The responsibility and dignity of our matron is of a different kind. The title is given to women's prison administrators, the head nurse in a hospital, and the woman in charge of students' living arrangements at boarding schools. As a dress-size classifier, matron is not associated with beauty or grace but rather with portliness. Mātrona, like mamma 'a breast' and mammāre 'to give suck,' has the root ma- 'making, measuring.' It is the root pa-, which appears in pastor, pabulum, pater, patron, that means 'feeding.' In contrast to the rather formidable connotations now associated with matron, a patron or patroness tends always to befriend.

With and despite the intrusion of women into formerly male spheres, the feminine suffix is falling into disuse. Poetess, sculptress and authoress are abandoned and their masculine counterparts are used for both sexes. Other job titles now seen as gender-free are doctor, reporter, worker, teacher, supervisor, and manager, which are now used commonly for both sexes. There is increasing use of chairperson and chairwoman in place of, or in addition to, chairman; but Madame Chairman may also be used in addressing the Chair. Another recent development is the title Ms. to replace both Miss and Mrs. because, like Mr., it does not differentiate between the married and the unmarried.

In French there is a strong tendency for male professional titles to be used for women coupled with the feminine address, e.g., Madame le ministre, Madame le docteur, le professeur, l'administrateur, le directeur, despite the efforts noted above to increase the use of the feminine form. Both putain (f.) and gigolo (m.), however, remain firmly attached to just one sex. 18c amatrice tried to obtain citizenship in France in vain: we adopted the masculine French noun, amateur, and, regardless of sex, so we all remain.

There is a tendency in language, perhaps due to patriarchal influence, to give pejorative meanings to feminine nouns, e.g., cow, bitch, sow sound different to the ear from their masculine counterparts; this might partly be because feminine nouns are specific while their masculine counterparts usually refer to the whole class e.g., pigs, Man. Perhaps with women's greater outspokenness and involvement in intellectual and political activities, we may see the emergence of more derogatory 'male' terms from the previously submerged, or ignored, half of our society.

We have still a long way to go to eliminate sexism in our language. However editor Susan Lloyd, as she revises Roget's Thesaurus, changes mankind to humankind, countryman to country dweller, rich man to rich person. She still retains master and mistress, perhaps essential because of the latter's pejorative connotation which is absent from the former.

LATIN NUMERALS

Latin numerals provide simple and compound derivatives and perhaps, most importantly, multiple-base compounds such as uniform, bilingual, trigenerational, quadripartite, quinquennium, sextuplets, septempartite, octogenarian, nonillion and decillion.

Cardinals		Ordinals	
ūnus	1	prīmus	'first'
duo (bi-)	2	secundus*	'second'
trēs (tri-)	3	tertius	'third'
quattuor (quadri-)	4	quārtus	'fourth'
quīnque	5	quīntus*	'fifth'
sex	6	sextus*	'sixth'
septem	7	septimus*	'seventh'
octō	8	octāvus	'eighth'
novem	9	nonus	'ninth'
decem	10	decimus*	'tenth'
centum	100	centē(n)simus	1/100
mīlle	1000	mīllē(n)simus	1/1000

* N.B. Asterisked ordinals were sometimes Latin praenomina 'first names.'

DISTRIBUTIVES

singulī*	'1 each'	novēnī	'9 each'
bīnī	'2 each'	dēnī	'10 each'
trīnī or ternī	'3 each'	quīnquāgēnī	'50 each'
quaternī	'4 each'	sexāgēnī	'60 each'
quīnī	'5 each'	septuāgēnī	'70 each'
senī	'6 each'	octōgēnī	'80 each'
septēnī	'7 each'	nōnāgēnī	'90 each'
octōnī	'8 each'	centēnī	'100 each'

mīllēnī '1,000 each'

NUMERAL ADVERBS

sēsqui	'one and a half times'**
bis	'twice'
ter	'three times, thrice'
quater	'four times'

---

* In all distributives, the final i is long.
** Torontonians know Seskwee Squirrēl at City Hall. See Ex. VI, I.10.

Etymological notes.

Like our Christian or given name, the Latin praenōmen was the first or personal name. Romans could be named Secundus, Quintus, Sextus, Decimus. From L. decem 'ten,' and L. decuria 'a military division of ten,' > ME. dycer we get dicker, meaning ten, or ten hides. Five pairs of gloves were once a dicker. To dicker meant to barter in respect to a lot of 10 furs. Now it is to haggle over a price or trade on a small scale. From L. decimus 'tenth,' > OF. disme 'a tithe, tenth,' > ME. dyme, disme, we get dime.

Siesta, from the Spanish nap taken at the hottest part of the day, comes from L. sexta hora 'sixth hour,' or midday since, from Roman times, the day started at 6 a.m.

A hospital* founded in Paris by St. Louis for 300 blind persons was called the Quinze Vingts when it was the custom to count by multiples of twenty.

From L. centum 'hundred,' F. has quintal, It., quintale, and Sp., quintal 'a hundredweight.' But when it is a metric unit of weight, it equals 100 kilograms or 220.46 pounds. Quintal does not derive from L. quīntus + ālis. What does come from quīntus is our quint, quintan (fever), quintessence, and quintet. Quint is colloquial for quintuplet. Roman public games celebrated every five years were the Quinquennalia. Rome's July was once mensis Quintilis, August, mensis Sextilis because the first month was then March.

EXERCISE VI

I.   Give etymological and current meanings (or fill in):

1.   Greeks made binary, not ternary, divisions of the objects of experience.

2.   Kissinger heads Reagan's bipartisan national commission on Central America.

3.   An Italian toast invites you to become a centenarian, a Polish toast, a millenarian.

---

* 11c F. hôtel 'abode' precedes F. hôpital by a good century. In 1190, F. hôpital meant charitable establishment, and did not minister exclusively to the sick. Hotel, hospital and hostel are triplets.

70

4. The future Golden Age of Millenarianism is as impossible a notion as the past Golden Age of Mythology. Julian Huxley

5. How many years transpire between one's having become a nonagenarian after having attained to the age of an octogenarian?

6. At age 66, Dodo Cheney is 14 years from reaching _____ status.

7. Of the students who wrote the examination, she placed in the second quartile.

8. September is the 9th month in the calendar, October, November and December the 10th, 11th, and 12th. What is inconsistent about this?

9. The Septuagint was the work of 72 Palestinian Jews in the 3c B.C. who completed it in seventy days.

10. In what year will Canada celebrate its sesquicentennial? Does it precede or postdate Toronto's for which sesquifestivities began on March 6, 1984?

11. Between the U.S. and the U.S.S.R. is that tertium quid, China.

12. Triennial elections or parliaments are not common. The quadrennial Olympics are de rigueur.

13. Trivial may derive not from très viae but from trivium, which, in the Middle Ages, meant the course of three arts, grammar, logic and rhetoric, a more ordinary curriculum than the more abstruse quadrivium which embraced music, arithmetic, geometry and astronomy.

14. "Church unity" sometimes resembles too closely that peculiar union which the boa-constrictor is so fond of consummating between itself and the goat. W. Matthews

15. A univocal word is opposed to a(n) _____, which has two or more significations.

II. a) To what category, figurative or literal use, does each word in the following pairs belong: limb, limbo, native, naive, onion, union, urban, urbane?

71

b) Separate the following words and pair them off as learned or popular: anile, bit, chubby, corpulent, depth, felicity, happiness, kingly, lonely, meal, modicum, profundity, repast, royal, secular, solitary, worldly, old-womanish.

III. In Lesson II, we became familiar with Latin adverbs which have made their way into English as nouns, adjectives or adverbs. Here are some adverbial expressions which you can introduce into your own English sentences: ā fortiōrī, ā posteriōrī, ā priōrī, circā, and prō formā.

Exercise VII

REVIEW

A. Men pass through infantile, puerile, juvenile, virile, anile, and senile stages. One of these words, _____, does not have a pejorative connotation. Fill in. Give the word's etymology and current meaning.

B. Distinguish between intramural and intermural athletics. What is meant by extramural activities?

C. Is ad hoc a noun, adjective or adverb in "He spoke ad hoc to the issue."?

D. What Latin word supplies the base in legal, loyal? in ordinal, ordinary? Is the meaning of the base reflected in the current meanings of each? If so, show how.

E. Three of the four "humors" or fluids are found in the human body; 'black bile' is imaginary. Name them. Give an equivalent English derivative for the Latin word.

F. Give 'popular' synonyms for equine, vulpine.

G. Give etymology and current meaning of plenary. What does the Russian Plenum imply in respect to expected attendance?

H. Distinguish between seminar and seminary. Give the root word's etymological meaning. Prove that crude and ecru are doublets.

I. The Office of None was said in Chapel. Analyze None. Give its etymology and current meaning.

J. She sent her CV to a potential employer.

K. What is the Latin for 'spark'? Give the triplets.

L.   Dryden's humor was <u>saturnine</u> and reserved.

M.   Though well conceived, it happens to be <u>otiose</u>.

N.   Every Roman male made sacrifice to his <u>Genius</u> on his birthday.

O.   For the 'learned' equivalent give the 'popular':

   a) digital _____   c) mundane _____
   b) germane to _____   d) febrile _____.

P.   Genteel forms quadruplets with:_____, _____, and _____.

Q.   Using an appropriate suffix, form an English derivative from the Latin compound adjective in each case:

   L. <u>vulgus</u> 'the crowd,'   L. <u>rēx, rēgis</u> 'king _____.
            'the masses' _____
   L. <u>carō, carnis</u> 'flesh' _____   L. <u>vetus, veteris</u> 'old' ___.

R.   Give the Latin origin of: doge, Duce L. _____, genre, gender L. _____, dainty, dignity L. _____, czar, Tsar, Kaiser L. _____.

S.   Things connected with the young are called _____.

T.   Select the words which have undergone specialization of meaning: album, coroner, humor, minister, nostrum, sane.

U.   From L. <u>quiētus</u> and VL. <u>quētus</u>, we have F. <u>coi</u>, <u>coite</u> 'calm, tranquil, peaceful' which gives E. _____.

V.   _____ are the symbols of a king or queen (insignia and decorations of an office or order). Show the word's components.

W.   Define amicus curiae, arbor vitae, dies irae dies illa,* jus naturae, mos majorum,** ultra vires, vox populi.

X.   Sir Thomas More used the _____ language to write his <u>Utopia</u>.

Y.   What forms provide our nouns optimum and vacuum?

Z.   Romans named the Mediterranean _____ _____. This means literally _____ _____.

---

* the <u>diēs īrae</u> ... is now often included in the Requiem Mass.
** see <u>vocabulary</u> under <u>majōres</u>.

73

EXERCISE VIII

I.   Analyze the following words by dividing them into segments
      and by giving the meaning of each segment; then, give the
      current definition as in the example provided.

      equinoctial   equ /i/noct/i/al   aequ-us 'equal'; -i,
      connecting vowel; nox, noct-is 'night;' -i, connecting
      vowel; -alis 'pertaining to,' 'having the character of,'
      'belonging to,' 'appropriate to'; current meaning:
      "characterized by equal length of days and nights."
      atrabilious, condign, impervious, inert, infirmary,
      nepotal, obliquity, plenilunar, security, supersonic,
      triumvirate, vermiform.

II.   Provide a synonym or synonymous expression for these
      adjectives: aboriginal, corporal, declivitous, devious,
      equivocal, jejune, penultimate, secular, semiobscure,
      terraqueous, ursine, vituline.

III. Separate these into segments. Define each segment and the
      word: binaural, contemporary, deity, paternity,
      semiferal, triform.

IV.   Determine contextual meaning or fill in blanks:

      1. To walk is to adopt the gait of a biped.

      2. His debility was extreme.

      3. Trujillo embarked on a grandiose project.

      4. The notion that artist or writer thrives best in
         poverty gives rise to the expression "angelic
         impecuniosity."

      5. It is fitting that a queen be Junoesque.

      6. He had a sudden moment of lucidity .... Conrad

      7. The quasi-dragon was a curious creature, a
         bare-breasted woman lupine from the waist down.

      8. The department's members approved the thesis topic by
         a formal vote, nem. con. (Clue: nemo = 'no one')

      9. Social legislation must be pro bono publico.

      10. Puisneship designates the office and function of a
          puisne judge. F. puis né derives from Latin _____
          natus (born).

74

11. Let it be named from the fishes that swim in it, the wild fowl or <u>quadrupeds</u> which frequent it. Thoreau

12. Corroborative detail is intended to give artistic <u>verisimilitude</u> to an unconvincing narrative. Gilbert

13. An <u>inter vivos</u> trust differs from a testementary trus<u>t</u>.

14. Anyone wishing to help the editor comb bibliographies may submit a <u>vita</u>.

15. The _____ inscription on the Rosetta Stone was <u>deciphered by</u> the Egyptologist, Champollion. (Clue: in three languages)

16. A child's tricycle is otherwise known as a _____. In French Canada this is a 'scooter.' (Clue: a grown-up rides a <u>vélo</u>)

17. When we show resemblance to a remote ancestor in some characteristic which nearer ancestors do not have we show an _____ trait.

18. The right of primogeniture is that of the _____ son to inherit his father's estate.

19. An archbishop, or the highest-ranking bishop in a province is a _____. The most highly developed order of mamma<u>ls are the</u> _____.

20. The French word for fortnight, based on the number 15, is _____.

Another name for a cat is a feline, for a cow, a bovine, for a sea bear or fur seal, the ursine seal. One who acts like a sheep is ovine.

V. a) Fill in the blanks in the following sentences by forming Latin derivatives from among the following words: <u>fēlis</u> 'cat, <u>taurus</u> 'bull,' <u>canis</u> 'dog,' <u>equus</u> 'horse,' <u>leo</u> 'lion,' <u>asīnus</u> 'donkey, ass,' <u>vulpēs</u> 'fox,' <u>simīa</u> 'monkey,' <u>lupus</u> 'wolf,' <u>piscis</u> 'fish,' <u>rana</u> 'frog,' <u>aquila</u> 'eagle,' <u>musca</u> 'fly.'

1) A curved or hooked nose is said to be _____.
2) If we are as silly as asses, we are _____.
3) The _____ burglar was a cat. 4) The care and management of the _____ is taught in equine care courses. 5) If we <u>wolf</u> our food down, we evince a _____ appetite. 6) A Spanish diminutive of our

ordinary housefly is the _____. 7) If we swim as fast as a fish, we have _____ speed. 8) Anyone who acts like a monkey displays _____ behavior. 9) If we are as strong as bulls we have _____ strength. 10) The zodiac sign, _____, has the shape of a bull. 11) Because they were full of wild dogs, explorers named them the _____ Islands. 12) Statues of men riding horses are called _____ statues. 13) The zodiac sign, Pisces, is shaped like _____. 14) A place where fish are kept, other than an aquarium, is a _____. 15) A bull-fighter in Spain is called a _____. 16) The genus Rana refers to _____. 17) Both a church dignitary and a small scarlet bird bear the same name, _____.* 18) If you are confronted with a foxy thief, you are dealing with a tricky, _____ person. 19) Cozzens says the prof. casts pearls before young simian primates. They are like _____. 20) Ursa Major is otherwise known as the _____ _____.

b) Determine the etymology of millepore, minuet, porpoise, quatrain, usher. c) Analyze and give the current meanings of aquamarine, duress, penumbra, sesquipedalian, supercilious. d) Analyze the underlined word: 'Muskox' is a misnomer, for muskoxen neither produce musk, nor are they bovines.

VI. Combine the appropriate forms (prefix, noun base, adjectival/noun ending) to form English words, as in the example provided.
suprā 'above' + norma 'standard' + -ālis 'pertaining to' = supranormal. N.B. In a few cases, a noun or adjective's base is altered by vowel gradation (Lesson XI) when compounded with a prefix.

bīnī 'two each'	+ oculus	+ -āris	_____
centum 'a hundred'	+ pēs, pedis (insert connecting vowel)		_____
cum (> co-)	+ aevum	+ -ālis	_____
cum (> coll-)	+ latus, lateris	+ -ālis	_____
cum (> con-)	+ genius	+ -ālis	_____
cum (> corr-)	+ ruptiō-ōnis (a breaking)		_____
dis (F. de-)	+ fāma		_____
in (> ill-)	+ lex, legis	+ -ālis	_____

---

* (Clue: think of the bird with the fine red plumage.)

* 21. If 17 was hard, try this one: St. Louis' Busch Stadium is called the 'aviary' for its players, the St. Louis _____.

in (> imm-)	+ mors, mortis	+ -alis
in (> im-)	+ pecūnia + -ōsus	+ -ītas _____
in (> im-)	+ pervius	
in (> im-)	+ pūrus	+ -itas _____
in	+ aptus (short a changes to e)	+ -ītudo _____
in	+ aequus	+ -itas _____
in	+ amīcus (short a changes to i)	+ -ālis _____
intra	+ urbs, urbis	+ -anus
medius	+ aevum	+ -ālis _____
per (> pell-)	+ lūcidus 'clear, shining	_____
per	+ annus (insert connecting vowel; short a changes to e)	+ -alis _____
prae	+ judicium	+ -alis _____
prae	+ marītus (adj. 'marriage-')	+ -ālis _____
primus	+ aevum	+ -alis _____
se	+ cūra	_____
sēmi (> sin-)	+ caput, capitis (short a changes to i)	_____
super	+ cilium 'eye lid'	+ -osus _____
super	+ faciēs (short a changes to i)	+ -ālis _____
ūnus + i-	+ camera	+ -alis _____

VII. Give the correct spelling of words composed of the following elements:

1) ad + nullus = _____, (verb) 2) cōntra + LL. bandum 'proclamation,' = _____, 3) cum + fortis 'strong,' = _____, 4) cum + fīnis, fīnis 'end,' = _____, 5) sub + tēla 'web,' = _____ (adjective).

VIII. Define: ē plūribus ūnum; nē plūs ultrā; post hoc, ergō propter hoc; prīmus inter parēs; sine* irā et studiō;* sine quā nōn; sub speciē.
*(Clues: sine 'without,' studiō, abl. of studium 'passion.')

IX. Define the underlined words in the context:

1. Old Bytowners tell of fights that ended conclusively in the cauldron beneath Chaudière Falls. Cdn Geog. Jl.

2. My heart is at your festival,
My head hath its coronal. Wordsworth

77

3. St. Augustine's philosophy of history ... leads, de facto though not de jure, to carelessness with detail. G.L. Keyes

4. Brooklyn ... became ... an asphalt herbarium for talent destined to cross the river. Mailer

5. There has always been something preternatural about paths .... Malcolm Lowry

6. And one keen pyramid with wedge sublime,
Pavilioning the dust of him who planned
This refuge for his memory, doth stand. Shelley

X. (a) Form a derivative for each of the following adjectival prefixes:

centi-, curvi-, lati-, longi-, milli-, multi-, nulli-, omni-, recti-.

(b) Find five negating particles in: It is listless prudery, a faint malaise of disrelish, a settled inappetency that finds ... eroticism unpleasant. Do these exhaust the list of negating particles?

(c) What factors have predetermined the development of franglais in Canada? e.g., la preuve is in le pudding.

(d) Is the blend or mixture apparent in franglais jocular?

(e) Form abstract nouns from the multiplicative numerals: simplex 'single,' duplex 'double, two-fold,' and multiplex 'manifold.'

XI. Match words in List A with appropriate counterparts in List B.

List A: 1) condign, 2) egregious, 3) illegitimate, 4) inaugural, 5) infamous, 6) injudicious, 7) inseparable, 8) interstellar, 9) obnoxious, 10) profane, 11) sovereign, 12) supersonic.

List B: a) traitor, b) speed, c) space, d) swearing, e) person, f) companion, g) ruler, h) choice, i) swearing-in ceremony, j) error, k) punishment, l) offspring.

XII. Determine the meaning of the prefix in: 1) aboriginal, 2) anteroom, 3) circumlocution, 4) consort, 5) inflammable, 6) interregnum, 7) promontory, 8) secure, 9) sinecure, 10) superficies.

XIII. Distinguish the meanings of the words in the following pairs:

a) declassify, subclassify   e) non-moral, immoral
b) international, intranational   f) Pacific power,
c) material, materiel   pacific power
d) median, average   g) rigid, sub-rigid

XIV. a) Which of the following are native (resident) words in English and which adopted:

canticle, die (verb), farrago, fish, incunabula, intercellular, jocular, primeval, sing, street, tendency, venture, word?

b) What do these prepositions mean: (in) re:, qua, pace?

XV. Give the etymology of the underlined words; explain their meanings or fill in the blanks (in 3 and 4, doubly underlined):

1. Artillery, basso, chiaroscuro, maestro, piano, soprano are borrowed words. Italian was felt to be superior to express these ideas.

2. A dicker of gloves involves _____ pairs.

3. Cognate with IE. *bhrāter, Greek phrater, Skt. bhratr, Romany Gypsy pral and our slang pal is L. ==========, a doublet of friar and Sp. Fray. (*conjectural form, hypothesized word)

4. Cognate with Skt. panca, Greek pente, Slavic (Russian) pyat', Latin quīnque, Oscan pump, Irish cuig, and Welsh pimp is English ================

5. What was the ancient Greek or Roman quadrireme?

6. Man is not a quadruped, but a _____ .

7. Men may securely sin, but safely never.   Ben Jonson

POPULAR OR FOLK-ETYMOLOGY

Nome, Alaska gets its name from the question "Name?" scrawled by a cartographer over a formerly undesignated area. But, by a reverse process, folks make up names for persons, places and things.

Popular etymology is the production of a new word by a speaker or writer who associates some foreign or unfamiliar term with one he knows on the basis of a fancied resemblance in the sounds of both. Analogously, he confuses the meaning of the old word and corrupts its spelling to form the new word. Posthumous, originally written without h, is derived from L. postumus, superlative of post 'after.' It means 'coming later or last.' The second element was mistakenly derived from its supposed etymon, humus 'earth, ground,' so the word came to be written with the h, identified with burial, later with death. Newfoundland's Baie d'Espoir is now Bay Despair. Buttery < ME. botery, botelrye < OF. boteillerie < L. botaria < bota (butta) 'cask' is not related to butter. It is a storeroom for liquor. Cutlas < F. coutelas < L. cultellus 'knife' owes its spelling to an imagined connection with cut, a Celtic verb.

Jeopardy < F. jeu parti > Chaucer: jupartie; this abstract noun meant 'even game, uncertain chance.' Now it means 'peril.' Salt-cellar < OF. salier 'salt-box' < L. salārium 'vessel for holding salt' gave salter. A redundant addition gave salt-saler, whence the corruption of salt-cellar. The original word had no relation to cellar. Surround < OF. suronder < L. super 'over + undāre 'to flow around,' the denominative verb of unda 'wave,' gave surround because of an erroneous pronunciation. The second element has nothing to do with round. Pantry derives from L. panis > OF. paneterie 'bread room;' it is falsely associated with pans. ML. lardārium < lar(i)dum 'the fat of bacon, lard, > OF. lardier > AF. larder illustrates how a word may retain its etymological meaning intact. As verb, it means to slaughter.

Ros marīnus, 'sea dew,' misunderstood, became rosemary. Sirloin is from a hypothetical OF. surloigne, frm sur 'over,' + longe 'loin'; there is a legend that the cut was knighted for its excellence, hence the misspelling 'sir.' After the Norman Conquest Greek kerasos 'cherry tree,' whence L. cerasus, cerasia, gave rise to AF. cherise. English speakers took this as plural, and back-formed a singular cherry. We do, however, retain a doublet cerise (the s is kept), later adopted from French. Similarly sg. L. pīsum 'pea,' became OE. pise and a singular pea was back-formed. Shay also lost an s (cf. F. chaise) because chaise was thought a plural. We do retain it in chaise longue (mispronounced lounge). Cognate with L. aqua is AS. īeg which, in combination with land, forms the basis of īgland ('water-land'). Island is contaminated by OF. isle (< L. insula) which supplies the s that replaces the original Anglo-Saxon g. The medial s showed up in 1546, a pedantic intrusion from L. insula. It was perhaps believed that isle was a dimin. of insula, so s comes into our spelling where g should have been.

Although sullen derives from solus + ānus, i.e., 'pertaining to one who remains alone,' hence, 'gloomy,' and solemn derives from sollus 'all, entire' and annus 'year,' and usually referred to something sacred or ceremonial, they may be falsely considered etymologically related. Shakespeare sensed that they were unrelated; Romeo & Juliet 4.5: 'Our solemn hymns to sullen dirges change.' Here solemn means ceremonial or festal.

Victor Hugo illustrates what happens when Latin-less Frenchmen attempt a haphazard meaning for "Tu Ora," "Pray Thou," under the window of the cell of Roland's tower in Paris. "The common people ... gave to this dark ... hole the name of Trou aux Rats." The second element of 'surround' has nothing to do with round. The Latin forms producing the word are super 'over' and undāre 'to flow.'

In earlier English, surround, quite logically, meant 'to overflow.' Its equivalent, F. suronder, influenced our spelling, and the spelling subsequently influenced the change in meaning. A legitimate derivation is that of the verb 'to sound' from LL. subundāre 'to go underwater,' whence F. sonder, E. sound (verb).

Dialectical and popular sparrow-grass, earlier sparagrass, is a corruption of sparagus (asparagus). Gk. asparagos, 'plant shoot, sprout,' is akin to Gk. spargan 'to swell.' When the sound, meaning or spelling of a word is affected by a haphazard association, the phenomenon produces unusual results.

Thanks to children's pronunciation, we end up with F. tante, 'aunt.' Our aunt is from L. amita; in OF. the word was pronounced ante-ante, but children said tante. The F. dent de lion became our dandelion. Chaise longue became chaise lounge because people wanted to relate F. longue to the better-known or better-understood word lounge. Thomas Muffet tells us that "Frenchmen think a Pheasant is called Faisain because it makes a sound man (il fait sain)." Humble-pie is really made of numbles, an OF. word for lumbulus, a small cut from the loin or lumbar (F. loigne) part of the animal.

Soldiers playing a practical joke may apple-pie your bed.

'In apple-pie order' derives from F. nappe pliée en ordre. F. plier < L. plicāre 'to fold' also gives 'pie' in 'pie your bed, and in 'apple-pie bed.' In neither case is the dessert a legitimate etymological source. L. pīca 'magpie' is the source of pie; it habitually collects oddments, a pie contains miscellaneous items.

Hocus pocus, a formula once used only by jugglers, is now generalized to refer to any nonsense cloaking deception. Some falsely think it comes from 'hoc est corpus meum,' = "this is my body," but it is really an abbreviation of a 16c imitation Latin phrase: 'hac pax max Deus adimax.'

Samuel Johnson mistakenly derived nincompoop, actually of Dutch origin, meaning a relative of a clown or fool, from nōn compos (mentis) 'not in possession of one's mind.'

A derivation based on popular tradition and hearsay evidence is that of Italia from Italus, an ancient king. L. vitulus 'calf' gave Vitalia (cf. Oscan Vitelliu), whence Italia, presumably for the excellence and abundance of its cattle. Another mistaken derivation is that of Rome from its legendary founder, Romulus. Nor is it convincing that Rome comes from Gk. rhōmē 'strength, force, army.' Both Romulus and Rome are probably Etruscan names.

Roman polishers of marble sometimes gave their stones a coat of wax which, melting and running, would leave a dull, rough finish on the unpolished stones. By contrast, polishers would label their wares as sine cēra 'without wax,' or 'unwaxed.' A fake etymology would derive our word sincere from this practice, but the word derives from IE. *sem- + *kero- which became sim-kero- and yielded sin-kero- 'of one growth, not adulterated or mixed.' Hence, L. sincērus 'clean, pure, sound, genuine, unadulterated' is the true origin of sincere. While neither Gk. kēros nor L. cēra 'wax' has anything to do with L. sincērus or English sincere, there is 'wax' in kerosene, a word a Haligonian, Dr. Abraham Gesner coined in 1852. He also invented the process which gave the world kerosene oil. Besides its use in lamps, stoves, and industry this oil helps preserve strawberries. At one time it was forced in large doses on truant boys (A Concise Dictionary of Canadianisms, 130). The -ene ending may come from L. -ēnus** (cf. -ānus) which, attached to a noun-base, indicates place, or origin: cf. L. terrēnus and modern L. Americānus.

---

* hypothetical IE. forms are so indicated.
** See 'place relationships' ending, #12, Lesson III

A QUIZ ON ABBREVIATIONS

Eric Partridge tells us that when an official uses ult., inst., and prox., he has been contaminated by commercialese. We are all familiar with the clipped show-biz, gent, prof, specs, sitcom, and vet. Nor do we have any trouble with the meaning of per cent.

A. What do the following abbreviations mean:

a) L.s.d. 2) 8vo, or 8° 3) duet 4) quartet 5) a.m.
6) p.m. 6) A.D. 7) ad lib 8) ca. 9) loc. cit.*
10) op. cit. 11) v.i. 12) v.t. 13) A.M.D.G. ?

B. Folio and quarto are ablatives from the phrases in folio, in quarto. The next smaller size of page is in octavo. 1) What is a history in ten volumes f.? 2) Write out the abbreviation for quarto. 3) Give the term for the centigrade system of division, graduated into a hundred equal parts. 4) What is the shortened form of U.S. slang 'oll correct?' 5) What does o.p. mean in a bookseller's catalogue?

---

* = 'in the place cited (quoted)' and 10) = 'in the work...'

LESSON VII

MORE COMPOUND NOUNS

We saw earlier how diminutives, a type of compound noun, the Latin endings for which were listed, are formed. One French ending we borrow is -et (-ette), sometimes attached to the base of a Latin noun, e.g., coronet, statuette, turret, tablet, calumet (originally, calam-). Italian gives us gazette, and cittadella 'little city' in citadel. We may contrast F. novelette and It. novella.

Another Latin ending which forms a compound noun is -ātus, > -ate 'office of,' 'group having a common purpose,' 'period or holder of office of,' e.g., principate. (Formed on a denominative verb base, however, is candidate. L. candidātus derives from L. candēre 'to be a glowing white.' Candidus, which gives us candid, means 'bright;' albus, whence album, is a lusterless white. A candidātus wore an artifically whitened toga to symbolize personal purity). Cf. electorate, magistrate, priorate, senate. The adjectives probate and reprobate also serve as verbs. Denominative verbs, which we look at later, give, e.g., abbreviate, elongate, inaugurate, officiate. From denominative verbs, we tend to form nouns by adding the agent ending -or; cf. dictator, testator, vitiator, denominator, equator. (See Lesson IX)

EXERCISE IX

Analyze the underlined words:

I.
1. 'False as a bulletin' became a proverb in Napoleon's time. Carlyle (N.B. It. diminutives may end in - ello, -ella, - etto, - etta (with this cf. F. - et, - ette), and -ino, -ina: cf. bollettino, signorina).

2. I'm very good at integral and differential calculus. Gilbert

3. Cartoon and cartouche are not diminutives, but augmentatives.* What about cartel?

4. Oxford has maisonnettes.

5. What type of flower is the noisette?

6. The German lady likes operettas.

7. The M.A. thesis may be an opuscule of 80 pages.

85

8. She was <u>pommeled</u> by her assailant.

9. They listened to a <u>sextet</u>.

10. How undesirable it is to build the <u>tabernacle</u> of our
brief lifetime out of <u>permanent</u> <u>materials</u>.
Hawthorne

   * suffixes or prefixes which increase in force the
   idea conveyed; by ext., words formed from such
   affixes, e.g., generalissimo, ultraconservative.

II.   Some words conceal their original spellings, e.g., acorn,
belfry, brandy, bus*, cab*, canter*, chum*, cockroach,
coed, crayfish, cute, gin (both drink and machine), mob*,
primrose, Romance (language), varsity*.

   a)   Trace the words to their original spellings.

   b)   Determine the meanings and spell out the underlined
   parts of prō and <u>con</u>., prō <u>tem</u>., vox <u>pop</u>.

   c)   Abbreviated L. ablatives are: <u>aet</u>., <u>m</u>., <u>no</u>., <u>prox</u>.,
   <u>ult</u>. Determine their meanings <u>and</u> their <u>original</u> L.
   <u>forms</u>.

   d)   What does condo abbreviate? co-op?

EUPHEMISM

A euphemism is a more pleasant-sounding word which has
been substituted for an offensive one. Many euphemisms derive
from Latin or Greek, but sometimes the ancient language
derivative has itself become offensive and is itself euphemized:
"A shorn crown... a euphemism for decapitation." Froude. We
have less distasteful words or expressions to correspond to and
substitute for those more exactly descriptive in expire for die,
viscera (or, in another sense, intestinal fortitude) for guts,
parlor for bar (or saloon), electroconvulsive therapy (or
electrostimulation) for shock treatment, mucus for snot,
expectorate for spit, perspire for sweat, courtesan for
prostitute, deuce for devil, footwear for shoes, funeral director
for undertaker, hairdresser for barber, inexpensive for cheap,
office cleaner for charwoman, unfit houses for slum and vendeuse
for shopgirl. Not to cause pain or embarrassment to ourselves
and others, we avoid plain speaking. Euphemisms occur in the
business world in less emotive and more aesthetic context, e.g.,

---

* Other clipped words: (stage-) prop, curio, wig.

to enhance one's mental state vis-à-vis a service offered. A barber shop becomes a tonsorial parlor and even a beauty shop becomes an Aphrodite or Venus salon. Beer saloons become taverns and groceries title themselves gourmet shops. Cemeteries come to be known as memorial parks.

Asylums have become mental hospitals. We feel uncomfortable about death and mental illness, the functions of the body, and sexual matters. We tend to avoid being too harsh in our censure, so we soften the blow when referring to others who offend us. The origin of the name euphemism is associated with religious practice. When worshipers in Greece might be inclined to disturb a religious ceremony by using words of ill omen they were told to speak fairly (eu 'fair' + phēmi 'I speak'). Sacred beings and objects are invested with great power and there is a fear that directly to name them would invoke their wrath and evoke harm.

There is a proverb: Give a dog a bad name and hang him. Euphemism reverses this. It gives a dog (or anything or anyone) a good name in the hope that it (or he) won't bite. By euphemism we avoid callously trampling on other people's susceptibilities. Its linguistic importance? (1) It causes certain words to fall out of use. (2) It underlines the importance of emotion in the functioning of language. (3) It permits us to speak without giving offence and without directly expressing discontent through the avoidance of highly emotional words.

Common and ordinary replace vulgar; homely replaces ugly or plain when describing a person's looks; lady replaces dame; follower, minion or satellite; country dweller, rustic; scholar, pedant. 'Golden age adults' may indeed be senile,* golden age, senility.* Help displaces menial and servile, and young girl, wench. The words displaced degenerate in meaning, or become obsolescent. Their dignity fades with their longevity. Wardens send prisoners not to solitary confinement, but to meditation rooms. A victim of homicide is "the alleged victim." Dying is "terminal living." A company's garbage dump is a "civic amenity site."

EXERCISE X

In previous lessons, we have seen how doublets are formed when, in addition to the direct borrowing of derivatives from the Latin, there is indirect borrowing through one of Latin's derivative languages; e.g., French, Spanish, Italian. The indirectly borrowed word would have undergone a transformation in the other language, so that not only the spelling but also the meaning might differ from that of the word which came directly from the Latin. Doublets, though different in spelling and meaning, are derived ultimately from the same parent word.

I.   Show how the following pairs are linguistically related:

1) beldam, belladonna, 2) camera, chamber, 3) cancer, chancre, 4) costume, custom, 5) dignity, dainty, 6) doge, duce, 7) ennui, annoy, 8) fabric, forge, 9) frail, fragile, 10) hostel, hospital (cf. hotel), 11) ministry, métier, 12) mister, maestro (cf. master), 13) monster, muster, 14) noyau, newel, 15) piety, pity, 16) property, propriety, 17) round, rotund, 18) sample, example (cf. exemplum), 19) Sir, senior, 20) species, spice.

II.   Pair off and separate the euphemisms from the more offensive words in the following: abstemious, cheap, childish, cowardice, criminal, crowd, deception, degree-factory, disbeliever, domestic engineer, dowdy, drunkenness, duplicity, entrails, greasy spoon, guts, histrionics, homely, housewife, inebriety, infidel, mob, parsimonious, pedant, play-acting, popular, posterior, puerile, pusillanimity, rear-end, restaurant, scholar, strait-laced, tight-fisted, ugly, university, vulgar, wrong-doer.

III.   Pair off the appropriate nouns in List II with the adjectives in List I. List I: arbitrary, Caesarian, capital, dismal, dulcet, fabulous, genial, interim (adjectival), libelous, marginal, mellifluous, native, penal, plebeian, scrupulous, special, spiritual, tenuous. List II: accuracy, attachment, committee, decision, defamation, description, farm, host, investment, land, privilege, profit, progress, prospects, section, taste, tones, voice.

N.B. Several of these are clichés, but some adjectives in List I are flexible enough to apply to two nouns in List II.

IV.   Analyze the underlined words (or fill in):

1. He paid no attention to the canaille.

2. Where is it that the Duce has led his trusting people...?   Churchill

---

* Not all oldsters are senile, of course. Senility results from the loss of intellectual faculties through a disease afflicting the aged.

3) Sandburg's 1959 address to Congress on Lincoln was neither ironic nor <u>facetious</u>.

4. Even if I could conceive that I had overcome my <u>pride</u>, I should probably be proud of my <u>humility</u>.   Franklin

5. Could we suppose that the lawyer would ... give plausibility to <u>iniquitous</u> decisions, no degree of intellect would <u>win for him</u> our respect.   John Ruskin

6. I took my rifle, ... too small to kill an elephant, but I thought the noise might be useful <u>in terrorem</u>. Orwell

7. Ontario's <u>peregrine</u> falcon risks extinction.

8. L. <u>piperīnus</u> > ML. <u>pipinella</u>, a plant of the primrose family, yields _____.

9. Who sits in _____ and is quiet hath escaped from three wars: hearing,   speaking,   seeing. The Abbot Antony

10. By what <u>subdolous</u> practices ... of this secret art Caxton <u>obtained</u> its mastery, we are not told. Disraeli

11. Referring to the ____ c of Italian art is <u>Trecento</u>, short for <u>mil trecento</u>.

12. That which has only one loculus, compartment, chamber, or cell is _____-locular.

13. In 1970, France declared war on <u>franglais</u> (3,000 Anglicisms and Americanisms). On the way out* are: blue jeans, charter, drug-store, fast food, jogging, jumbo-jet, marketing, package tour, parking, peep show, pipeline, sex shop, trade show, le weekend. (*Four of the above show no sign of going. Which four have remained firmly entrenched)?

14. <u>Patrimony</u> is not the counter-term of matrimony.

15. Originally a tax-gatherer, 18c E. publican came to mean one who kept a _____.

V.   Which word in the following pairs is obsolete, or archaic: beneficent, beneficient; maleficent, maleficiation; missal, missive; begat, begot; yclad, clothed; yclept, named?

VI.   Define the Latin expressions: 1. ad maiorem Dei gloriam;
       2. de profundis; 3. extra muros; 4. mens sana in corpore
       sano; 5. sub silentio; 6. sui generis.

LESSON VIII

LATIN VERB CONJUGATIONS

There are four Latin verb-conjugations whose respective endings are 1) -āre 2) -ēre 3)-ere and 4) -īre. English has adopted as nouns a) certain first person singular present indicative active forms: veto (1st conj.), video (2nd conj.), credo (3rd conj.), and audio (4th conj.); b) some third person singular active forms: caret, deficit, exit, habitat, interest, introit, Magnificat (Luke 1.46-55), tenet and transit; c) the L. future, placebo; and d) the L. infinitives posse and nolle prosequi.

A defendant who will not plead guilty may say 'nolo contendere.' First person plural present indicatives which we have taken over as nouns are ignoramus, mandamus and mittimus. The perfect indicative has given us the nouns affidavit and ipse dixit. More nouns come from the subjunctive mood: caveat, fiat, habeas corpus, imprimatur, and imperatives: Memento, Miserere, plaudit < plaudite, and recipe.

The present participle gives us locum tenens and delirium tremens (absit omen!). An imperative with object is carpe diem. The gerundive or future passive participle provides addendum, agendum, Amanda, corrigendum, QED - quod erat demonstrandum, deodand, habendum, memorandum, Miranda, mutatis mutandis, modus operandi, modus vivendi, propaganda and pudenda.

Exercise XI

I.   Determine the etymological and current meanings of: floruit, non sequitur*, scilicet**, lavabo, sic transit gloria mundi, tempus fugit, videlicet; veni, vidi, vici.

   *   sequitur is the 3rd person sg. present tense of sequī, secutus 'to follow,' a deponent verb. Deponent verbs are passive in form, but active in meaning. Examples from each conjugation are: fārī, fātus 'to speak; having spoken;' fatērī, fassus 'to admit; having admitted;' loquī, locutus 'to speak; having spoken;' and partīrī, partītus 'to share; having shared.' They do not conform to the pattern of active verbs. The first and last items are verbs in the perfect (i.e., past) tense, as their meanings indicate.

   **   From scīre + licet, as vidēlicet is from vidēre + licet 'it is permitted (to ...)' (Clues: floruit is a 3rd pers. sg.; vēni ... is a 1st pers. sg.)

91

II.   Explain the use of the underlined words:

1) <u>Cogito</u>, ergo sum. <u>Errare</u> humanum est.

2) The emigrant's motto is 'ubi panis ibi patria.' What verb is missing but understood?

3) Virtus <u>est</u> ordo amoris.   St. Augustine

4) Homo <u>sum</u>.   Terence

5) Planck disproved 'natura non <u>facit</u> saltus.' (Clue: the form is the 3rd person singular present tense)

6) Paris' heraldic motto is '<u>fluctuat</u> nec mergitur.'

7) The Royal Mountain may be the original <u>habitat</u> of the Fameuses, a great fruit. <u>Dominion Illus.</u>

8) Tennyson wrote of the cold <u>hic jacets</u> of the dead.

9) Clough entitled a poem <u>Qui laborat</u>, <u>orat</u>.

10) 'Te igitur clementissime Pater ... <u>rogamus</u>' opens the first prayer in the Canon of the Mass.

11) In medio <u>stat</u> virtus.

12. Christianity inherited from Judaism the <u>tenet</u> of an initial perfection followed by a catastrophic fall. T. Dobzhansky

13. Verba <u>volant</u>, scripta manent. (Clue: both verbs are in the present 3rd person plural)

14. Nil <u>admirari</u>.   Horace

15. Kirk Douglas cast himself as the <u>posse</u> leader.

16. O seinte Marie, <u>benedicite</u>!   Chaucer

17. <u>Memento</u> mori.

18. I hereby enter my <u>caveat</u> against this piece of raillery.   Addison

19. Nothing can be concluded without the King's <u>Fiat</u>.

20. The book was issued with the committee's <u>Imprimatur.</u>

21. The American Numismatic Society's motto is Parva Nē Pereant.

22. Stet* , a printer's term, indicates that matter previously struck out is to remain.

23. Our species is rather Homō faber than Homō sapiens.

24. Old-fashioned gentlemen in Scotland use sedērunt jocularly to mean an informal chat over a bottle. A sederunt is a sitting of a deliberative or judicial body, especially an ecclesiastical assembly. (Clue: the verb is in the perfect tense, 3rd person plural)

25. In this brief transit where the dreams cross
The dreamcrossed twilight between birth and dying ...
Eliot

26. A Paduan woman's Italian-Latin poem begins:

Te saluto, alma dea
O dea generosa,
O gloria nostra
        Italica....

27. The Acadians adopted 'Ave, maris stella,' the first words of a Latin hymn, as a 'national' hymn.

---

* Latin has three verbal moods: indicative, subjunctive, imperative. Stet is in the subjunctive mood. Cf. sentences 18 through 21. This mood indicates, among other things, a wish or command, e.g., May you praise God: Deum laudes (1st conj.); let us sing: canamus (3rd conj.). Note that in the personal endings, in the -ēs of laudēs and in the -amus of canamus, the -ā- of the 1st conjugation's indicative (laudās 'you praise') becomes -ē-, but that -a- is consistently the sign of the 2nd, 3rd and 4th conjugations. Dūcere 'to lead,' 3rd conj., appears in the historian Livy's 'ratiō dūcat, nōn fortūna.' Catullus, to his sweetheart: 'vīvāmus, mea Lesbia, atque amēmus.' In paragraph 3 of this lesson, 'absit omen' means 'may there be no harm (from the word just used)!'

COMPOUND NOUNS AND ADJECTIVES FORMED FROM VERBS - 1

Compound nouns are formed from verbs by adding various suffixes to the present infinitive base or the perfect-participial base as shown in the following tables. Except in the case of deponent verbs, the p. pple is passive in meaning, e.g., rēctus = 'having been straightened,' or simply 'straightened.'

a)   The suffix -iō (gen. -ionis) > E. -ion, meaning 'state of, act of, result of the act of,' may be added to either the present infinitive or the perfect-participial base.

PRESENT INFINITIVE	PERFECT PARTICIPLE*	BASE	LATIN COMPOUND NOUN	ENGLISH LOAN WORD
opinārī 'to think, suppose'		opin-	opinio	opinion
regere 'to rule, straighten'	rēctus	reg-	regio	region
serere 'to sow'	satus	sat-	satio	season (borrowed through Fr.)
sedēre 'to sit'	sessus	sess-	sessio	session

* In form, a 1st and 2nd decl. adj. whose neuter may be used as a noun, e.g., datum, stratum, dictum.

b)   The noun-forming suffix -mentum ('act of, means, result of the act of') is added to only the present infinitive base.

integere 'to cover'	integ- + -u	integumentum	integument
docēre 'to teach'	doc- + -u	documentum	document

(Cf. also filament, impediment, instrument and monument)

c)   The noun-forming suffix -men ('act of, means, result of the act of') is also added only to the present infinitive base.

clināre 'to lean'	clin- + -a	clinamen	clinamen
stāre 'to stand'	st- + -a	stamen	stamen

(Cf. also foramen, regimen and semen)

d)   -ium is also added only to the present infinitive base. It means 'act of, place, means, result of the act of.'

auspicor 'to take   auspic-   auspicium   auspice
the auspices'

studēre 'to be   stud-   studium   study,
eager'   studio

e)   -bulum, -bula, or -culum is added only to the present infinitive base. It means 'place, means, instrument, or result of the act of.'

stāre 'to stand'   st- + -a   stabulum   stable

spectāre 'to   spect + -a   spectaculum   spectacle
keep looking'

(Cf. also dirigible, mandible, tentacle and vocable)

f)   -īna is also added to the present infinitive base; it may either mean, if the result is an abstract noun, 'act of,' or 'result of the act of' or 'that which has been _____.' The idea in the verb's base is added.

pangere 'to   pag-*   pagina   page
fasten, strike'

ruere 'to tumble   ru-   ruina   ruin
down'

g)   -or, if added to the present infinitive base, means 'state of, result of the act of,' and forms abstract nouns.*

	BASE	LATIN COMPOUND NOUN	ENGLISH LOAN WORD
furere 'to be mad' rage'	fur-	furor	furor
candēre 'to be white'	cand-	candor	candor

* Note the exception: liquor, < liquēre 'to be fluid or liquid.'

---

* because from an older verb, pacere, pagere (3rd conj.) 'to fix, come to an agreement;' pagina exceptionally has a short i.

h) -or may, however, be added to the perfect-participial base to form an agent noun, and then it usually means 'the person who' performs the action indicated in the base. This ending must be distinguished from the one which forms abstract nouns when added to the present infinitive base.

	PAST-PARTI-CIPIAL BASE	L. DERIVATIVE	E. DERIVATIVE
ōrāre 'to speak, pray'	orat-	orator	orator
docēre 'to teach'	doct-	doctor	doctor

i) -rīx, is the feminine equivalent of -or when added to the past-participial base, and forms agent nouns.

vincere 'to win'	vict-	victrix	victrix, victress

j) -ūra is added to the perfect-participial base to form an abstract noun. It means 'act of,' 'result of the act of.'

nāscī 'to be born'	nat-	natura	nature
scrībere 'to write'	script-	scriptura	scripture
tondere 'to shear, shave'	tons-	tonsura	tonsure

Exercise XII

I. For each of the following words, determine whether the present infinitive or perfect-participial base has been used. Define the present infinitive of the verb used.

divisor, executrix, fissure, governor, oration, picture, reason, supplement, tentacle, treason.

II. Distinguish between the meanings of the suffixes in

(1) candor, cantor; (2) spectacle, spectacles; (3) studio, study; (4) temperament, temperature; (5) investiture, vestibule.

III. Determine the Latin word from which the following are derived:

artifice, augury, cuisine, doctrine, firmament, interrupter, latrine, obstacle.

97

IV.   Give the etymological and current meanings of:

        fraction, gesture, languor, miracle, section, suasion, suspicion, venison.

V.   Distinguish between the meanings of these doublet pairs:

        pigment, pimento, ratio, ration, regimen, regime, tradition, treason.

VI.   Analyze the following words; determine which are learned and which are popular, and the meaning of the suffix in each.

        animadversion, defection, escalator, executor, nurture, orison, preceptor, pronunciamento, suture, testatrix.

VII.   Distinguish between: connotation, denotation; counteraction, contravention; election, selection; impediment, obstruction; procuratrix, procuress.

VIII.   The following list contains eight (8) pairs of linguistically related words. Identify the pairs and show how the members of each pair are related. advocate, alliance, collide, colloquial, delirium, docent, elision, fabulous, illicit, indoctrinate, infancy, inter, leisure, ligament, memento, native, obloquy, renascence, terror, vocabulary.

IX.   Analyze the underlined words and determine their contextual meaning:

        1) Ablutions in the East, ... a part of religious worship
           Stanley

        2) Leo blushed ...., regretting all he had revealed ...
           in a curriculum vitae he had sent to (a commercial
           cupid) Salzman. Malamud

        3) Vesuvius had made lately a terrible irruption.
           Luttrell

        4) That which is correct in miniature will be true in the
           large.

        5) That gallery of monumental men.   Swinburne

        6) Come, come, be every one officious
           To make this banquet.   Shakespeare

7) That <u>opprobrium</u> of mankind now calls himself our Protector.   Clarendon

8) This bird is a <u>prodigy</u> of understanding.   Goldsmith

9) Fields, where summer spreads <u>profusion</u> round   <u>idem.</u>

10) He had but to cover this material with a <u>vitrification</u> of transparent glaze.

X.   What is the meaning of the prefix in: accession, contortion,   conviction,   intercession,   intersession, obfuscation,   obsequious,   persuasion,   preposition, recondite,   redintegration,   sedition,   subsidization, transubstantiation?

XI.   -ūra > -ure, when attached to a perfect-participial base, denotes an action or condition resulting from an action, i.e., 'act, result of the act of.'   It often forms an abstract noun. We have seen above how nature, scripture and tonsure were formed.   The model below shows how rapture and rupture are developed.

Model:

Infinitive	Past Participle	P.p. base	L. Noun (if existent)	E. derivative
<u>rapere</u> 'to seize, drag, plunder'	<u>raptus</u>	<u>rapt-</u>		rapture
<u>rumpere</u> 'to break'	<u>ruptus</u>	<u>rupt-</u>	ruptūra 'fracture, breach'	rupture

List the following words in the right-hand column, then, following the model given above, work back to the left-hand column to give the L. infinitive.

aperture, armature, caesura, capture, censure, cincture, creature, culture, facture, feature, fissure, fixture, fracture, juncture, lecture, ligature, measure, mixture, nomenclature, overture, picture, pressure, puncture, sculpture, sepulture, signature, stature, stricture, structure, temperature, tincture, torture, venture, vesture.

Determine the etymologies of: acupuncture, adventure, aperture, architecture, agri-, arbori-, flori-, horti-, pisci-, vini-, and viti-culture, caricature, ceinture, composure, confiture, conjecture, couture, curvature, (de) pasture, disclosure, discomfiture, (en)tablature, erasure, filature, flexure, foliature, forfeiture, future, geniture, imposture, investiture, literature, miniature, mis(ad)venture, portraiture, posture, prefecture, primogeniture, procedure, rasure, serrature, tenure.

N.B. Many of our words ending in -ure are French: e.g., furniture, garniture, ordure, pleasure.

Editorial note

-or or -our?

An honorable end is sought to a spelling controversy. Is it misdirected nationalism for Canadians to believe they are threatened in their honour by the -or ending? This -or ending is not just an Americanism. Ardor, color, favor, honor, labor and valor are Latin spellings which were changed in medieval French to -eur, and then came into English as -our. It was therefore common English practice to write governour, since it came out of OF. governeor, gouvernour. Tremour, likewise, was influenced by OF. tremour. Whether you prefer to spell these words with -or or -our depends on how you were trained at an early age. Your location in the English-speaking and -writing world may also have been influential. -our came into English from Norman French and became dominant at a time when spelling was at best idiosyncratic. The American-Latin spelling saves space and time and does not seem to threaten Canadian honour. The Canadian who opts for -our is not necessarily slavishly aping British practice which has its own consistency; cf. creator, creditor, debtor, hallucinator with the abstract nouns ardour, candour, honour, humour.

Standardization of English spelling, even if desirable, would only be possible through international cooperation. If all publishing houses agreed to a uniform spelling, this spelling could then be implemented world-wide. Habit is the strongest determinant in language, and habit dictates that we go to our respective authorities, Webster's or Funk and Wagnall's in the U.S.; Oxford in Britain; Oxford or Webster's, as we wish, in Canada, or Gage's Dictionary of Canadianisms.

NOUNS AND ADJECTIVES FORMED FROM VERBS - 2

Compound adjectives are formed from verbs by adding an adjectival suffix to the present infinitive base or the perfect-participial base.

A) Some adjectival endings may be added to either base to form compound adjectives, e.g., -bilis › -ble and -ilis › -ile. Both these endings express passive capacity, meaning 'able to be, capable of being;' but they also sometimes convey the notion of active capability in which case they mean 'suitable for, able to, given to, causing.' When attached to a first-conjugation verbal base the connecting vowel -a- is used in front of -bilis, as in mūt-ā-bilis and trāct-ā-bilis. To verbal bases of other conjugations -i- is the usual connecting vowel e.g., audible, from audīre and fusible, from fundere, fūsus, except that -a- may be found in words borrowed through French, e.g., tenable and capable. There are exceptions to this, however, in English formations where -a- seems to be used almost indiscriminately, e.g., creditable, chargeable, datable. In formidable and palatable, however, the -bilis has been added to a noun base. The use of -īlis as an adjectival suffix has led to our words agile, missile, docile and volatile.

B) Other suffixes used in forming compound adjectives are added only to the present infinitive base: -āx (› -ac-), -uus, (› -u-) -ulus, (› -ul-), and -idus (› -id-). Adjectival formations using these suffixes tend to mean 'inclined to.' Both -āx and -uus most often appear in English in combination with the suffix -ōsus › -ous. -ulus always combines with the suffix -ōsus › -ous. Examples of the above are tenēre 'to hold,' ten-āx + -ōsus › tenacious 'inclined to hold;' vacāre 'to be empty,' vac-uus + -ōsus › vacuous 'tending to be empty;' bibere 'to drink,' bib-ulus + -ōsus › bibulous 'addicted to drink;' stupēre 'to be struck senseless,' stup-idus, › stupid 'foolish.'

C) Another suffix often attached to -āx (gen. -ācis) is -itās) › -ity, which is used to form abstract nouns, so that, e.g., parallel to tenacious, we have tenacity. Similarly, we have capacious and capacity, veracious and veracity, audacious and audacity, voracious and voracity.

101

D) Certain adjective-forming suffixes are attached only to the perfect-participial base, namely, -ōrius, -īvus, and -īcius. The English endings in the case of the first two are -ory and -ive, but the -īcius ending always combines with the suffix -ōsus, whence E. -icious (c and t were often confused in later Latin), meaning 'characterized by.' Examples of the above are conservatory and laboratory, captive and tentative, factitious and fictitious.

-ōrius means 'pertaining to' as in our circulatory and gustatory, compulsory and dilatory. It also means 'given to' or 'characterized by.' The neuter counterpart of -ōrius, -ōrium, as in sanatorium, auditorium indicates the place for or of the activity in question, healing and hearing, for example. -īvus = 'given or tending to' also provides nouns such as initiative, prerogative, palliative.

Exercise XIII.

I. 1. Compare the meanings of the following pairs and draw a conclusion as to why we may say there is a relationship. languor, languid, pallor, pallid, stupor, stupid, valor, valid.

2. What is the opposite of a deciduous tree?

3. When would florid language be used?

4. Give a synonym of inflexible ending in -id.

5. By combining the present infinitive base of the L. verb 'to harm' with -uus, we come up with _____.

6. When would one's face become livid?

7. Colors that are lively may be referred to as _____.

8. What is the force or meaning of the prefix in perfervid, preternatural, surreptitious, survive, transliteration?

9. What do we mean by a sensible person? a sensuous person? one who has sensibility? a sensitive person?

10. One who writes in a grandiloquent, pompous or inflated way displays a _____ style. (The word ends in -id).

11. The musical term borrowed from Italian, tremolo, is the doublet of _____.

102

12. A synonym of valetudinarian ending in -id is _____.

II.   What is the force or meaning of the suffixes in assiduous, creditable, fictitious, garrulity, habiliments, incisor, omnivorous, perfervid, suggestible, tractable, valorous, vestry?

III.   Analyze collusive, competition, effusive, fallible, imperative, imponderable, pendulous, perfectible, vacuity.

IV.   Find eight pairs of words etymologically related and show how they are related: accessory, artifact, compassionate, compulsion, concede, convent, diffusive, dispel, efficacious, fracture, impassive, incapacitate, incisor, inexorable, oratorio, partition, peremptory, provide, pugnacious, receptacle, remission, triturate, video, souvenir. (N.B. Eight words in this list do not apply).

V.   Analyze the underlined words: determine contextual meanings.

1. For help is something you have to give/When daughters are faced with the <u>ablative</u>... Phyllis McGinley

2. Mind is not <u>commensurable</u> with Space. Dove

3. The elephant's <u>docility</u> is exhibited unto us in the theaters. Holland

4. Language is <u>fossil</u> poetry. Emerson

5. A rugged attire, hirsute head, <u>horrid</u> beard Burton

6. In a meane man prodigalitie and pride are faultes more <u>reprehensible</u> than in Princes. Puttenham

7. The Saxon language received little or no <u>tincture</u> from the Welsh. Burke

8. It is a man's own fault if his mind grows <u>torpid</u> in old age. Johnson

9. The nature of Justice consisteth in keeping of <u>valid</u> covenants. Hobbes

10. The imperiall <u>Votress</u> passed on,
In maiden meditation, fancy-free. Shakespeare

VI.   More versatile than Latin, English possesses some built-in
        processes for creating words or extending meanings. Among
        these is conversion or functional shift whereby we make
        nouns out of verbs, and vice-versa. The verb 'go' may be
        put in use as a noun as in slangy 'on the go,' 'make a go
        of it,' and 'no go.' Go is a shifted form.

        Determine which of the following may be used as both noun
        and verb: caricature, credit, feature, picture, portrait,
        portraiture, portray, service, square, summer, weekend,
        winter. Select from these a word which can be used as
        three parts of speech. In what order does a dictionary
        list conversion meanings?

ETYMOLOGICAL NOTE

        Culture is a 16c, civilization, a late 18c word. Culture
was first used in English, as L. cultūra 'cultivation of the
soil,' in an agricultural sense.   Cicero first used the
expression, cultūra animi. Francis Bacon employed culture in the
same sense as mental cultivation. By the 18c, in France and
England, it meant formation of the mind, emotions, manners,
taste. Both in Germany and in Latin America, Kultur and cultura
are articulated so that they encompass both culture and
civilization. In English, because there is felt to be a
dichotomy, culture and civilization are not used interchangeably.

        Civilization is a noun-formation from 'to civilize.' F.
civiliser appears at the end of the 16c, our verb, slightly after
the first third of the 17c. The noun appears in France in 1734;
in England, in 1772. Johnson objected to civilization, admitting
only civility. The English tradition tends to develop the notion
of civilization as a characteristic of "superior" societies,
opposing cīvis, cīvīlis and cīvitās to barbarus (by which Greeks
meant those not speaking Greek, hence savage), barbarian and
barbarity. By the end of the 19c, culture came to be favored
over civilization in England, but American anthropologists use
the   words   'culture'   and   'civilization'   indifferently.
Civilization is the ensemble of social values of which culture is
a part. The latter is the effort, result or state of the
cultivated person. It is also the ideal of the life of the
mind. We speak of a man's culture, but a community has both a
culture and a civilization. Although it seems impossible, many
'cultured' people lack civilized characteristics, and a
'civilized' society may be hostile to culture, the ideal of the
life of the mind. The problem is how to articulate culture and
civilization.

LESSON XI

INFINITIVAL AND PAST-PARTICIPIAL BASES

Memorize the bases of the present infinitive and the past participle* as underlined in the following Latin verbs. Note the derivatives from the respective bases.

PRESENT INFINITIVE	PAST PARTICIPLE	MEANING	E. DERIVATIVES
habitāre,	habitātus	'to dwell, reside'	inhabit; habitation
mutāre,	mutātus	'to change, alter'	commute; mutate
portāre,	portātus	'to carry'	deport; portative
stāre,	statum	'to stand'	stable; status quo
augēre,	auctus	'to increase'	augment; auction
mordēre,	morsus	'to bite'	mordant; morsel
movēre,	motus	'to move'	remove; motion
tenēre,	tentus	'to hold'	tenor; tentacle
vidēre,	vīsus	'to see'	provide; revise
agere	actus	'to do, act, drive'	agent; actor
capere,	captus	'to take, grasp, hold'	capable; capture
cēdere,	cessus	'to go, yield'	accede; recess
dūcere,	ductus	'to lead'	induce; deduct
jacere,	jactus	'to throw'	jaculate; reject
legere,	lēctus	'to gather, read, choose'	legible, collect
pellere,	pulsus	'to drive'	impel, compulsion
scrībere,	scriptus	'to write'	describe; conscription

105

| specere, | spectus | 'to look at' | despicable; respect |
| solvere, | solūtus | 'to loosen, free' | resolve; dissolute |

* The past or perfect participle is declined like a first or second declension noun.

Exercise XIV.

1. Fill in each blank space with a Latin-derived English word formed from a Latin verbal base and appropriate prefix and / or suffix. NB: your answers will be in alphabetical order.

   a) Legible material under a cartoon is a _____.

   b) One who travels a long distance to and from work is a _____.

   c) The fire-cracker was <u>thrown out</u> or _____.

   d) A desk or stand from which a minister reads scripture lessons is a _____.

   e) A thing which stands in the way (e.g., of progress) is an _____.

   f) Because of her accomplishments, she was <u>moved forward</u> or _____.

   g) Expressions of a will to change made on New Year's Eve are _____.

   h) She was <u>chosen apart</u> or _____ as ambassadress to France.

   i) One who oversees the work of employees is a _____.

   j) When the earth shakes, people experience the _____.

II. Analyze, by segmenting, the following words; define each segment; then give the current definition of the word. Example: adjective

   segment: ad   prefix 'to, toward, for'
   verbal base: ject-   from past participle of <u>jacere</u>, jactus 'to throw'
   suffix: -ive < -īvus, 'tending to, connected with'
   current definition: 'a word which modifies a noun or pronoun.'

anfractuous, commutation, deciduous,* frontispiece, interjection, predecessor, receptacle, secession, traduce, trajectory.

* ‹ <u>cad</u>ere (-<u>cid</u>ere), <u>cās</u>us (-<u>cās</u>us) 'to fall'

III. List the corresponding action-nouns for verbs ending in -tain:

abstain, attain, contain, detain, entertain, maintain, obtain, pertain, retain, sustain.

IV. Classify the following -ject compounds as nouns, adjectives or verbs (NB: Some can be more than one part of speech):

abject, deject, eject, inject, object, project, reject, subject.

V. Fill in the blank spaces with Latin-derived words. NB: your answers will be in alphabetical order.

1. Educational materials used to assist hearing and sight are called _____.

2. Anxiety about WW III has not been driven away or _____.

3. We refer to a socially superior group as an _____.

4. The salesman held salable goods for viewing at his _____.

5. Problems that cannot be disentangled are referred to as _____.

6. Psychoanalysis leads to an act of looking within oneself or _____.

7. One who reads at a worship service is called a _____.

8. Biologists refer to sudden changes in heredity as _____.

9. One who holds a post before another is the latter's _____.

10. One goes to a pharmacist to have a _____ filled.

107

11. The process of surveying the past or looking back is called _____ .

12. Avaunt! and quit my sight! let the earth hide thee! Thy bones are marrowless, thy blood is cold; / Thou hast no _____ in those eyes / Which thou dost glare with! (Clue: base verb is _speculāri_, or see Macbeth 3.4.95)

13. An endorsement made on a passport by proper authorities allowing the bearer to proceed into a country is a _____ .

VI. The following list contains eight (8) pairs of words that are linguistically related. Select the pairs and show how, in each case, the words are related. Example: the words capacity and reception both derive in part from _capere_, _captus_ (-ceptus) 'to take.' Capacity contains _cap-_, present-infinitive base of _capere_, and reception contains _cept-_, the perfect-participial base of the same verb:

absolution, aqueduct, compel, concede, constant, continent, immutable, improvise, impulse, irresolvability, legendary, lesson, nihil obstat, prevent, seduce, success, tenacious, video.
(_Nota bene_: two of the words do not apply)

VII. In each of the following groups of words, find the one that is not appropriate, because it is not related to the others. Explain why it does not fit. Example: In the group cadenza, motorcade, occasional, occident, and pre-decease, all the words are based on the L. verb _cadere_ 'to fall' except for motorcade which is combined of _motor_ + -cade. -cade is a combining form meaning 'procession,' cf. cavalcade; motorcade is a procession of motor vehicles. The other words all contain the idea of falling, either literally or figuratively.

a) dispel, expulsion, pellucid, pulsate, repellent

b) dissolve, insoluble, resolution, salutary, solvent

c) auspices, despise, frontispiece, introspection, recipe, spectre

d) abstain, content, tangent, detention, impertinent, sustenance

e) conduit, ductile, educe, inducement, reduce, refuse.

VIII. Determine the contextual meaning of the underlined words:

1. Grief joys, joy grieves, on slender <u>accident</u>. Shakespeare

2. The average boy and a good sized lump of maple candy allow us to <u>deduct</u> self-evident conclusion regarding the facility <u>with</u> which attachments are formed in early life.

3. Even in <u>destitution</u> and exile they retained their punctilious <u>national</u> pride.   Macauley

4. ... the perturbation of conscious guilt confusing itself in attempted <u>exculpation</u>, even before a mute accuser   Scott

5. He cared little for wine or beauty; but he desired riches with an ungovernable and <u>insatiable</u> desire. Macauley

6. Having finished his lectures for the year, the professor recited a <u>Magnificat</u>.

7. The Rough Riders pressed for a new definition of <u>non-imports</u>.

8. Be rich, but of your wealth make no <u>parade</u>.   Swift

9. This enemy, permafrost, the Russians call "<u>perennially</u> frozen ground."

10. To receive <u>perks</u> makes a job more attractive.   (See <u>perquirere</u>)

11. Plays and poems, hunting and dancing, were <u>proscribed</u> by ... his saintly family.   Macauley

12. ... eyes which glowed with a perpetual <u>salutat</u> to the world   Cather

13. <u>Emortality</u> will not come all at once. We cannot conquer death without a knowledge of life. A. Silverstein (Clue: <u>morior</u> 'I die;' <u>mori</u>, <u>mortuus</u> 'to die')

14. We know the (ēditio) <u>vulgāta</u> as the <u>Vulgate</u>, St. Jerome's 4c publication.

15. The British Admiralty fixes the nautical mile at 6,080 ft. The statute mile is 1,760 yds. The nautical mile is 800 ft. longer than the statute mile.

IX. From the verbs listed at the beginning of the lesson, form words with these etymological meanings:

a) result of the act of leading together

b) act, or result of the act of being moved down

c) act, or result of the act of driving out

d) act of residing in

e) not able to be gathered (chosen, read)

f) unable to hold (grasp)

g) to throw in

h) not able to be freed (loosened)

i) act, or result of the act of holding in

j) to change (alter) thoroughly

k) of, made by, or of the nature of a throwing forth

l) tending to go back

m) able to be looked back at

n) act, or result of the act of holding back

o) to carry under.

VOWEL GRADATION*

You noted earlier that in the formation of compound adjectives, e.g., inimical, perennial, superficial, the noun's base was slightly altered so that a in the base became i or e. The same principle of vowel gradation holds when you attach a Latin prepositional prefix to a Latin verb-root or stem. English derivatives reflect these changes. Three variations are observable: (a) before a single consonant (except r), a short a or e in the base usually changes to i:

Latin Word	English Derivation	Prefixed Latin Word	English Derivation
cadere 'to fall'	caducity, caducous, cadaver, cadence	decidere 'to fall down'	deciduous
		recidere 'to fall back'	recidivist
facere 'to do, make'	rubifacient	deficere 'to fail, be wanting'	deficient, defect
habēre 'to have'	habit	inhibēre 'to curb, restrain'	inhibit
sedēre 'to sit'	sediment	insidēre 'to adhere to, occupy'	insidious
tenēre 'to hold'	tenant	continēre 'to enclose, preserve'	continent

(b) before two consonants, a short a in the base usually changes to e:

factus 'done'	factual	infectus 'spoiled'	infection
		inficere 'to dip in, stain, spoil'	
sacrāre 'to declare sacred, condemn'	sacral, sacrament, sacre (vb.)	consecrāre 'to consecrate'	consecrate

(c) ae changes to i, and au changes to ū:

caesum 'cut'	caesura	incīsus 'cut into'	incision
causa 'motive'	cause	accūsāre 'to blame'	accuse
clausum 'closed'	clauster	inclūsus 'locked in'	inclusion

---

* Vowel gradation shows variations in both quantity and quality of the vowel. It results from accentual variations of (1) intonation (pitch), and of (2) stress (depending on force of expiration). We find it in strong verbs, e.g., sing, sang, sung and in colloquial ablaut-rows, e.g., chit-chat, knick-knack, see-saw.

111

X.   Give the correct spelling of words composed of the following elements:

1) ad + -cession = _____ , 2) ad + -scandere = _____ ,

3) ad + -nihilate = _____ , 4) ad + -traction = _____ ,

5) sub + -gestive = _____ , 6) super + -undāre = _____ .

DENOMINATIVE VERBS

In Latin the denominative verb is formed from a noun, adjective or adverb, e.g., frustrā, whence frustrāre. From the base and the addition of -āre* verbs are formed which convey the meaning residing in the base, e.g., locus 'place' gives loc- + -āre, locāre 'to place,' and medius 'middle' + -āre, mediāre 'to be in the middle.' The base of pāx, pācis + -āre yields pācāre, which, via F. payer, is the origin of 'to pay.' LL. mātrix 'womb, source, public register' has a diminutive, mātrīcula. A University matriculates you when it enrolls your name in the official register.

L. ēdux 'guide' led to the denominative verb ēducāre, 'to act as guide, bring up, rear, train, nurture,' whence ēducātiō 'a bringing up, rearing, education.' From ēducātus, Romans also made the agent nouns: ēducātor 'foster-father, tutor, one who guides' and its female counterpart ēducātrix 'foster-mother, nurse.'
* An exception, among several, is finīre, from L. finis 'boundary, end.'

Exercise XV

I.   To form L. denominative verbs, use the bases of these nouns and adjectives: arbiter, arbitri, 'judge,' arma 'weapons,' genus, generis, 'race,' litera-ae, 'letter,' mīles, mīlitis, 'soldier,' ōs, oris, 'mouth,' publicus 'pertaining to the people,' radius, 'ray,' scintilla 'spark,' vōx, vōcis 'voice:' 'to (be a) judge' (N.B.: deponent verb), 'to equip with arms,' 'to (produce a) race,' 'to letter,' 'to (be a) soldier,' 'to mouth,' 'to (make for the) people,' 'to (make a) ray,' 'to spark(le),' 'to voice.'

II. Form simple derivatives from the denominative verbs above.

III. Analyze these compound derivatives: corrugate, deactivate, definite, descriptive, designate, importunate, indoctrinate, pernoctate, prospectus, relocate.

IV. Analyze the underlined words:

     1. We cannot meet without your trying to plant a temperamental left jab on my spiritual solar plexus. I think you understand that we are affinities. Wodehouse

113

2. To <u>audition</u> a ballet dancer? To <u>audit</u> the books of account?

3. Snoring? A monosonorous nocturnal <u>cantata</u>.

4. Bell-ringing signaled the <u>curfew</u>.

5. We <u>decimated</u> almost half the enemy.

6. The rhetorical figure of <u>descriptio ad vestitum</u> depends on the assumption that a man's character may be observed from his _____.

7. The presence of a king engenders love
   Amongst his subjects and his loyal friends,
   And it <u>disanimates</u> his enemies.   Shakespeare

8. Chicago's ward 22 was involved in "<u>eratication</u>."*

9. The Romans in their levies enrolled first names of good omen: Victor, Valerius, Salvius, Felix, Faustus. <u>Fausta</u> is the latter's counterpart.

10. The <u>invisibilia</u> are of infinitely greater power than the <u>visibilia</u>.

11. She obligingly consented to be a <u>mediatrix</u> in the matter.

12. They endeavoured to <u>palliate</u> what they could not justify.

13. When his wings' wax melted, Icarus <u>plummeted</u> into the sea.

14. A child must be 13 to do <u>pointe</u> work in ballet.

15. Scientists declare scientific revolutions <u>post factum</u>.

16. Wolves, cougars, foxes, coyotes, raccoons and suburban dogs are <u>predators</u>.

17. <u>Redemptor Hominis</u> is a papal encyclical addressed to <u>800 million Roman</u> Catholics.

---

* N.B.: not to be found in your dictionary, since it's a very recent coinage.

18. The outer layer of skin is the stratum corneum. Beneath it is the stratum granulosum, a dehydrated layer that may be a willing receiver for the incoming drug.

19. The Evangelist John saith, He tabernacled among us.

20. Benefits are conditional upon the spouse living with the testator at the time of his death.

21. Matrimony leads to acrimony leads to testimony leads to alimony.

22. Liberty without wisdom or virtue is folly, vice and madness, without tuition or restraint.

23. Virilocal residence, rather than uxorilocal or bilocal, is more common in hunting societies and our own.

V. a) Form agent nouns by using the perfect participle base of the following verbs: adjūdicāre - 'to judge,' adulāri - 'to flatter, fawn upon,' audīre - 'to hear,' capere - 'to take,' censēre - 'to reckon,' defalcāre - 'to deduct,' dēficere - 'to fail, be wanting,' legere - 'to read,' movēre - 'to move,' ōrāre - 'to speak, pray,' regere - 'to direct,' vincere - 'to defeat, conquer.' Cf. also creator, fabricator, monitor. The Spanish derivatives Ecuador, matador, San Salvador, toreador and the French derivatives amateur, directeur, facteur, littérateur are similarly formed.

    b) Define these Italian derivatives: conduttore, elettore, esibitore, inventore, peccatore, pescatore, pittore, portatore.

    c) Analyze the F. agent provocateur, animateur, auteur, menteur, pasteur, traducteur.

    d) Analyze the underlined words: actuarial tables, arrogated powers, attenuated leaf, exacerbated pain, laminated plywood, marinated salad, patriated constitution, probate court, reprobated sinner, striated shell.

VI. Show how the underlined words differ in function and meaning in these sentences:

    a) The museum accessioned the Rideau Chapel as an art object;

    b) The accession of a new president took place; and

115

c) Following the <u>accession</u> of the territory came the <u>accession</u> of wealth.

WORD NOTES

The perfect-participial feminine or neuter plural ending of first conjugation verbs may be so changed as to produce an unusual ending. A case in point is F. <u>-é</u>, <u>-ée</u> which English adopts as is or changes to -y, or -ey.

F. <u>-ée</u> comes out of L. <u>-ata</u>, e.g., L. <u>armata</u> gives F. <u>armée</u>, via <u>Sp</u>. English may adopt the ending <u>wholesale</u>, as in <u>fricassee</u>, but usually changes it to -y, or -ey. <u>Gelata</u> 'frozen' gives jelly; hypothetical <u>coriata</u> 'skinned' via <u>F. curée</u> gives quarry; <u>jurata</u> 'sworn' gives, via F. <u>jurée</u>, jury. <u>Volata</u> 'flown' gives volley. LL. <u>parabolata</u> via F. <u>parlé</u> gives parley.

All these noun-formations from verbal bases tend to indicate the result of the action implicit in the verb as in army, result of the act of arming. -ee appears in addressee, consignee, devotee, draftee, employee, enrollee, inductee, invitee, legatee, levee (a sovereign's morning reception; a river embankment), parolee, payee, referee, retiree, trustee.

English ignores F. formations on the noun base: <u>becquée</u>, <u>cuillerée</u>, <u>pelletée</u>, favoring the suffix -ful: <u>beakful</u>, <u>spoonful</u>, <u>shovelful</u>. <u>Feuillée</u>, <u>nuée</u>, <u>onglée</u>* are others.

Exceptionally, a noun or adjectival base may be responsible for a derivation containing the -ee, -ey, or -y affix, e.g., L. <u>diurnum (spatium)</u> 'period of a day' gives It. giorno, F. <u>jour</u>. A hypothetical or popular LL. <u>diurnata</u> gives It. <u>giornata</u>, F. <u>journée</u> 'day, day's work, day's pay.' Journey, formerly a day's work, a day's traveling, is now specialized to suggest somewhat prolonged travel.

French and English sometimes diverge in the formation of derivatives from the L. <u>-ata</u> (n. pl.) suffix. L. <u>dictata</u> 'things dictated, lessons, commands' comes into English as a dictate or command, but into French as dictée 'the action of reading a passage which someone is to write down.' E. dictate and F. <u>dicter</u> 'to suggest, to ask to write down, to inspire' do not necessarily differ, since one may dictate in a school, or office.

---

* <u>Rangée</u>, of Germanic origin and related to F. <u>rang</u>, is the tier <u>familiar</u> to sports fans.

MORE WORDS FROM VERBAL BASES

In Exercise XIV, question VI, we met with capacity and tenacious. Both are formed from the base of the present infinitive plus the adjective-forming suffix -āx (genitive -ācis). The resulting adjective and noun draws to it the suffix -ous (< ōsus), and -ity (< -itās) respectively. The compound suffix -acīous produces adjectives meaning 'inclined to,' and 'abounding in;' -acity makes abstract nouns meaning 'the quality of being inclined to' and 'the quality of abounding in.'

Examples are the adjectives audacious, pugnacious, and rapacious, from audēre, 'to dare,' pugnāre 'to fight,' and rapere 'to seize' respectively. Cf. contumacious, efficacious, fallacious.

As mentioned before, -uus followed by -ōsus > -ous may be suffixed to the present infinitive base. It produces adjectives meaning 'inclined to,' e.g., assiduous, conspicuous.

A third suffix -ulus produces the adjectives bibulous, credulous, garrulous, pendulous, querulous and tremulous. -ulus bears the meaning 'inclined to,' 'tending to.'

A fourth suffix -idus is added to the present infinitive base to form adjectives meaning 'inclined to.' Some words containing this suffix are arid, fervid, humid, livid, lucid, pallid, perfervid, rigid, squalid, stupid, valid and vivid. Can you add others?

The addition of -or, 'state of' to the base of some of the latter verbs, e.g., fervēre, humēre, pallēre, rigēre, squalēre, stupēre and valēre produces abstract nouns* which parallel the adjectives formed with -id; fervor is etymologically 'the state of boiling' and rigor 'the state of being stiff.' What is the etymological meaning of candor and candid, fulgor and fulgid, horror and horrid, languor and languid, torpor and torpid?

In Lesson IX, -bulum, -bula or -culum was shown as a suffix added to the present infinitive base. This is not a diminutive ending. Examples are binnacle, cubicle, miracle, obstacle, receptacle, tentacle, and vocable.

---

* but see the note at Lesson IX, g).

EXERCISE XVI

I. Determine the conjugation to which these verbs belong: audire, auditus 'to hear,' cavere, cautus 'to beware, take care,' credere, creditus 'to believe,' currere, cursum 'to run,' ducere, ductus 'to lead,' ferre, latus 'to bring, bear,' (NB: irregular verb), jungere, junctus 'to join,' manere, mansum 'to remain,' plicare, plicatus (plicitus) 'to fold,' rogare, rogatus 'to ask, propose a law,' servare, servatus 'to save, preserve,' trahere, tractus 'to draw.'

II. Identify these forms by gender and number: acta, capti, lati, lecta, portatae, pulsum, scripti, solutum, tractae.

III. Determine the meaning of alea jacta est, equo ne credite, non liquet, placet, recipe; Sanguis est semen Christianorum.

IV. What is the etymological meaning of audio, video, caveat, confer, id est, quod erat demonstrandum, quo vadis?, quod vide, stabat mater, tenet, videlicet?

V. How do we abbreviate: anno Domini, circa, confer, denarius (think of the English pence), post scriptum, quod erat demonstrandum, recipe, scilicet, stet, videlicet?

VI. Fill in or substitute derivatives from Latin to complete the sentences:

1. The CPA made a final statement of account (an _____).

2. A common Latin inscription "to beware of the dog" was _____ _____.

3. The underdog (yields) to the topdog.

4. The instructions were (thoroughly folded up).

5. A mutual promise, upon lawful consideration or cause, which binds the parties to an obligation, engagement, or performance, usually written up and signed, is a _____.

6. In undertaking a risky business, it is well to take _____.

7. A spectator inclined to fight 'with his fists' is _____.

8. Give every man thy ear, but few thy voice;
Take each man's _____, but reserve thy
judgement. <u>Haml.</u> I.3.68

9. The annual 'Caveat Emptor' Award takes its name from
the Latin phrase which means "____ ____ ____ ____."

VII. Determine which of the following are diminutives and which
are non-diminutives formed on the present infinitive base:
armadillo, cavil, constable, cupola, curricle, fallible,
inexorable, pinnacle, tintinnabulum, vestibule.

MILTONIC LATINISMS

VIII. Define the underlined words:

1. I oft <u>admire</u> / How Nature wise and frugal could commit
Such <u>disproportions</u> with superfluous hand.
<u>PL</u> 8.25

2. Wouldst thou approve thy constancy, <u>approve</u>
First thy obedience. <u>PL</u> 9. 367-68

3. That undisturbed song of pure <u>concent</u>
<u>At a Solemn Music</u> 9

4. How charming is divine philosophy,
... a perpetual feast of nectared sweets,
Where no <u>crude</u> surfeit reigns.
<u>PR</u> 4.328

5. No voice <u>exempt</u>, no voice but well could join
Melodious <u>part</u>; such concord is in Heaven.
<u>PL</u> 3.370-71

6.   In Stygian cave forlorn
'Mongst <u>horrid</u> shapes, and shrieks, and sights unholy.
<u>L'Allegro</u> 4

7. And strictly <u>meditate</u> the thankless Muse?
<u>Lycidas</u> 66
(cf. <u>Comus</u> 547)

8. ... such prompt eloquence
Flowed from their lips, in prose or <u>numerous</u> verse.
<u>PL</u> 5.150

9. Round this opacous Earth, this <u>punctual</u> spot
<u>PL</u> 8.23

10. She proving false, the next I took to wife...
    Was in the vale of Sorec, Dalila,
    That <u>specious</u> monster, my accomplisht snare.
                                        <u>SA</u> 230

MEMORIZING VERB-BASES

As in the previous list of verbs, memorize the bases of the present infinitive and the past participle of the following. Note the derivatives from the respective bases.

mandāre, mandātus	'to commit, enjoin, entrust'	command; mandate
plicāre, plicātus (or plicitus)	'to fold'	display; explicate
rogāre, rogātus	'to ask, propose a law'	prorogue; interrogation
servāre, servātus	'to save'	preserve; conservation
censēre, census	'to assess, judge'	censure; census
haerēre, haesus	'to stick'	cohere; adhesion
pendēre, pēnsus	'to hang'	depend; suspense
sedēre, sessus	'to sit'	supersede; session
currere, cursum	'to run'	incur; excursion
facere, factus (-fectus)	'to make, do'	facsimile; artifact
mittere, missus	'to send, let go'	manumit; transmission
rōdere, rōsus	'to gnaw'	rodent; erosion
sistere, status	'to set, cause to stand'	persist; interstices
stringere, strictus	'to draw tight'	stringency; stricture
tendere, tēnsus (or tentus)	'to stretch'	distend; pretence extent
terere, trītus	'to rub, wear'	teredo; contrition
vertere, versus	'to turn'	vertebra; verse
volvere, volutus	'to roll'	evolve; convolution

audīre, audītus	'to hear'	audio-visual; auditory
finīre, finītus	'to end' 'to limit'	define; infinite
īre, itum (pres. ptc. base -ient-)	'to go'	transient; initial
venīre, ventum	'to come, go'	intervene; event

Deponent Verbs (having passive forms and active meanings):

mirārī, mirātus	'to admire, wonder at'	admire; admiration
fārī, fātus	'to speak'	infant; fatal, prefatory
memorārī, memorātus	'to remember'	immemorial; commemorate
testārī, testātus	'to witness'	protest; intestate
verērī, veritus	'to fear'	revere
gradī, gressus	'to step'	grade; aggression
lābī, lapsus	'to slip, fall'	lability; lapse
loquī,* locūtus	'to speak'	eloquent; locution
nāscī, nātus	'to be born'	nascent; nation
patī, passus	'to suffer'	patient; passion
sequī, secūtus	'to follow'	sequence; execute
ūtī, ūsus	'to use'	inutile; abuse
partīrī, partītus	'to share'	impartible; partitive

---

* Romance comes from a Latin adverbial phrase, loquī Romanicē 'to speak in the Roman manner,' i.e., colloquial Latin: French. Romanicē became the noun romance, which in the 12c meant a French poem appealing to aristocrats in which love was at first the main feature. The English romance of the 13c rather emphasized adventures and exploits of English heroes.

EXERCISE XVII

I. Determine the current meanings:

absit omen, caveat venditor, fabula de te narratur, fiat lux, lapsus calami (linguae), in loco parentis, in memoriam, in situ, locum tenens, memoranda, mutatis mutandis, non sequitur, obiter dicta, per diem, per se, per capita, sic transit gloria mundi, tabula rasa, viva voce, vox populi, prosit, peccavi.

II. Form an Engl. derivative from the present infinitive base of

armāre 'to equip with weapons,' cavillārī 'to mock,' clamāre 'to shout,' crēscere 'to increase,' errāre 'to wander,' laudāre 'to praise,' nocēre 'to harm,' quaerere 'to seek,' regere 'to rule, straighten,' scindere 'to cut, split,' struere 'to build,' tingere 'to dye, stain.'

III. Select the inappropriate word in the following groups and explain your choice:

censor - censure - incense - recension

artifact - artificial - feasible - forfeit - sacrifice - transfix

aggressive - congress - digitigrade - egress - exaggerate

allocation - colloquy - elocution - loquacious - soliloquy

admirable - miracle - Miranda - mire

complicate - duplex - explicate - imply - reply - supply

elocutionary - execute - prosecute - sequential - suitor

ambience - circumambient - deviation - initiate - transit

IV. a) Show how the following words have undergone semantic change (elevation or degeneration of meaning):

amateur	constable
artificial	fabulist
egregious	marshal
urbane	puritanical

123

b) Distinguish the meanings of demise when used as a noun and a verb. Pronounce and define animate when used as adj. and verb.

c) Distinguish between labile and labial.

V. Analyze the underlined words:

1. Our prison.../... immures us round
   Ninefold, and gates of burning adamant,
   Barred over us, prohibit all egress. Milton

2. The refectory was a great, low-ceiled, gloomy room;
   on two long tables smoked basins of something hot.
   C. Brontë

3. In times of public danger, the dull claims of age and
   rank are sometimes superseded. Gibbon

4. Anything which masquerades as another thing, e.g., a
   prostitute appearing as a Salvation Army lassie, is
   ipso facto laughable.

5. Caution is the eldest child of wisdom. Hugo

6. Emulation* lives so near to envy that it is difficult
   to establish the boundary-lines. H. Giles

   * (Clue: aemulāri, -ātus 'to rival')

7. ... Nice from the Greek Nike, goddess of victory;...
   and the Alsatian towns ending in dorf....* But what
   to make of the place names... Noisy, His, Condom,
   and Void?   More   incursions   of   Franglais?
   S. de Gramont

   * dorf equals G. Dorf. Germans capitalize all nouns.

8. ... the mind in creation is as a fading coal, which
   some invisible influence, like an inconstant wind,
   awakens to transitory brightness...   Shelley

9. Common in early Christian and Byzantine art is the
   orant Virgin.

10. Tenured professors helped to select a rector.

11. For ditty and amorous ode, I find Sir Walter Raleigh's vein most lofty, <u>insolent</u> and passionate. Puttenham
(N.B.: Renaissance Latinizers tried to restore insolent's pristine meaning and dignity)

VI. Define the underlined words:

1. It must indeed be a <u>captious</u> critic who can find a pretext to make a quarrel out of that. Churchill

2. You can hardly <u>conceive</u> this man to have been bred in the same climate. Swift

3. This singular accident, by a strange <u>confluence</u> of emotions in him, was felt as the sharpest sting of all. Hardy.

4. There is no <u>convenience</u> between Christ and Belial. Sampson

5. That <u>conversion</u> will be suspected that apparently concurs with interest. Johnson

6. At length <u>convinced</u> with the heavinesse of sleep... he turned him to the wall. Munday

7. The <u>convolutions</u> of a smooth-lipped shell Wordsworth

8. After a week of soulless dissipation, I invited a small party of the most <u>dissolute</u> students to a secret carousal in my chambers. Poe

9. God had <u>pretended</u> a remedie in that behalfe which was Manna. Carew

10. Abate the edge of traitors, gracious Lord,
That would <u>reduce</u> these bloody days again.
Richard III

VII. a) What are the four elements in the word <u>independentia</u>*?

---

* There is in fact no Latin word <u>independentia</u>. The four elements were put together by some English writer. Pope says: "Let fortune do her worst, whatever she makes us lose, as long as she never makes us lose our honesty and our independence." Similarly, interdependence is formed from a hypothetical Latin <u>interdependentia</u>.

b)   An intervening or intermediate time may be referred to as the _____ .

c)   The word you used to answer b) appears adjectivally in the expression _____ meeting.

d)   In astronomy, the planets between the earth's orbit and the sun are referred to as _____ planets.

e)   What is the name of the doctor who serves as an assistant resident in a hospital shortly after his graduation from medical school?

f)   What does the prefix mean in internecine, interregnum and interstellar?

g)   What is the action of detaining or confining aliens within a country in time of war?

THE PRESENT PARTICIPLE

The present participle of Latin verbs provides many English derivatives. To obtain it, one adds to the verb's base -āns (1st conjugation), -ēns (2nd), -ens or -iēns* (3rd) or -iēns (4th), e.g., amāns, terrēns, loquēns and faciēns, and audiēns. The genitive is -antis (1st), entis (2nd), -entis or -ientis* (3rd) and -ientis (4th). The participle, which functions as an adjective, is declined as a 3rd declension adjective.

One may sometimes form an abstract noun by adding -ia to the present participle's base. The result yielded in English is the ending -ce or -cy as in decadence and leniency.

CONJUGATION	PRES. INFIN.	BASE	PRES. PTC. BASE	ENGLISH DERIVATIVE
I	clāmāre 'to shout'	clam-	clamant-	clamant
II	dēterrēre 'to frighten from'	deterr-	deterrent- (+ -ia, ending added)	deterrence
III	remittere 'to let go back, send back'	remitt-	remittent-	remittent
IV	sentīre 'to feel'	sent-	sentient-	sentient
	orīrī 'to rise'	or-	orient-	orient

WORD NOTES

All present-participial endings in OF. were leveled to -ant. English derivatives through French usually produce this same ending. Witness ascendant, confidant, covenant, lieutenant, mordant, pendant, recreant, resistant, sergeant, servant, tenant.

---

* in the case of -iō verbs only, e.g., capiō, faciō, fugiō, rapiō, speciō

Absens and praesens, participles of abesse and praeesse, show the participle sens; the other participle of esse, essens, is found in quintessence. When Aristotle postulated a fifth element in the universe, he called it pemptê ousia. L. quinta essentia (the most essential part of anything) was coined to express this idea. The participle ens developed later. It gives us entity (anything real). F. sans is altered from L. absentia, with the influence of sine 'without.' Sans is archaic or poetic.

Fame, a prize much striven for, goes back to L. fāma (from fāri, 'to speak') and meant originally only 'rumor, report, common talk.' Infant is derived from L. infans 'one who is not speaking.' Italians meant also by infante a young boy who served as an attendant to a knight, on foot. Infanteria came to mean 'a band of foot-attendants,' whence our word infantry. It. fantaccino, from It. fante, shortened form of infante, originally a valet, and then, a foot-soldier, led to F. fantassin.

11c enfant, 'non-speaking child,' came to mean the child up to age seven. In Imperial Latin înfāns was replacing puer and meant the child from seven to fifteen years of age. Still later, it came to mean the child in relationship to its parents. Enfanter, enfantement, enfantin, enfance were all 12c words. None of them is reflected in English except infancy (< L. înfāntia). Infancy first meant 'inability to speak,' 'want of eloquence.' It was then transferred in meaning to 'infancy, early childhood, second childhood,' and the collective notion of 'children.' Colloquial F. fanfan developed in the 16c. 19c F. Fanfan la Tulipe, a character created by songsters, designated a type of French soldier who loves life as much as military glory. He always defends causes which he feels are just. In 1792 Rouget de Lisle composed the Marseillaise for the army of the Rhine. It became the French national anthem. "Allons enfants de la patrie" reveals the word in its military denotation. Enfants perdus, a military term which developed later, meant 'forlorn hope.' It referred to troops in a hopelessly dangerous position. In quite another context, the expression enfant terrible developed. He is either a mischievous child, or one who causes trouble by making inappropriate, frank, bold remarks.

In law, infancy is a technical term which may refer to the period before the age of legal majority, usually twenty-one. Infant and infancy, infantry and infantryman are all related etymologically.

A patient is automatically 'one who suffers;' it derives from L. patiens, -entis. 16c F. developed impatienter 'to be impatient.' English has not been so versatile. Our tangent is also from the base of a present participle, tangens, -entis 'touching.' It is used largely in geometry. Tangential as adjective signifies not dealing with a subject at length, digressing.

Cognate with Gk. kalein 'to call' is L. clamāre, whence OF. claimer 'to cry out, claim.' Claimant's doublet is clamant. L. convenīre 'to agree, to be of one mind' gives OF covenir whence OF. covenant 'an agreement.' We transform it into a transitive and intransitive verb, and retain it as a noun, its doublet being convenient.

Astrologers attributed influenza to the influence of the stars. LL. influentia meant a flowing in, from L. īnfluēns -tis + -ia, pres. ptc. of īnfluere 'to flow in.' Credenza, cadenza, extravaganza, influenza and stanza all show Italian influence. LL. stantia 'abode' became It. stanza, 'stopping place, room,' and our word meaning a verse of four or more lines.

F. croissant 'a crescent' comes from the baking of breakfast rolls in this shape in Vienna after the Turks lifted the siege in 1689. The crescent moon was adopted in 1453 as the emblem of the former Turkish Empire after the taking of Constantinople. What can equal eating your Hörnchen, symbolic of your city's occupiers over many years, at breakfast?

L. serviens, from servīre gave OF. serjent, 'a servant,' whence sergeant. A feudal servant who attended his master in battle is now a non-commissioned officer in the army, or the police. 13c OF. lieutenant is from locum + tenēns -tis 'one holding the place of another.'

L. unguentum is from unguere 'to anoint.' F. oindre derives from this, as does OF. oignement, ME. oinement, E. ointment. L. obedīre 'to obey,' really L. oboedīre, (obaudire),

gives obedientia, whence OF. obeissance and ME. obeisaunce, whence obeisance, shown by a curtsy. Obedience is its doublet.

L. nocēre 'to harm, annoy' gives OF. nuisir, noisir, whence 12c OF. nuisance, ME. nusance, and our word which has reverted to the OF. spelling. L. connīvere 'to wink, close one's eyes,' gave 5c LL. connīventia, 16c F. connivence and E. connivance. Connivency is obsolete, but consent or pretended ignorance in wrong-doing survives as connivance.

Chance, from popular L. cadentia (n. pl. used as a fem. sg. noun) entered 12c F. as chute, 'a fall.' 17c chute de dés led to its meaning as 'heureux hasard.' Chance is therefore an early legacy from the dice-box.

Renaissance is formed on the base of L. nāsci, nātus 'to be born.' The word appears in 14c Miracles de Notre-Dame, but we now use it primarily to mean the rebirth of Greco-Roman culture and its concomitant intellectual and artistic activities or, indeed, revolution, for it was a period of rapid, and often violent, cultural change. Naissance is attested in the 12c. Formed on the past-participial base of the same Latin verb is native. 12c F. naïf is followed by 14c F. natif. 17c naïf, the source of our 'naïve,' meant one without tact or finesse, a little silly. Naive, used neutrally, indicates one who is artless or unsophisticated, but it too tends to be used pejoratively to suggest the simple-minded.

Native is used by a patriot proudly speaking of his own land, or by a person who considers himself superior to another he considers racially inferior. The 17c used it of inhabitants of countries considered savage, or of inhabitants of a country as distinguished from visitors to it. It may be used pejoratively to refer to a primitive or uncivilized person.

A peculiar suffix in English is the -acy, -cy found in advocacy, primacy, lieutenancy, etc. We have 'importance' and 'consequence' but also 'candidacy,' 'efficiency,' 'militancy,' 'presidency.' An -ia noun-ending added to the present-participial base allows us to see the formation of 'evidence,' but also 'super-intendency.' The ML. pronunciation of -atia helps to explain our pronunciation of 'adequacy' and 'conspiracy,' 'curacy' and 'procuracy,' which we know in its short form 'proxy.' This refractory suffix tends to take an unpredictable and independent course whether added to nouns, adjectives or participles (cf. captaincy, supremacy and intimacy, efficiency, militancy and privacy).*

Latin has verbal adjectives which are participial in meaning. They are formed with the suffixes -ndus, -bundus, -cundus. -ndus, the same as the gerundive ending, which we will soon look at, forms an active or reflexive adjective: rotundus 'round, whirling,' comes from rotāre to whirl.' From sequī 'to follow,' Latin forms the adjective secundus 'second, favorable.' -bundus and -cundus denote a continuance of the act or quality expressed by the verb, e.g., from florēre 'to bloom,' floribundus 'flowering', from mori 'to die,' morībundus, 'dying' and from vagāri 'to roam,' vagābundus 'wandering.' Fecund comes from a Latin root fē- 'nourish,' whence fēcundus. From the base of īrascī 'to be angry,' L. has īrācundus 'irascible.'

---

* See J.D. Sadler, "A Peculiar Suffix," The Classical Journal, May, 1970, pp. 364-65.

The present participle indicates progress or continuity. Purely adjectival, it provides us with the gardening terms frutescens, patens, procumbens, repens or reptans, semperflorens, sempervirens, scandens and vacillans.** In accordance with Linnaeus' binomial system of nomenclature, these participles are used as adjectives to indicate a plant's or a flower's species. By now, about a million species of plants have been named and described by this system.***

Exercise XVIIa.

I. 1. Some words enter the language before others. Which word came first in the following pairs: peynture, picture, parfait, perfect, aventure, adventure, ceinture, cincture, overture, aperture, sure, secure? Deduce the principle governing the adoption of the two types of borrowings, those words that have come into English through a derivative language of Latin, and those formations made from the Latin full form.

    2. Count the prefixes, infixes and suffixes in incomprehensible. What is the root?

    3. What linguistic phenomenon is at work when retarded children are called exceptional and classes for slow learners become "opportunity classes?"

    4. What do the underlined words in the following expressions have in common: Bacchic revelry, cereal products, Junoesque stateliness, mercurial nature, venereal disease, volcanic ash?

    5. Distinguish between caitiff and captive, missile and missive, motif and motive, stationary and stationery, plaintiff and plaintive. Indicate which pairs are doublets. Define all words.

    6. The antonym of senescence is _____, the 'state of burgeoning vigor, of pure youth.'

** On technical names for plants see J.D. Sadler's "Horticultural Classics," The Clasical Journal, 65.6 (Mar., 1970) pp. 267-69.

*** Cf. Linnaeus, Critica Botanica, 1737. For matters pertaining to botany's rules of nomenclature, see O.E. Nybakken, Greek and Latin in Scientific Terminology, Iowa, 1962, pp. 302-7.

7. Homō ludens implies that the proper designation for our species is not Homō sapiens, "man the intelligent," or Homō faber, "man the contriver," but "man the _____."   M. Hadas

8. What is the difference between a reticent and a taciturn person?   between an abstemious and an abstinent person?

9. Differentiate the meanings of cogitate, contemplate, meditate, ruminate and speculate.

10. Which category of people are more submissive: the amenable, or the acquiescent?

11. One with introverted and extroverted tendencies, turning his mind both inward and outward, is an _____.   Having a character trait or condition midway between introversion and extroversion, he displays _____.

12. One who has unwarranted pride and displays haughtiness is _____.

13. One who presumptuously lays claim _____ power or dignity to himself.

14. To alter, enlarge, or corrupt a book, manuscript, etc. by putting in new words, subject matter, etc., is to _____, whereas to estimate a value or quantity on the basis of certain variables within the known range, from which the estimated value is assumed to follow, is to _____.

15. Latin-derived words (Col. C) correspond in meaning to current definitions (Col. A) and to etymological meanings (Col. B).

Col. A	B	C
1) to occur simultaneously	'to fall in with'	
2) disgraceful, contemptible	'able to be looked down at, despised'	
3) show, detailed explanation; exhibition	'result of a setting out'	
4) excessive dislike, aversion	'a fighting back'	

132

5) to occur as something   'to come in
    extraneous; to come   addition'
    after something else

6) common, customary,   'pertaining to
    habitual, regular,   custom, use'
    normal

III. Analyze the underlined words:

1) They have not enough of <u>coherence</u> among them-
    selves.... Burke

2) The Anglo-Normans, moved to name a pub for the
    <u>Infanta</u> di Castile the never quite bride of James I,
    came up with The Elephant and Castle.   J. Ciardi

3) I don't ask you to trust me, without offering a
    respectable <u>reference</u>.   Dickens

4) The <u>remonstrances</u> of peace groups are disregarded.

5) That branch of belief in him was <u>supervenient</u> to
    Christian practice.   Hammond

IV. Translate a) vox clamantis* in deserto,
               b) verbum sat** sapienti.

     * of one who is crying (= shouting)
     ** <u>sat</u> is for <u>satis</u> 'sufficient, enough'

The Gerundive

     The Gerundive is formed by adding the endings -andus,
-endus, -endus (-iendus in the case of -io* verbs) and -iendus to
the present-infinitive base of verbs of the 1st, 2nd, 3rd, and
4th conjugations, respectively. -andus agrees with a singular
masculine noun, as does -endus or -iendus; -anda, -enda, -ienda
agree with sg. feminine nouns; -andum, -endum, -iendum agree with
neuter sg. nouns. Memorāre gives memorandum, "the thing which
must be related, brought to memory, mentioned." Amanda (given
name) means "she who must be loved;" armandus would mean "he who
must be furnished with weapons." (The given name Armand is from
German and not related to L. armāre). York University gets its
motto tentanda via from Vergil's Georgics 3.8:   temptanda via
est: 'the path must be essayed.'

* e.g., capiō, faciō, fugiō, rapiō, speciō

Like the perfect participle, the gerundive is passive in meaning. It expresses fitness, necessity, or obligation. "Carthagō dēlenda est" paraphrases what Cato the Censor said repeatedly in 153 B.C. about an African city. Obsessed, he would end all his speeches in the senate with this statement (cf. dēlēre 'to destroy'). Agatha Christie's Miss Marple quotes the Horatian 'nil desperandum' when intent upon solving a mysterious crime.

WORD NOTES

In proof-reading, we use the neuter plurals addenda, corrigenda, delenda. We singularize agenda, though it is neuter plural. Propaganda, a feminine singular, is derived from a committee of cardinals formed by Pope Gregory XV to supervise the work of foreign missions. The group's name was 'Congregatio de Propaganda Fide' or 'Committee for the Propagation of the Faith.' Parenthetically, the neuter of the gerundive, the gerund is used as a noun in Latin, e.g., ars equitandi, ars loquendi, ars scribendi, modus operandi, modus vivendi, finis vivendi.

Referendum, from L. referre 'to bring back,' is the submission of a proposed law, or one already in effect, to a direct vote of the people to determine whether it shall stand or be abrogated. This popular vote supersedes or overrules the legislature. A reprimand, < OF. réprimande, from L. reprimenda 'a thing that ought to be repressed,' is a formal rebuke by a person in authority, e.g., a dean at University. A court may order an officer of the law to be reprimanded for neglect of duty. We are all familiar with multiplicand, radicand, and subtrahend in arithmetic, with dividends (money divided among stockholders, creditors, or members of a co-op), and legend (OF. légende, from LL. legenda 'a story'), something to be read. Miranda must be admired. Mutatis mutandis tells us the necessary changes have been made. A reverend member of the clergy is 'very much to be fearèd.' When we say that we are tremendously impressed, do we realize that L. tremendus 'to be trembled at, dreadful' is at the adverb's base? A stupendous lie is by all rights one which strikes us senseless (< L. stupēre 'to be amazed').

From L. lavandus, gerundive of lavāre 'to wash,' we get LL. lavandārius, and lavandāria 'a washer.' From OF. lavandier and ME. lavander and lavendrie, we derive laundry. From lavander 'a washerwoman,' comes ME. launder, whence our verb. As we get reminisce from reminiscentia (a plural in Tertullian and Arnobius) by back-formation, so we get launder from lavandāria. Our color and flower lavender are not related. A lavabo (see Lesson VIII, Exercise XI, literally 'I shall wash,') is a) a ritual of washing the celebrant's hands after the offertory, b) vs. 6-12 of Psalm 25 in the Vulgate (26 in the Authorized and

Revised Versions), c) the washbowl, laver < LL. lavātōrium, or basin used, d) the room containing this in monasteries, or e) the small bowl used in the rite for drying the celebrant's hands.

The n. pl. gerundive of facere 'to do' became Sp. hacienda 'estate, plantation, country house.' From "things to be done," there is a transference of meaning to "a place where things are done." Hacienda is attested in 18c E. and 20c F. Its F. doublet, facende, is a 16c loan word from P. fazenda. It. faccenda is a business, job, matter.

Words may go contrary to pedantic rules and undergo transformation by fiat, e.g., the publication board of the American Institute of Electrical and Electronics Engineers recommended (Nov., 1969) that "plurals ... derived from Greek and Latin be formed by adding -s (or sometimes -es) to singular forms." Agenda, plural in Latin, but singular in English, is pluralized to agendas, but individual items on the list (of the agenda) are agendums, the IEEE stated. Agenda, like data, is seen as a collective noun, the whole rather than its component parts being envisioned. As we know, this has already happened to media, so that medias will become the normal plural form. Pedantry cannot halt the evolution of language. Descending to a somewhat more prosaic matter, we find that in arithmetic terminology, wherever we may have expected an -um ending, there is none. The gender indicator does not exist in addend + addend = sum, minuend - subtrahend = difference, dividend divided by divisor = quotient, and multiplicand x multiplier = product. However, in mechanics, we have the addendum circle; in music, through Italian, diminuendo or decrescendo, and crescendo, but not minuendo. Innuendo is from the abl. of the gerund of innuere 'to nod to, intimate, hint.' Italian rallentando, with gradually slowing tempo, has its counterpart, accelerando. Another direction to the performer, this time to become plaintive, is lacrimando.

MEMORIZING ALL VERB BASES

Memorize the four bases of the verbs given below, as illustrated.

EXAMPLE: dare, datus 'to give' dans, dantis; dandus-a-um (NB:
only the base of the verb forms is underlined)

ambulāre, -ātus 'to walk'
ligāre, -ātus 'to bind'
delēre, -ētus 'to destroy'
docēre, doctus 'to teach'
*fervēre, _____ 'to
seethe, boil'
cadere, cāsum 'to fall'
caedere, caesus 'to cut, kill'
cernere, crētus 'to sift,
decide'
claudere, clausus 'to close'
colere, cultus 'to till,
cultivate'
dēficere, dēfectus 'to fail,
be wanting'
frangere, frāctus 'to break
fugere, fugitus 'to flee'
fundere, fūsus 'to pour'
petere, petītus 'to aim at,
seek'
premere, pressus 'to press'
scandere, scānsum 'to climb'

fallere, falsus 'to deceive,
dupe'
fīdere, fīsus 'to trust'
findere, fīssus 'to split'
fluere, fluxus (fluctus) 'to
flow'
scīre, scītus 'to know'
sentīre, sēnsum 'to feel'
servīre, servītus 'to serve'
migrāre, -ātus 'to rove'
sēdāre, -ātus 'to settle,
cause to sit'
habēre, -itus 'to have,
hold' (or -hibitus)
jacēre, _____ 'to lie,
recline'
ta(n)gere, tāctus 'to touch'
trahere, tractus 'to draw'
trudere, trusus 'to push'
posse, _____ 'to be
able, powerful' (pres. ptc.
base pot-)

EXERCISE XVIII

I.   Etymologize, and pick out derivatives from
     present-participial bases which have undergone French
     spelling influence:

     armipotent, arrant, cadent, confidant, descendant,
     dormant, mordant, pendant, persistent, prebend,
     provenance, reprimand, revenant, savant, sequence,
     sergeant, servant, subjacent.

---

* Like fervēre are candēre, dolēre, fetēre, fulgēre, humēre,
  horrēre, languēre, liquēre, nitēre, pallēre, rancēre, rigēre,
  squalēre, torpēre, valēre, vigēre. One may form abstract nouns
  by adding -or (-our, British spelling) to their present-
  infinitive base. All these are second conjugation verbs.

II.	Form English derivatives from Latin which have the following meanings. Note that your answers will be in alphabetical sequence:

things which must be done, running together with, (spirits) boiling out, wandering (e.g., knight), stepping, not seeing beforehand, shedding tears (musical direction), licking (e.g., flames), she who must be admired, all-knowing (God), going before, (the faith) which has to be spread, as in Pope Gregory's Congregatio de ____ Fide, 1622), the receiver (e.g., of a benefit), state of ruling, state of serving under.

III.	Give the meanings of the prefixes in: abreaction, adhere, antepenultimate, deduct, disservice, exponent, interstellar, occident, peremptory, pervert, prejudice, protrude, remorse, replica, secrete, secure, subside, traverse, ultramundane.

IV.	Fill in the blank spaces with an English word derived from a Latin present participle (NB: your answers will be in alphabetical order):

1)	Simultaneous attraction toward and repulsion from an object, person or action is _____ .
2)	A thing which climbs towards its summit is in its _____ .
3)	A circumstance which follows as a result of something preceding is a _____ .
4)	A person who lacks trust in himself is _____ .
5)	One who cannot wait for want of endurance is _____ .
6)	A powerless person is _____ .
7)	As a seminary student, he was a beginning or _____ priest.
8)	The educated portion of the population is its _____ .
9)	An all-powerful ruler is _____ .
10)	The East or Levant where the sun rises is also called the _____ .
11)	Castor canadensis, the beaver, is an aquatic _____ .
12)	That of which a physical thing consists is its _____ .
13)	One who rents or holds an apartment or house is a _____ .
14)	In 1865, the U.S. adopted the Spanish-derived word _____ to denote a member of a vigilance committee.

V. Separate the following words into their segments and define each segment as illustrated:

Example: word: reverential
          segments: re- prefix with intensive meaning
                     verēns-tis, pres.-ptc. base of
                         verērī, veritus 'to fear, feel
                         awe for'
                     -i- connecting vowel derived from
                         -ia, a noun-forming suffix
                         meaning   'result of'
                     -alis adjective-forming suffix
                         meaning 'connected with,
                         pertaining to, having the
                         character of'
          meaning: characterized by or inspiring
                     reverence

abstraction, defoliant, digitigrade, equivalence, horticultural, preliminary, prodigal, substitution, suffuse, tendentious, uncircumcised, valedictorian.

VI. Select the inappropriate word in the following groups; explain your choice:

confuse, effusion, fund, fission, profuse, transfusion;
consent, decent, nonsense, resent, sensuous, sentiment;
contingent, intact, intangible, sustain, tangential;
abstract, detractor, distrait, entr'acte, portrait;
competition, impetuous, petal, petulant, repeat;
fraction, frangible, frail, irrefutable, refrain (noun).

VII. Analyze the underlined words:

1) In England the bear who ate a Napoleonic veteran would have been shot, a deodand levied. In France, they caricatured the incident and called the bear by the veteran's name. S. de Gramont
2) His fluency betrayed him into verbiage, and his descriptions are more diffuse than vigorous. Symonds
3) Juvenal's Graeculus esuriens, whence 'esurient,' shrinks from no task that will bring him money.
4) Neither Gaia nor Pandora has a progenitrix.
5) A Jesuit motto is Repetitio mater studiorum.
6) A bagel is more than a doughnut with rigor mortis. G. Goliger
7) And you above the city, scintillant,
    Mount Royal, are my spirit's mother. A.M. Klein

VIII.   The following list contains eight (8) pairs of words that are linguistically related. Identify the pairs, and in each case show how the words are related. N.B.: four words do not apply.

avoirdupois, concede, digress, elect, fulsome, inhibit, legend, legitimate, process, refulgent, retrograde, scansion, sediment, sedition, subtrahend, tact, tangent, tractor, transcend, transient.

IX.   Give the doublets of cadenza, confident, convenient, crescent, unguent, penance, poignant, prudent, sergeant, stanza.

X.   Which of the following are not derived from present participles: complaisance, deference, difference, ebullience, flatulence, incidence, opulence, radiance, reticence, succulence?

XI.   Analyze affluence, emergence, mendicant, petulance, strident, vagrant.

XII.   Show where the present infinitive base or the perfect-participial base has been used in the following words. Give the present infinitive and the meaning of the verb that has supplied the base in each instance:

clause, cohabitation, compulsion, creditable, discern, docile, doctor, emigrate, fallible, incredulous, indelible, intangible, pressure, profusion, prospectus, protrusion, reactor, repetition, repository, sedative, sentiment, vertebrate.

XIII. The following words are either derived from the present-participial base or the gerundive base. Distinguish them and give the meaning of the verb that has supplied the base in each case:

addendum, audience, competent, confidence, convenience, current, deodand, desiderandum, diffidence, dividend, equivalent, horrendous, inherent, legendary, memorandum, multiplicand, patience, prescient, stringent, stupendous.

XIV.   Form an English derivative from each of the four bases of ferre (bases fer-, lātus 'to bring,' 'to bear,') and of crēscere, crētus 'to grow,' an inchoative* or inceptive* verb.

---

* Both L. inchoāre and L. incipere mean 'to begin.'

XV.   Determine from which part of the verb these words are formed: ascension, circumvent, confide, declamatory, deletion, dissent, edit, elocution, eloquence, exposure, impend, influx, injection, native, proscribe, regent, retract, transmute.

XVI. Using participial bases and the appropriate adverbial prefixes, adjectives, suffixes forming abstract nouns, agent nouns, fill in the following descriptive sentences:

1. One who does good for people is a _____.
2. A public performance at a theatre, a dance, a bazaar, etc. the proceeds of which are given in aid of some individual, group, or cause is a _____.
3. One who wishes people well is _____.
4. One who enjoys good food and other pleasant things is a _____.
5. The condition of trusting thoroughly, or firm belief in the trust-worthiness of another is _____.
6. The condition or state of awaiting or looking forward to an event or someone's arrival is _____.
7. The condition or state of flowing, as of a speech, is _____.
8. One who perpetrates an evil deed is a _____.
9. Something harmful, causing evil is _____.
10. One who has ill will towards others is _____.
11. Formed on the base of nocēre 'to harm,' a _____ is an act, condition, thing or person causing trouble, annoyance, or inconvenience.
12. As people who are engaged in the cultural process, we don't need more missiles and H-bombs so much as we need more specific knowledge of ourselves as _____ in culture.
13. Feeling regret for an offence committed, or sorrow, accompanied with the desire to atone for a sin, is _____.
14. A meeting (or sitting) of spiritualists at which they try to communicate with the spirits of the dead is a _____.
15. Any obscure, visionary or idealistic philosophy which proposes to discover the nature of reality by investigating the process of thought rather than the objects of sense experience is _____.

XVII. Determine the etymological meaning of reluctance. What semantic change is illustrated by its modern use as distinct from its use in Milton, where it means strife?

WORD NOTES

Besides verbs of 'seeing' as a source of knowledge, L. has many verbs of knowing which range from sapere 'to have sense, be prudent' through metīrī 'to measure,' prehendere 'to grasp,' sagīre 'to discern acutely,' to cognoscere and scīre 'to know.' Verbal activity which leads to knowledge is contained in the verbs cogitāre, intellegere, opinārī, putāre, rērī, studēre, etc. Let us dwell on what has happened to some derivatives of one of these verbs.

A F.-derived word illustrates how a word may come to mean or suggest virtually the opposite of an earlier meaning. From L. cognitum, past participle of cognoscere, there develops the OF. queinte, cointe. ME. queynte reflects the OF. pronunciation of the time. In reference to persons, it meant 'wise, clever, ingenious;' applied to things, 'ingeniously or cunningly devised or contrived.' Later specialized, it meant 'beautiful, pretty, fine, dainty' 1671. Of people, it meant 'elegant or foppish' 1784; later restricted in meaning, 'strange, odd, curious' in character or appearance 1808. Recently, it took on the meaning of 'picturesque or pleasing in an old-fashioned way.' This led to its colloquial derogatory use in the sense of 'odd, ludicrous.' Through semantic shift, the original meaning is now obscured. It. cognoscente and F. connaisseur, synonymous agent-nouns, derive from the verb's present participle and present infinitive base respectively. They mean 'one who knows a subject thoroughly.'

Recognizance was probably formed on the noun cognizance ‹ OF. conis(s)ance. Its doublet, reconnaissance, is a military or scientific survey of a district.

Cdn. F. inconnu 'unknown' is a fresh water food fish native to the rivers and lakes of the Yukon. English reduces this to 'conny.' Ferguson, Tuktoyaktuk, mentions "the large fish--inconnu or connie." Inconnu's doublet stems from It. incognito, which we use as adverb or adjective. In "The motif of the incognito king given hospitality by a man of low rank seems ... a universal one in the ... Middle Ages" (E. Walsh, Folklore), it is adjectival. Henri Peyre uses it in its Latin form as he "plunges into the terrae incognitae of literature." An 1855 map of Canada bears the legend Terra Incognita to the north of Frobisher Strait.

***   ***

L. datum 'given', becomes F. dé and E. die (pl. dice). L. fātum, 'that which has been spoken,' gives E. fate. Fata were the three dread goddesses, the Fates. LL. fata 'goddess of

142

fate,' gave OF. fae, F. fée which became fay, no longer the utterance of a divinity, nor the divinity itself.

Fairy was originally spelt faerie. It represents the magic powers of which the fay was capable. The correct name for the individual fairy is fay, but because faerie came to be spelled fairy, we speak of a fairy as the one who practises magic and not the magic or enchantment itself. It. Fata Morgana is a mirage seen in the Straits of Messina. It is attributed to the fairy Morgana (cf. Morgan le Fay of Arthurian legend). Morgan-le-Fey is Anglo-French.

F. vers came from the masculine form of the past participle versus of vertere 'to turn.' This was used as a noun. Vertigo is from the same verb; it appears in 16c English as a medical term, then in France. A dizzy person is one affected by vertigo, hence vertiginous. Balzac uses vertigineux connotatively as 'tending to cause vertigo.' By the end of the 15c F. vertigineux meant 'one affected by dizziness.'

From versus we also get verse, meaning literally 'a turning to the beginning of the next line.' Prōsa (oratiō), from proversa 'turned forward,' is straightforward (speech) without turnings. Prōversa became prorsa then prōsa, leading to 13c F. prose and to our prose.*

L. tractus 'pull of the scale' gives trait, and a doublet tract, land area. From jactātus comes jetty, that which juts out. (Cf. Word notes in Lesson XII). Jactāre is a frequentative verb (see Lesson XIX). Giving rise to popular L. jēctare, it is the source of F. jeter. It. iettatura, 'the evil eye,' is the act of putting a hex on someone; cf. F. 'jeter un sort.'

F. jongleur 'minstrel' is from L. joculātor 'joker,' from joculāri 'to joke.' We get juggler, and by back-formation, the verb 'to juggle.' A Middle Ages minstrel who sang songs, usually of his own composition, was a jongleur.

When Italians answer the phone, they say pronto (< L. promptum 'brought forth, at hand,' < L. prōmere 'to take, buy'). Probably under Mexican influence, Americans adopted it** in 1918. Pronto's doublet is prompt. Early L. praesto, adverb, 'here before your eyes, at hand to help,' gives our presto, a word favored by magicians.

---

* In Molière's Le Bourgeois Gentilhomme Monsieur Jourdain says: "Il y a plus de quarante ans que je dis de la prose, sans que j'en susse rien..."
** Sp. pronto means 'on the double.'

Prestige comes from a French word meaning essentially 'magic' or 'illusion' attributed to wizards; it is derived from praestringere, 'to bind before,' 'to blindfold.' Prestigious used to mean 'full of deceitful tricks' but it now means 'having or imparting distinction.' Distinction itself goes back to a L. verb which meant 'to prick off, separate, adorn.' The latter notion now marks its meaning, since it can mean a sign of eminence, superiority or fame.

A Frenchman in the eleventh century broke his fast by the disner (< LL. disjunāre 'to break fast'). In the twelfth century, he broke his fast by the déjeuner, since popular Latin disjunāre still meant 'to take a light meal upon arising.' One notes that the primitive form developing out of Latin is shorter in French than the learned word later borrowed.* In the nineteenth century, petit déjeuner was adopted so that the morning meal might be distinguished from the later meal, the dîner.

---

* For more details, see The Classical Bulletin 60.3 (Summer, 1984), pp. 49-50.

Learn the bases of the following verbs.

amāre, -ātus 'to love'
clīnāre, -ātus 'to lean'
jurāre, -ātus 'to swear'
LL. pausāre, 'to cease'
(whence F. poser)
putāre, -ātus 'to reckon, think'
secāre, sectus 'to cut'
spīrāre, -ātus 'to breathe'
cavēre, cautus 'to beware'
horrēre, _____ 'to shrink, shudder'
licēre, licitum 'to be permitted'
manēre, mānsus 'to remain'
placēre, placitus 'to please,
-plēre, -plētus 'to fill'
rērī, ratus 'to calculate, think'
torquēre, tortus 'to twist'
valēre, _____ 'to be strong, worth'
vovēre, vōtus 'to vow'
mētīrī, mensus 'to measure'
ordīrī, orsus 'to begin'
orīrī, ortus 'to arise'
acuere, acūtus 'to sharpen'
condere, -itus 'to hide, store'
crēscere, crētus 'to grow'
cupere, cupītus 'to desire'
dīvidere, dīvīsus 'to divide'

emere, ēmptus 'to buy' 'to take'
ferre, lātus 'to bear, bring'
fingere, fictus 'to fashion, alter'
gerere, gestus 'to bear, wage'
jungere, jūnctus 'to join'
lūdere, lūsus 'to play'
parere, partus 'to give birth'
pāscere, pāstus 'to feed, graze'
pōnere, positus 'to place, put'
serere, satus 'to sow'
sūmere, sūmptus 'to take'
vendere, venditus 'to sell'
haurīre, haustus 'to draw out'
polīre, polītus 'to polish, smooth'
salīre, saltus 'to leap'
sancīre, sānctus 'to make holy'
sortīrī, sortītus 'to draw lots'

EXERCISE XIX

I.   Determine the etymology of acumen, belligerent, competition, doctorate, figment, fissure, invigilator, leisure, obverse, prefer, rancor, season, specimen, supply, torment, transgression.

II.   Fill in the blank spaces with words composed in part from bases of the verbs listed above:

      1. Feticide is another word for _____.
      2. One who does not receive payment for participation in sport is a(n) _____.
      3. A love affair of illicit or secret nature is a(n) _____.

4. Those who plot against the government a criminal, illegal or reprehensible act are _____.
5. Venus' son, counterpart of Aphrodite's Eros, is _____.
6. An _____ study is a comprehensive survey of a subject.
7. An offering performed or made in pursuance of a vow is an _____.
8. Prose novels are in the realm of invented or imaginary _____.
9. The forming of a conclusion by reasoning from evidence is a(n) _____.
10. One who has taken an oath or swears allegiance is a(n) _____.
11. That which is capable of being measured or being assigned limits is _____.
12. A woman who has borne one child and is bearing a second is (a) _____.
13. A measure taken beforehand to avert evil or secure good results is a _____.
14. Triplets formed from the perfect-participial base of the verb 'to think' are _____, _____ and _____. (Clue: add -ĩō)
15. The action, or an act, of cutting or dividing is a _____.
16. Selection, choice or determination by the casting or drawing of lots is _____.

III. Give the English words that mean etymologically: 'breathing toward,' 'growing,' 'giving birth or bringing forth young,' 'leaping back,' 'to take together with,' 'to cut apart,' 'to jump on,' 'to swear away from,' 'to gather together,' 'to place together,' 'to place down,' 'to place between,' 'to place next to,' 'to place opposite,' 'to write upon,' 'to write down,' 'to write on,' 'to write beforehand,' 'to write in front of (forth).'

IV. Select from the following eight (8) linguistically related pairs of words, showing in each case how the words are related: accretion, collusion, competent, coniferous, consume, decision, diffident, elate, elude, excrescence, immanent, fission, mansion, mission, petition, regicide, resumption, sedate, stringency, strict.
N.B.: four words do not apply.

V. Analyze the underlined words by indicating the Latin segments from which they are composed; then, give the current meaning: to curate an exhibition, a cursory reading, to enjoin silence, execrable dishonesty, immanent Deity, inexorable fate, intransigent radicalism, to undergo obloquy, a peremptory tone, a juggler's prestidigitation, puissant empire, wanton rapacity, a reductio ad absurdum, reiterated requests, Hamlet's soliloquy, terra sigillata, the textus receptus of the NT, a ventriloquial sound.

VI.   Select the inappropriate word in each of the following groups and explain your choice:

   a)   course, cursory, curt, precursor, recourse, succor
   b)   affluent, confluence, flatulent, fluent, influenza, mellifluous
   c)   amputate, compute, deputation, disputant, Lilliputian, repute
   d)   aspire, conspiracy, inspiration, sprite, spry, transpire
   e)   contortionist, distort, extortion, torrefaction, torticollis
   f)   circumvent, convenient, convent, invent, revenue, ventral
   g)   assumption, consume, presumable, resumption, summer, sumptuary

VII.   Determine the contextual meaning of the underlined words:

   1.   Tangu boys learned ... in a generally permissive ambience the skills required of a male. K. Burridge
   2.   ... picturesque costume of the voyageur ... handkerchief ..., moccasins, ... and L'Assomption sash. Beaver
   3.   The pattern in the ceintures consisted of a wide red band in the centre barbed along the edges, like a series of continuous arrow points. Beaver
   4.   He made his way now through the vast congeries of rooms ... V. Woolf
   5.   The words figure and fictitious both derive from the same Latin root, fingere. Beware! M.J. Moroney
   6.   As a soldier he incurred ... the degrading imputation of cowardice. Macaulay
   7.   The monkey ... with a thick tail curling out into preposterous prolixity. Hawthorne
   8.   You gave them a cognovit for the amount of your costs after the trial ... Dickens
   9.   What is refractory to explanation cannot ipso facto serve as explanation.
   10. For Rousseau natural man is reborn in each child who must go through the same stages of imperfect denaturation. J. Shklar

SHAKESPEAREAN REMINISCENCES

VIII. Define the underligned Latinisms in:

147

1. Then, soul, live thou upon thy servant's loss,
   And let that pine to <u>aggravate</u> thy store.
                              Sonnet 146.10
2. Gaunt: As near as I could sift <u>him</u> on that <u>argument</u>,
           On some apparent danger seen in him
           Aim'd at your Highness, no inveterate malice.
                              Rich. II. 1.1.12
3. (Let her child) with <u>cadent</u> tears fret channels in
   her cheeks.
                              Lear 1.4.293
4. Like as the waves make towards <u>the</u> pebbled shore,
   So do our minutes hasten to their end ...
   In sequent toil all forwards do <u>contend</u>.
                              Sonnet 60.4
5. He was then of a <u>crescent</u> note.
                              Cymbeline 1.4.2
6. The <u>extravagant</u> and erring spirit hies
   To his confine.
                              Haml. 1.1.154-55
7. Advise the duke, where you are going, to / a most
   <u>festinate</u> preparation; we are bound to the like.
                              Lear 3.7.10
8. Beauty <u>provoketh</u> thieves sooner than gold.
                              As You Like It 1.3.109
9. O thou, the earthly author of my blood,
   Whose youthful spirit, in me <u>regenerate</u>,
   Doth with a twofold vigour lift me up ...
                              Rich. II. 1.3.70
10. ... but once put out thy light,
    Thou cunningst pattern of excelling nature,
    I know not where is that Promethean heat
    That can thy light <u>relume</u> ...
                              Othello 5.2.13

(Clues: attract, call forth; falling; growing; hasten;
hurried, immediate; increase; reborn; rekindle; roving,
traveling widely; subject.)

MORE LATINISMS IN ENGLISH

IX. Etymologize the underlined words and determine their
    meanings in the context:

    1. Stieglitz' camera registered what his <u>animal</u> eye
       perceived.
    2. <u>Dolours</u> of death into his soule did dart. Spenser
    3. A French nun in blue tugged at a rope <u>depending</u> from
       the belfry. F. Obrien
    4. Through all art there is a <u>filiation</u>.
    5. <u>Redundant</u> are thy locks ... Wordsworth, Laodamia 59

6. Fierce rain with lightning mixed, water
   With fire in ruin reconcil'd. Milton, PR 4.413
7. Orpheus could lead the savage race,
   And trees uprooted left their place,
   Sequacious of the lyre ... Dryden
8. Give up your breath in sleep's subaqueous shade,
   Hold to oblivion; are you afraid ...? E. Wylie
9. A joke is not to be translated about like an old
   trunk from one nation ... or language into another.
   M. Eastman
10. Where did the learned Héloisa vade ...? John Payne
    (Villon translation)

WORD NOTES

By Shakespeare's time, credulous, which had meant
'disposed to believe,' extended its meaning to 'apt to believe on
weak or insufficient grounds.' Cf. Othello 4.1.46: credulous
Fooles. Since then, it has been used in this derisive or
insulting sense; e.g., by Marlowe:

> Love is too full of faith, too credulous,
> With folly and false hope deluding us
> (Hero and Leander)

and Milton:

> So glistered the dire snake, and into fraud
> Led Eve our credulous mother, to the tree
> Of prohibition ... (PL 9.643-5)

Bearing in mind that the base of this word has given such
derivatives as credence, credible,* credit and creed, we are
faced with the paradox that even belief may carry its dangers,
especially when it is on slight and uncertain evidence. Such is
the nature of credulity. L. crēdulus is not formed with the
-ōsus 'full of, given to' as are such words as copious, curious,
fabulous and, from the Italian, grandiose; hence, credulous does
not have the etymological meaning 'full of belief,' but rather,
'easy of belief, confiding, trusting.' Latin authors used
crēdulus in its sense of trusting foolishly. Ovid mentions
fishes trusting to the hook and speaks of amor as a crēdula rēs.
But then, to Ovid, 'nos in vitium credula turba sumus'

---

* Of this word's derivative, credibility, now so overused, P.
   Howard says: "Its meaningless versatility would be
   incredible if its profligate career were not a common one for
   vogue words."

149

(F. 4.312).* It. credenza** (lit. faith) gives F. crédence 'sideboard' and the ecclesiastical credence table. As a precaution against poisoning, meats were first tasted.

When Sterne (Sentimental Journey, 1768) used the word sentimental, it meant pertaining to a delicate sensibility. Now degenerated, it may mean affectedly tender, mawkishly emotional, having an excess of sentiment or sensibility.

Familiar F. expressions are: 'femme de ménage,' 'nom de ménage,' and 'ménage à trois.' A derivative from the verbal base of manēre 'to dwell, to remain,' ménage developed, and then menagerie.

Post-Augustan mansiō, -ōnis 'dwelling' gives mansion and maison (cf. m. de santé). The lord mayor of London lives in the Mansion house. Manse, from ML. mansum, or mansa, is a parsonage or minister's residence. VL. mansionāticum gave ménage, whence menagerie, originally a collection of household animals. VL. mansionāta 'a houseful' has as one of its derivatives a menial (cf. OF. mesnial). F. manant was a dweller.***

From nocēre 'to harm' comes L. nocentia, an abstract noun giving rise to 12c OF. nuisance, ME. nusance. Nōlens volens, 'willy-nilly,' is equivalent to F. bon gré mal gré 'voluntarily, effortlessly.' Willy-nilly, contracted from will I, nill I, may mean indecisively.

---

* "We, the credulous crowd, incline to believe another is at fault."
** A cabinet so called because you "entrust" possessions to it.
*** It now means 'clodhopper.' In its specialized meaning, an habitant is a resident of Canada of French descent.

REVIEW

EXERCISE XX.

I.   Analyze all underlined words; give etymological and
       current meanings:

       a)   "... to distrust one's impulses is to be recreant to
             Pan."
             R.L. Stevenson
       b)   "... agreeing to differ with every ceremony of
             politeness is the only 'one undisturbed song of pure
             consent ...'" idem. (Cf. Milton's verse, p. 119)
       c)   "Let it be enough for faith that the whole creation
             groans in mortal frailty, strives with unconquerable
             constancy ..." idem.

II.   Give Latin-derived words for

       a)   a body of persons assembled for religious worship,
       b)   a composition, literary, musical, or dramatic of a
             fantastic character or theme,
       c)   a Latin version of the Bible authorized and used by
             the Roman Catholic Church.

III.   The following list contains five (5) pairs of words that
       are linguistically related. Identify the pairs and show
       the relationship in each case: accessories, gentry,
       peruse, summary, scurry, reactor, assumption, occasion,
       occlusion, sedentary, excoriate, presume, deciduous,
       quarry, agenda, ancestor. N.B.:   six words are not
       applicable.

IV.   Analyze five (5) of the following words. Separate them
       into their elements, define each element, and give the
       word's current meaning: contortionist, atrabilious,
       procrastinator, pestilential, traduce, counterfeit,
       fetish, reverberate.

V.   As in the previous question, analyze five (5) of the
       following underlined words: cogent reasons, dissident
       views, internecine strife, obfuscate the issue, a writer
       inclined to prolixity, proscribe one's enemies, purvey
       quack remedies, recondite words.

VI.   "Cost-conscious consumers can comparison-shop to avoid a
       R.I.P. - off in funeral purchase." Reproduce the Latin
       inscription; give its English counterpart. Comment on the
       rhetorical device in the first four words.

151

VII. Define the first underlined imperative in: "The fundamental proposition on whose content all philosophers of ethics are actually at one: neminem laede, immo omnes, quantum potes, juvā." Schopenhauer (NB: neminem, accus. case, 'nobody,' q.p. 'as much as you can,' juvā 'help').

VIII. a) Distinguez entre la pré-science et la prescience.
b) Faites la distinction entre l'emploi du verbe dans:
1) un joueur de baseball qui encaisse les huées de la foule,
2) un caissier qui encaisse les montants d'argent payés.

152

LESSON XVIII

MEMORIZING VERBS

MEMORIZE THE FOLLOWING VERBS.

solārī, solātus 'to comfort, console'
vorāre, vorātus 'to devour'
vocāre, vocātus 'to call'
calēre 'to be warm'*
tuērī, tutus 'to protect'
alere, alitus 'to nourish'
bibere, _____ 'to drink'
canere, cantus 'to sing'
dīcere, dictus 'to say'
flectere, flexus 'to bend'
fodere, fossus 'to dig'
gignere, genitus 'to beget'
garrīre, _____ 'to chatter'
pacīscī, pactus 'to make an agreement'
rēpere, rēptus 'to creep, crawl'
ruere, rutus 'to tumble down'
scindere, scissus 'to cut, split'
serere, sertus 'to bind, join'
spargere, sparsus 'to scatter'
sternere, strātus 'to spread'
tegere, tectus 'to cover'
incendere, incēnsus 'to set fire to'
linquere, _____ (-lictus) 'to leave'
luere, _____ (-lūtum) 'to wash, atone for'

mergere, mersus 'to dip, plunge'
nectere, nexus 'to bind'
nōscere, nōtus 'to know'
pendere, pēnsus 'to weigh, pay'
pingere, pictus 'to paint'
prehendere, prehensus 'to grasp'
pungere, punctus 'to prick'
querī, questus 'to complain'
ferīre 'to strike'
texere, textus 'to weave'
unguere, ūnctus 'to smear, anoint'
vādere, _____ 'to go, walk'
vehere, vectus 'to carry'
vellere, _____ (-vulsus) 'to pluck'
vincere, victus 'to conquer'
vīvere, vīctum 'to live'
volvere, volutus 'to roll'
prūrīre 'to itch'
saepīre, saeptus 'to enclose'
sāgīre 'to discern acutely'
tergiversārī 'to decline, refuse, turn one's back'

EXERCISE XXI

I. Determine the etymology and current meaning of:

bibulous, concomitant, concupiscence, convalescent, derelict, evince, expunge, garrulous, interlocutor, intersperse, pinto, prelate, reprehensible, retrogression, revulsion, svelte, textile, victress.

II. Analyze the underlined words and determine their current meanings:

---

* See note in Lesson IX about forming abstract nouns.

deliberate opinion, gestation period, gestatorial chair, irredentist Italians, Portuguese immersion course, terra incognita, prurient Pentheus, a punctuated reading.

III. Analyze and determine the current meaning of each underlined word.

1. Shakespeare's writings abound in classical allusions.
2. Calor, dolor, rubor, and tumor are Galen's four signs of illness.
3. Differing political and economic needs are the stuff of casus belli.
4. L. postumus, 'latest born,' falsely associated with L. humus 'ground, earth,' came to be used of a child born after his sire expired, or a work published after its author's demise.
5. Hunting is more sporting when dependent on skill of bow and arrow.
6. Equivocation begins early in Macbeth in the midnight hags' chanting their ambiguous words: "Fair is foul and foul is fair ..."
7. Very young ..., I had ... exultant vigor. T. Wolfe
8. Aeneas had his fidus Achates.
9. The emoluments and honoraria of physicians.
10. Or will God incense his ire
    For such a petty trespass ...? Milton
11. I propose that we deal with literary works as if they were living things, and that we apply some of the same criteria, mutatis mutandis, to them.
    Egon Schwarz
12. The Iliadic Zeus is by no means omnipotent.
13. While the song continues, they remain in a state of petrifaction. Goldsmith
14. Parents' sanctions often consist mainly of strong verbal criticism.
15. The old-fashioned bicycle is now undergoing a renaissance not seen since Tiffany glass returned to vogue. S. Browder
16. The man who never alters his opinion breeds reptiles of the mind. W. Blake

IV. a) Explain the tendency to use the word media with singular incorrectness.
    b) Is English descended from Latin?
    c) Did Romans know our mini-, midi-, and maxi- prefixes?
    d) What is the antonym of the adjective, 'compact?'

e) Snow in Mexico, a butterfly in winter, an escapee from Devil's Island are examples of a _____.*
f) A fish-fin, like a pass in football, may be _____.
g) Which is the annulary finger?
h) A light appearing at night over marshy grounds or a misleading influence or thing (friar's lantern, "will o' the wisp") is an _____.**
i) A room in a monastery set aside for scribes or copyists is a _____.
j) Archaeologists know entrance or exit passages leading to or from seats in an ancient theatre as _____. (Clue: L. vomitōrius < vomere 'to discharge')
k) Five persons have respective hourly wages of 6, 8, 10, 14 and 22 dollars. Do you prefer to have the average or the median wage?
l) Newton contributed to Latin centrifugus and centripetus (though the centr- base is Greek). What are our derivatives?
m) Does the etymology of dividend differ in
   1) a $400. free dividend to every Canadian,
   2) eight as dividend of four gives two?
n) Whereas intelligence seeks to grasp, manipulate, reorder, adjust, intellect examines, ponders, wonders, theorizes, criticizes, imagines.
   R. Hofstadter
   Which is the more praiseworthy quality?
o) Sternere, strātum 'to lay low, to pave' is at the base of strāta vīa. What common noun derives from this?
p) In "The man is white," "man" is a word, "man" is a species; hence, the word man is 'systematic ambiguous' in that it supposits for the man.
   R. Bosley

V. Analyze and define the underlined words:

1. If they will represent an history, they must not (as Horace saith) begin ab ovo ... Sidney
2. They laugh at auguries ... More
3. A newly coined word is co-vivant for a person enjoying a quasi-conjugal relationship.
4. Theological dicta were, to the thinkers of those days (the Middle Ages), that which the axioms and definitions of Euclid are to the geometers of these. T.H. Huxley

---

* Answer by a Latin phrase; think of Michigan's Kirtland's warbler, or the whooping crane.
** This translates the Latin for "silly fire."

155

5. We enjoy the gibes at women, pedants and warmongers (in Aristophanes), none of whom are yet <u>extinct</u>. D.H. Monro
6. A benefactor bestowed on the library his ... collection of <u>incunabula</u>. J.G. Cozzens
7. Durrell is <u>the only</u> person I know who has the <u>indomitable</u> guts to walk in (Horace's) footsteps. K. Rexroth
8. The three-year-old's precocious display of verbal <u>invective</u>*
9. <u>It is</u> Othello's pleasure, our noble and valiant general, that upon certain tidings now arrived, importing the <u>mere</u> perdition of the Turkish fleet ... <u>Othello</u> 2.2
10. His style <u>was as</u> <u>meretricious</u> as his thoughts were natural. Hazlitt
11. Heyerdahl sets down in Kon-Tiki the shift of color in <u>moribund</u> dorados.
12. <u>There is</u> written, her fair neck round about, Noli me <u>tangere</u>, for Caesar's I am, ... T. Wyatt
13. <u>Against the</u> feelings of compassion and humanity forever resistant, she remained <u>obdurate</u>.
14. Humour ... must always be <u>plausible</u>. D.H. Monro
15. On a large table a number <u>of</u> objects were lying together in a <u>promiscuous</u> jumble. W.H. Hudson

VI. Form Latin denominative compound verbs having the following etymological meanings and give an English derivative from each: 'to put care to,' 'to bind with,' 'to grasp with,' 'to paint down,' 'to lengthen out,' 'to follow out,' 'to prick out,' 'to dip (plunge in),' 'to go (walk) through,' 'to stretch before,' 'to cut (split) back.'

VII. For each of the following words say whether the present infinitive or the perfect-participial base has been used, and give the present infinitive and its meaning: accretion, apprehension, aspersion, congestion, illusion, inclination, mediation, region, resumption, suspicion.

VIII. a) The following words are synonymous, element for element, with Latin-derived words: output, outstanding, forego, foreplay, foresee, undertake, overview. Give the Latin-derived words that have the same meanings. (Clue: they are in alphabetical order)

---

* -ive, < L. -īvus 'given to,' 'tending to.' It is added to a perfect-pple <u>base</u>; recidivist in Lesson XI is an exception.

b) What is common to the following expressions: <u>caveat</u>, <u>habeas corpus</u>, <u>ne exeat regno</u>, <u>cedant arma togae</u>, <u>indocti discant</u>, <u>paulo maiora canamus?</u> (Clue: mood)

c) Three of the following abbreviations are used by the biographer, three by the artist; determine which is which and write out the words in full: fec., fl., n., ob., pxt., sculp.

IX. Form antonyms for each of the following words by changing the prefix. Example: converge - diverge.

assent, conjoin, decline,* desecrate, dissociate, dissuade, include, prelude, retract, segregate.
* the etymological antonym is called for in this instance.

X.
1. Distinguish between evolutionary and devolutionary changes.
2. Distinguish between the etymological and current meanings of expire; between 'the patient expired' and 'the lease expired.'
3. Explain how a Chicano in Texas is an <u>in-migrant</u> and not an immigrant.
4. The French applied the term <u>miscreants</u> to their Mohammedan enemies. What verb <u>is concealed</u> in the word?
5. Does one word not fit: confuse, defuse, diffuse, effuse, infuse, suffuse, transfuse?
6. What Latin verbs are concealed in congé, elite, exhibit?
7. Instead of AS. fare, relegated to the poetical style, we say travel, adopted from a foreign source; instead of cleave, we say divide, instead of hearten, encourage. What do we say instead of gainsay? Why do we not say divider for cleaver?
8. Which two Latin words are concealed in trammel which originally meant 'triple mesh' and now means 'something which confines or hampers?'
9. From LL. <u>dīrectum</u> 'right, justice,' we get droit meaning '<u>that to</u> which one has legal claim;' cf. droits of the Admiralty. Distinguish between F. <u>garder le droit</u> and étudier le droit.
10. The second person singular imperative of <u>meminisse</u> 'to remember' appears in two prayers in the Canon of the Mass, one for the living, one for the dead. It is also a noun meaning 'anything serving as a reminder, warning or souvenir' and is spelled _____.
11. Show how oratorio and oratory (small chapel) are doublets; disprove that oratory (art of speaking) forms a triplet.
12. Distinguish between palmar as in 'palmar slap' and palmary as in 'palmary' emendations.

157

XI.   Analyze the underlined words in the following sentences.

1. The Order of Canada changed its motto from 'Desiderantes Meliorem Patriam' to 'Acer Gerendo.' (Clue: see Word Notes at end of Lesson XV)
2. The bitter clamour of two eager tongues
   Richard II, 1.1.49
3. Itinerant crop-pickers differ toto caelo from itinerant Latin teachers.
4. Postman: "Mam, is this card for you? The name is obliterated." Woman: "Then it can't be for me; my name is O'Reilly."
5. Rhino horns in powdered form are falsely believed to be a sexual stimulant.
6. Here lies _____ _____, who died after eating a surfeit of sausages.

WORD NOTES

To adlib is 'to improvise.' It derives from the adverbial ad libitum, 'at one's pleasure.' The phrase ad lib is also used adjectivally as in 'ad lib jokes interpolated into a comic skit.' To speak ad lib should mean 'as much as you like,' but it has come to mean improvising. A broadcaster who adlibs is an adlibber. He spontaneously introduces new material into the script. A women's libber is similarly related linguistically to the basic meaning in L. libet, 'it pleases,' and libīdo, pleasure. An adlibber is one who primarily improvises, and one who secondarily speaks "to his pleasure."

L. ad hoc 'to this thing' is used both adjectivally and adverbially: ad hoc committee, to speak ad hoc, i.e., to the object or purpose for which speech is necessary or desirable. An adhocker sticks to the point; he is more valuable in discussion than even the most amusing adlibber. However, the adhocker who cannot fit an isolated fact into his theory and then proceeds to dismiss it with some farfetched ad hoc explanation is a vexatious person.

A dictionary < ML. dictionārium, n. of dictionārius liber, is literally 'a word-book' < L. dictio 'word, saying' + -ārium. In medieval days it was a collection of 'dictions' or phrases compiled for Latin students. The first Latin-English dictionary, the work of Thomas Elyot, appeared in 1538. It was intended to explain largely difficult words. In 1539 Robert Estienne published the Dictionnaire François-Latin.

F. diction, 1165, bore the meaning 'expression' up until the 17c. It also came to mean 'way of speaking' in French. In 1771 Diderot published his Encyclopédie, establishing a bi-partition between dictionaries and encyclopedias. The latter define words and add a description of things. An encyclopedia is not etymologically oriented. French etymology students can refer to Dauzat et al., Nouveau dictionnaire étymologique et historique, Paris: Larousse, 1964. The OED, Oxford, Clarendon, 1933 is best for students of English etymology. Here, denotative and connotative meanings are given; quotations show words in context; many entries show dates of first appearance, or of last, if the word is obsolete. Webster's Ninth New Collegiate, 1983, is another excellent source.

L. dōs, dōtis 'dowry' gave rise to a denominative verb, dōtāre 'to endow, portion.' LL. indōtāre > OF. endouer leads to endow. Endue comes from L. indūcere 'to lead in,' which gives ME. endewen and MF. enduire. Endue means provide with something; specifically, it is to endow with qualities, talents, etc. Because endue and endow have dissimilar origins, they are not doublets.

L. rīpa is concealed in arrive, but L. rīvus is in derive. To arrive is etymologically to come to the bank,* shore; to derive is to flow down stream. Both are denominative verbs. F. arriver in the sense of aborder comes from its use in the late Middle Ages. 12c F. has dériver, 14c F. has dérivation, and 15c F. produces dérivatif.

* Sp. arribar refers to a ship's coming into port, as does the noun, arribada. L. plicāre developed from 'to fold' into 'to tie up a boat,' hence, 'to arrive,' Sp. llegar.

DENOMINATIVE AND FREQUENTATIVE VERBS

Latin denominative verbs, formed from a noun, adjective, or adverb, are usually formed by adding -āre to the respective base, e.g., armāre, aequāre, locāre, ōrāre, pācāre. We saw how these are formed in Lesson XII.

Less common than the denominative verb is the frequentative verb. Latin frequentative verbs are formed by adding -āre to the base of a verb's past participle. They express repeated or intensive action in Latin, but usually lack intensive force when taken over into English.

Present infinitive	Frequentative verb	English loan word
canere 'to sing	cantāre 'to keep singing'	cantabile; cantata
salīre, saltus 'to leap'	saltāre 'to dance'	saltatory

The ancestor of chase is captāre. Note the origins of chase and purchase: captāre > VL.* captiāre > F. chasser > E. chase; prō + captiāre > OF. porchacier, purchacier 'to pursue, seek eagerly' > purchase. NB: pursue is not a doublet of purchase. It comes from VL. prōsequere, via F. poursuivre.

EXERCISE XXII

I.   Form Latin denominative verbs from:

arcus 'arch,' circus 'ring,' frustrā 'in vain,' granulum 'little grain,' index, indicis 'index-finger,' jus, juris 'oath,' medicus 'physician, surgeon,' nex, necis 'murder,' solidus 'solid,' vitium 'blemish, fault.'

II.   Form Latin denominative verbs meaning 'to place to,' 'to liken to,' 'to swear together,' 'to make full of wrinkles,' 'to make (turn) into ice,' 'to work,' 'to (be a) beggar,' 'to number,' 'to wheel,' 'to make public or common.'

---

* VL. = Vulgar Latin, i.e., popular Latin, the everyday speech of the Roman people, from which the Romance languages developed. VL. dates from the 3rd to the 6th centuries and is followed by Medieval Latin.

III.   Analyze by segmentation; give current meanings:

corroborate, defalcate, exacerbate, excoriate, extirpate, infatuate, militate, oscillate, reverberate, tessellate.

IV.   With or without the use of prefixes, form a derivative from these frequentative verbs: dictāre, pensāre, pressāre, pulsāre, tractāre, versāre.

V.   Underline the misplaced word; explain your choice:

intend pretense superintendent tennis; elect legendary illegible sublet; correct erection gentry regent; deterrent interment terrify terrorize; aggression gradual greed progress; armature armistice armoury arrear; valiant valid valley valour; abuse clause inclusion recluse; deficit factotum forfeiture ventricle; pause positive postscript postpone; datum debit deodand editor; inquiry quest question quire.

VI.   Give the Latin verb, with its meaning, which has supplied the base of each of the following: additive, adhesive, correlative, effusive, exhaustive, inquisitive, passive, prospective, selective, votive.

VII.   Match items in both columns by determining which Latin verb in its past-participial base has given rise to which derivative:

1)	enactment	a)	trūdere, trūsus
2)	intrusion	b)	cēdere, cessus
3)	distortion	c)	agere, actus
4)	projector	d)	condere, conditus
5)	collusive	e)	jacere, jactus
6)	commensurate	f)	metīrī, mensus
7)	condition	g)	orīrī, ortus
8)	pasture	h)	pāscere, pāstus
9)	abort	i)	lūdere, lūsus
10)	accession	j)	torquēre, tortus

VIII.   Identify the Latin prefix concealed in each of the following words: enemy, forfeit, hors d'oeuvre, pellucid, purchase, scamper, sewer, soufflé, sovereign, trespass.

IX.   By changing the prefix, form antonyms of:
associate, concord, decelerate, demote, disculpate, dissent, dissonant, eject, inflate, intramural, post-bellum, pre-nuptial, retrogression, subject (noun), subsonic.

162

X. Analyze the following underlined words:
1. Media is becoming an <u>aggregate</u> singular.
2. To <u>appropriate</u> wrongfully by purloining is frowned upon.
3. The quadrumane, an ape, <u>brachiates</u> from branch to branch.
4. The intrepid pursuers of perpetrators of perfidy intend to <u>eradicate</u> them.
5. Perhaps luck is the way the life puts history into bas-relief, and <u>differentiates</u> moments and people; the way that the universe <u>punctuates</u> time. L. Morrow
6. To <u>estivate,</u> the antonym of <u>hibernate</u>, is to spend the _____ in a dormant condition.
7. An atom absorbs units of <u>radiation</u> called quanta.
8. The <u>bella di notte</u> intends to <u>rejuvenate</u> her client.
9. Nature hates calculators; her methods are <u>saltatory</u> and impulsive. Emerson
10. Good posture reduces the spinal <u>subluxation</u> complex, chiropractors say.
11. You can winter in Bermuda and summer in Ottawa, but you cannot spring and fall with the same seasonal pleasure. If in those seasons you stay put, you may <u>vegetate</u>.
12. Man <u>vacillates</u> between different opinions or courses of action.
13. The plot was designed in a light vein that somehow became <u>varicose</u>. D. Lardner
14. For Adrian Beverland (<u>Peccatum originale</u>, 1679) the apple in Genesis was <u>amoris symbolum</u>, <u>donare</u> was equivalent to <u>coire</u>, and ramus, flos and <u>arbor</u> to membrum virile.

XI. For each of the words in the left-hand column, select the word in the right-hand group which best defines it.

1) comprehensive   a) corroborant, inclusive, tractable
2) consternation   b) condensation, panic, resolution
3) digression   c) depreciation, entrance, a going aside
4) fallible   d) able to fall, false, able to err
5) inconcinnity   e) lack of elegance, quarrelsomeness, loquacity
6) ineffable   f) gullible, inexpressible, inefficient
7) labile   g) connected with lips, remarkable, tending to slip

163

8)	nubile	h)	castigating, cloudlike, marriageable
9)	prelusory	i)	aimless, introductory, deceptive
10)	punctual	j)	dilatory, reputable, prompt
11)	querulous	k)	plaintive, concupiscent, questionable
12)	tenacious	l)	having a dwelling, retentive, thin
13)	tortuous	m)	illegal, punitive, winding
14)	ultracredulous	n)	not gullible, critical, too gullible
15)	valedictory	o)	saying goodbye, saying hello, valetudinarian

XII. (a) Retract and retreat are doublets which derive from retrahere, retractus 'to draw back.' Distinguish between them, then illustrate two uses of retreat as a noun.

(b) Distinguish between the prefixes and meanings of avocation, advocation.

(c) What English words mean etymologically: 'a result of speaking around,' 'an examination or scrutiny for the purpose of finding a person or thing,' 'mutually destructive, aiming at the slaughter of each other,' 'the action or process of trying, testing, or proving,' 'an inciting to evil with the prospect of some pleasure or advantage,' 'the action of turning one's back on, i.e., forsaking a cause, a duty, a party, etc.'

(d) Distinguish between Twain's uses of levee:
1) ... he talked ... about the great event of the day, the levee of the distinguished foreigners at Aunt Patsy Cooper's.
2) When the boat touched the levee at New Orleans she bade goodbye to her comrades.

(e) Distinguish between 'the literate' and 'literati.' What semantic change does the current meaning of the latter reveal? What would the coinage glitterati mean?

(f) Which statement is literal and which figurative in:
1) ... the cake left after the expression of the oil,
2) ... the fullest expression of public feeling.

(g) Distinguish 1) "likeness is a tricky property," from Shakespeare's "I will draw a bill of property, such as our play wants;"
2) the early name for a church was oratorium, from Victor Borge's enchanting oratories on punctuation.

XIII. Pronounce and define the Latin phrases.
a) On Madame Eglantine's golden brooch was written Amor vincit omnia.
b) His position as arbiter elegantiarum may imply ... that of a mentor and guide, an older man ... than Nero. Bagnani
c) Cato, censor morum, exhibited a stern traditional morality.
d) Dominus, illuminatio mea is Oxford University's motto.
e) Idaho's motto is esto perpetua.
f) The fibula Praenestina bears the earliest specimen of Latin, written from right to left.
g) So plesant was his In principio. Chaucer
h) Ipsa sui pretium virtus sibi. Browne
i) To maintain mens sana in corpore sano we need not avoid lapsus calami but we must avoid spiritus frumenti.
j) Mulier est hominis confusio. Chaucer
k) All those words of scholarship, ... to our ancestors the ne plus ultra of refinement, are now relegated to the lumberroom of erudition ... Symonds
l) My lady came in like a nolle prosequi and stopped the proceedings. Congreve
m) Lady: My nephew was non compos (mentis), and could not make his addresses. Congreve
n) Sir John A. Macdonald was called fox populi on account of his cunning and popularity.
o) Radix malorum est cupiditas. Chaucer
p) Amid confusion the legislature adjourned sine die. A. Nevins
q) Our summum bonum is commodity, and the goddess we adore Dea Moneta. Burton
r) The fault lies in ... Seneca, Nero himself, in the crass materialism of the time. What can one expect of mankind, which demands a society ubi sola pecunia regnat? Bagnani
s) What is turpe lucrum in medieval canon law?

XIV. Analyze the underlined words; give their contextual meanings.
1) One person simply adores a certain odor which another just as simply abominates. R. Bedicheck

165

2) The difference between the great and less man is ... chiefly ... alterability.
3) Titus Andronicus, the people of Rome / Send thee, by me, their tribune and their trust, / This palliament of white and spotless hue, / Be candidatus then ... T.A. 1.1
4) Morality is a duenna to be circumvented. Meredith
5) A shorn crown ... a euphemism for decapitation. J. Froude
6) Under the influence of love's delusion Thackeray
7) We ignore the artificial smells of petrol fumes and industrial effluents .   J. Gloag
8) The donkey was dying of hunger between two equidistant bundles of hay. A. Fremantle
9) What is there in tobogganing to so fascinate both sexes in our 1886 humanity? Toronto Grip
10) The termagant fulminates criticisms.
11) Malraux's Katov, prepared, chose a terrifying immolation. A. Kazin
12) The medicine man, the angakok, was repeating incantations to bring good weather, to ensure a catch of seals, to speed the recovery of a sick woman. Leechman
13) My parents tried in vain to inoculate me with wisdom. W. Irving
14) Des Esseintes could detect no trace of prevarication in the old man's expressionless face. Huysmans
15) The man who procrastinates struggles with ruin. Hesiod
16) The nonagenarian, a bag of recalcitrant bones, feels the stirrings of desire and recalls her former love.
17) The combatives swayed to and fro, a revulsive trinity. Beerbohm
18) Gladstone viewed Victoria ... as a sacrosanct embodiment of venerable traditions. Strachey
19) Before one generation has passed, an Encyclopedia is superannuated. DeQuincey
20) Transhumant cattle-herders ... held the whole apparatus of urban living in contempt. Lienhardt

WORD NOTES

Captāre, frequentative of capere, captus 'to take' gives us the verb, captate and captation, i.e., the making of ad captandum appeals. A blight on the society in Rome was the captātor, a legacy-hunter who cajoled his victims. The rhythmic dilatation and contraction of the heart or artery is pulsation < pulsāre, the frequentative of pellere, pulsus 'to beat, drive, strike.' Pulsāre gave 14c F. pousser 'to grow,' perhaps because one of its tropical meanings is 'to move.' Saltatorial and saltatory are based on saltāre 'to dance,' frequentative of salīre, saltus 'to jump.' Cf. F. sauter.

Enchant is from a compound of the frequentative verb cantāre 'to keep singing.' L. incantāre meant 'to say over, mutter, chant a magic formula (against someone), bewitch.' When introduced, a French person says 'enchanté(e),' "charmed."

Spectator is from the frequentative verb, spectāre 'to keep looking at.' It is formed, however, on the base of the past participle, spectāt-. Some compound derivatives formed on the present infinitive's base of this frequentative are aspectant (in heraldry and art, facing each other), expectant, respectable, respectant (in heraldry, designating two animals borne face to face).

Pensāre 'to weigh out carefully, consider' is a frequentative of pendere, pēnsus 'to weigh.' (Do not confuse this verb with pendēre (-pēnsus) 'to hang.') The past (or perfect) participle of L. compensāre 'to balance one thing against another' gives us compensate.

The frequentative of tuēri "to gaze upon, watch; look to, defend,' is tūtāri. Early L. uses it of a slave who watches his master's property, or of anyone who 'keeps an eye on' the house. By transference, L. tūtāri developed the meaning 'to avert, ward off an evil.' A tutor was a legal guardian who protected minors, women, the insane, estates, and, later, by extension, eloquence, the republic. 12c F. tuer 'to kill' began innocently. VL. tūtāre (< L. tūtāri 'to protect') meant to stanch, extinguish, e.g., one's thirst. F. s'entre-tuer, 12c, was followed by tueur, 13c, tuerie, 14c, and papier tue-mouches, 1872. A tue-mouches is a fly-swatter, but l'amanite tue-mouches is a deadly mushroom.

A Final Note on Doublets

Let us look at some pairs of words that have been miscon-strued as doublets. Our first example is abbreviate and abridge. LL. abbreviāre, in its perfect-participial base abbreviatus to which a silent -e has been added, gives abbre-viate. F. abréger, whence abridge, and LL. abbreviāre, whence abbreviate, are cognates. Assemble and assimilate are not doublets. Assemble is partly composed of L. simul 'together,' whereas assimilate contains L. similis 'like; it is formed on the perfect-participial base as is abbreviate. It is incorrect to pair off aggravate and aggrieve (< L. aggravāre 'to burden, make heavy'). Defeat is from OF. desfait, pp. of desfaire 'to undo' derivative of dis + facere. Defect is from L. deficere, dēfectum 'to desert, fail, be wanting' (< L. dē + facere).

167

Avow (not a triplet of advocate and avouch) is a doublet of avouch. Both originate in L. advocāre. Avow derives from OF. avouer. Avouch comes out of OF. avochier 'to affirm positively' (< L. advocāre). They are all cognates. Advocate is from advocāt-, the past-participial base which has been formed into a noun, advocātus.

Appreciate (not a triplet of appraise and apprise) is formed from the past participle of appretiāre 'to value, estimate.' Implicate (not a triplet of employ and imply), like appreciate, comes from the base of a past participle, in this case, of implicāre 'to enfold, involve.' Challenge derives from L. calumniāri 'to attack with false accusations' whence OF. chalengier, ME chalengen. Calumny, its cognate, is from L. calumnia 'trickery, slander,' (< L. calvi 'to deceive'). It becomes F. calomnie. Calumniate is not a doublet of challenge. Monetary and monitory are not doublets, even though both derive from monere 'to warn.' The Latin sources are, respectively, monētārius and monitōrius. Monētārius is from the noun-base monēta; monitōrius develops out of the verb-base monit-. A monitor warns or admonishes.

Deliver and deliberate are not doublets. Our 'deliver' is from LL. dēlīberāre and ME. deliveren 'to release, pass from one to another.' This is to be distinguished from 'deliberate' which has lībra 'the Roman pound, balance' in it and is formed on lībrāre 'to poise, weigh, make equal.'

LESSON XX

INCEPTIVE VERBS

Latin inceptive verbs are formed by adding -scere to the base of present infinitives, -ēscere to the bases of nouns or adjectives, e.g.,
quiēs, quiētis > quiēscere 'to rest, keep quiet'
ruber, rubrī > rubēscere 'to grow or turn red, redden, blush'
valēre > valēscere 'to begin to be well'
vānus > vānēscere 'to pass away, disappear, vanish'

These verbs often denote the beginning of an action or state, but the inceptive force is not always evident in our translation of the Latin and is only occasionally retained in their English derivatives, e.g., convalescent, obsolescent.

The verbs agere, capere, and facere are altered when used to form certain multiple-base compounds to -igāre, -cipāre and -ficāre, e.g., in navigāre, participāre, clarificāre, 'to sail,' 'to impart, inform,' and 'to make famous,' respectively. -ficāre became F. -fier, E. -fy, e.g., magnificāre 'to value greatly, extol,' F. magnifier 'to glorify,' E. magnify. Related to -ficāre is the adjectival ending -ficus, 'causing, making ...' A medicāmentum somnificum causes sleep; somnific is synonymous with soporific. Somniferous and soporiferous are formed from the noun's base + the connecting vowel -i- + -ferous 'bearing, producing;' -ferous comes from -fer, base of ferre, and -ous from -ōsus ('full of,'). Cf. auriferous, coniferous, luminiferous, nuciferous, penniferous.

EXERCISE XXIII

I.   Give the etymological meanings of adolescency, albescent, canescent, crescendo, deliquescent, effervescence, efflorescence, frutescent, iridescent, pubescent.

II.   a)   Give examples of obsolete and obsolescent words.
      b)   List four verbs ending in -ish whose ultimate source is Latin.
      c)   What happened to the Latin ending of the verb in the formation of connect, discern, feign, succumb?
      d)   How has the Latin verb-ending been reduced in cede, move, reduce, serve?
      e)   What provocation resulted in Niobe's lapidescence?

III. a)   What are carboniferous and cupriferous deposits?
      b)   The doublet of colloquy is _____ .
      c)   The antonym of decrescendo is _____ .
      d)   A wart is a type of _____ on the skin.
      e)   The process of becoming black is _____ .

169

f) Magellan found the _____ to be relatively free from violent storms and Keats' Cortez stared at it.
g) Participant has not undergone F. influence. Participaction combines the meanings of two words. It is a _____ word (Clue: it is formed like Cdn E. permafrost).

IV. Analyze; give current meanings:
bacciferous, certify, coalesce, concupiscence, diamondiferous, emancipate, fustigate, incandescent, laticiferous, morbific, recrudescence, senescent, stultify, variegated, vilification.

V. Analyze the underlined words; give contextual meanings:
1. Surgeon and scalpel, clergyman and Christ, psychiatrist and subconscious probings, all work toward the ablation of cancer.
2. The confirmed Hi-Fi addict glories in his own distress.
3. By means of a classical allusion Yeats takes us back to ancient legend or myth.
4. Teens are a major consuming audience for tobacco manufacturers. Find a more appropriate word.
5. There was a gentle, cautious confabulation about the young vicar. M. Craven
6. He was kind, cordial, open, even convivial and jocose. Macauley
7. Arraigned for a crime was the culprit.
8. The speaker is desultory.
9. There is husband-wife dissensus.
10. Running water, glaciers and wind are erosional agents.
11. She makes attempts at augury and extispicy.
12. This book makes vocabulary learning a less formidable task.
13. ... one Lawrence Whitaker in his merry humour doubted not to call me Furcifer only for using a fork. T. Coryate
14. We love characters in proportion as they are impulsive and spontaneous. Emerson
15. The ballgown is of iridescent silk taffeta with gold-faced ruffles.
16. My English text is chaste; all licentious passages are left in the decent obscurity of a learned language. Gibbon
17. The nascent state of an element at liberation from a compound is exemplified by that of nascent chlorine.
18. The neomort can be preserved as 'organ farm' for transplants. N.B. Gk. neos 'new.'
19. ... about (the sun) shone a faintly opalescent halo. G. Sutton

170

20. He is the putative author.
21. Fish are phallic symbols; cigars, tumescent cigarettes.
22. The sable younkers (chimney-sweepers) lick in the unctuous meat. Lamb
23. A vector has magnitude and a direction in space.
24. The top cervical vertebra, articulating with the occipital bone and thus supporting the head, is the atlas.
25. Antivivisectionists would like to see the number (60 million animals killed yearly in U.S. labs) reduced.

VI. Determine which words are either obsolescent or obsolete: anent, buss, eke, exequies, hight, laminable, maugre, ossicle, pox, silentiary, silicify, vild, warth, wight.

LESSON XXI

DEPENDENT MULTIPLE-BASE COMPOUNDS

Dependent multiple-base compound nouns and ajectives are formed by using any verb base as the second element, e.g., belligerent, 'waging war," arboricolous, 'living in trees,' and liquefaction, 'reduction to a liquid state.' The first member in these dependent compounds depends upon, or serves as object of, the verbal idea contained in the second member. Agere, capere and facere were mentioned in Lesson XX; four more examples are given below.

1. Caedere, caesus 'to cut, kill' (base: -cid-)
   agent noun: suicida 'one who kills himself', suicide;
   abstract noun: suicidium 'the act of self-murder,' i.e.,
   as neuter noun, 'a killing of ...,'
   suicide.

2. Colere, cultus 'to inhabit' (base: -col-)
   adjective: arenicolous, 'inhabiting sand.'

3. Parere, partus 'to give birth, bear' (base: -par-)
   adjective: oviparous, applied to animals that produce
   young by means of eggs. A nullipara is a
   woman who has not borne any offspring.

4. Vorāre, -ātus 'to eat' (base: -vor-)
   agent noun: herbivora (sc. animalia) animals, especially
   mammals, that feed on herbage or plants (sg.
   herbivore);
   adjective: frugivorous, eating or feeding on fruit.

EXERCISE XXIV

I.   What Latin-derived word expresses the notion of: living
     in trees, flesh-eating animals, brother-murder, bringing
     (producing death), a woman bearing for the first time,
     inhabiting the earth (land), one who kills his wife,
     producing live young?

II. Analyze and give current meanings for insectivorous,
     Lucifer, mortification, omnivore, post-partum,
     stagnicolous.

III. Form English derivatives with these etymological meanings:
     to drive a ship around, to make clear, bearing light, to
     make peace, the murder of a king, one who kills his
     sister.

IV.   Analyze the underlined words and give current meanings:
adventitious adventures, anticipatory democracy, assiduous
money-borrower, bona fide expression, corrective
castigation, contentious opponents, contumacious monks,
blinded by emotion, eviscerate a sacrificial animal,
excerpted passages, out of bounds exuberance, fluctuant
muscle tonus, intricate enigmas, multinational
corporation, coronary occlusion, recidivous tendencies,
restive horse, sudoriferous glands, surreptitious
curiosity, verificatory testimony.

V.   Analyze the underlined words, giving their contextual
meanings.
1.   'Society' as an abstraction may function in beatific
bliss, but its component numbers go about heavy-
hearted. R.A. Hall Jr.
2.   The effect of literary works (especially of poetry)
is largely dependent on ... intonation, stress,
juncture ... incompletely represented in writing.
idem
3.   The white beach was a havoc of lava boulders ...
sleek with spray and lambent as brass in the sinking
sun. A. Dillard
4.   What leaf-fringed legend haunts about thy shape
Of deities or mortals, or of both,
In Tempe or the dales of Arcady? Keats
5.   Self-abnegation is the higher road; we should mortify
the flesh. Hardy
6.   Airport terminals and other commercial places are
sociofugal public spaces. Is sociofugal unintelligi-
ble jargon?
7.   The Indians attach superstition to the chiploquorgan,
the stick on which the kettle is suspended over the
camp fire. Newfoundland Quarterly
8.   Verbicide was committed when we exchanged Whig and
Tory for Liberal and Conservative. C.S. Lewis

VI.   Complete the following sentences with words composed from
verbal bases and / or compounding elements. Your answers
will be in alphabetical order.
a)   _____ strata contain or yield gold.
b)   The point or time at which the moon is furthest north
or south in her monthly course is the _____ .
c)   The process of preparing an army or fleet for active
service is _____ .
d)   A female whose age admits of, or is suitable for
marriage is _____ .
e)   That which brings disease or plague, or bears moral
contagion is _____ .
f)   One who or that which is abundantly productive of
offspring is _____ .

174

g) To convert something abstract into a material thing or to regard an abstraction as a substance is the same as to _____ .

h) To establish the truth, accuracy or reality of a thing or a circumstance is to _____ .

i) Nearly all mammals which produce living young instead of eggs from within the body are _____ .

j) A shouting or calling out which is vehement and deafening is clamorous or _____ .

VII. Identify the items in List B with those in List A.
List A: 1) commensurate, 2) digression, 3) imprecator, 4) intuition, 5) a lapsus calami, 6) a non sequitur, 7) rationale, 8) revolution, 9) sortition, 10) tutelage, 11) ventriloquist, 12) verbification.

List B: a) one who speaks for himself and a dummy; b) conversion of a noun, etc. into a verb; c) immediate cognition; ready insight; d) the act of casting lots; e) an explanation of belief or practice, or, an underlying reason; f) guardianship, instruction, guiding, influence; g) a slip of the pen; h) one who puts a hex on a person, society, etc.; i) a statement which does not logically follow; j) equal in extent; k) a wandering from the subject; l) a radical change.

VIII. Which noun or adjective supplies the base of these words, derived from denominative verbs? alliteration, annihilation, confirmation, delineation, demonstration, deprivation, designation, formation, imprecation, incantation, probation, summation.

IX. Does Nash distort the facts in:
   Whenever I behold an asp,
I can't suppress a startled gasp.
I do not charge the asp with matricide,
But what about his Cleopatricide? O. Nash

X. a) Using a word coming from L. fenestra 'window, an opening to admit the light,' fill in the blank: New schools should introduce _____ and avoid our incandescent and fluorescent heritage.

b) When we compose smog from smoke + fog, we form a portmanteau. Do likewise for permanent + frost.

EXERCISE XXV

I. True or False:
1. There is no difference between 'an exponent of socialism' and 'a proponent of socialism.'

175

2. Much of our everyday vocabulary was firmly establish-ed some five hundred years ago.
3. Language tends to be stationary in that words do not develop new meanings.
4. Distinctions between sensual and sensuous, emotional and emotive, etc., tend to be abstract or academic.
5. Ad hoc formations, e.g., petrodollar, petrocrat and multiversity do not usually find their way into a dictionary.
6. Several names of our months derive from Roman religion.
7. The carnation, State flower of Ohio, was so called because of its resemblance in color to a white person's skin.
8. The largest number of Latin words were introduced into English between 1550-1650, and the smallest between 1750-1800.
9. English is a composite language not descended from Latin; rather, its evolution may be diagrammed as follows: Primitive Germanic > Old Norse > Old English (Anglo-Saxon) > Middle English > Modern English.
10. When one reads a poem, emotional reverberations from a past which may have nothing to do with the poem tend to interfere and hence, to enrich its meaning.
11. Funnybone is a pun on the anatomical name - humerus 'shoulder, bone of the upper arm.'
12. Hybridization refers only to the mixture of Greek and Latin elements in one word.
13. The words movable and mobile are doublets.
14. Rational and rationale are doublets.
15. A learned word, if widely enough used, becomes popular.
16. A man who gives his salary to the poor is an altruist.
17. Transliteration and translation are synonymous.
18. Absit nomen, absit omen refers to a supersitition that the mere saying of a bad thing may bring it to pass, hence that if we avoid the 'name,' we avoid the misfortune which it implies.
19. Acute and cute are doublets.
20. When Shakespeare has Cassius say of Caesar, "... he doth bestride the narrow world / Like a Colossus ..." he is alluding to the statue of Apollo which stood astride the harbor of Rhodes in antiquity.
21. English is a composite language which descends from Latin and Greek.
22. Much of our everyday vocabulary was established only in the last two centuries.
23. Retreat and retract are doublets.

24. The words figure and fictitious both derive from the same L. verb fingere, which means 'to fix.'
25. 'Cupid' is linguistically related to 'covetous.'
26. An indolent tumor causes no pain.
27.   A criminal caught in flagrante delicto is one detected and apprehended 'red-handed.'
28. Synonyms of 'to denigrate' are 'to blacken' and 'to defame.'
29. Sanskrit, Greek, Latin and German have all influenced some English words.
30. L. spectāre 'to keep looking' is the frequentative verb formed from spect-, past-participial base of specere.
31. In 'to retort a humiliation' and 'to retort mercury,' the verb has the same etymology.
32. A volcano neither active nor extinct, but going through a long cessation of activity, is dormant.

EXERCISE XXVI

I. Underline the misplaced word; explain your choice:
    a) clause, inclusion, recluse, usury
    b) armature, armistice, armoury, forearm (noun)
    c) decide, excide, excise, reside
    d) allocate, colloquy, elocution, obloquy
    e) retract, retreat, substract, tradition

II. Form Latin compound verbs having the following etymological meanings: 'to pour together,' 'to stand against,' 'to cut asunder,' 'to hold in,' 'to swear to the bad.'

III. Analyze and define each underlined word:
    contingency plans; execrate one's enemy; Medea, the infanticide and senecide; the munificence of private charity; her obsequious manner.

IV. Analyze and define each underlined word:
    1. A medieval work, the Christus Patiens, shows a parallel between Dionysus and Christ.
    2. The face of the presiding magistrate, clean shaved and impassible looked at him. Conrad
    3. The mystic sees the ineffable, and the psychopathologist the unspeakable. Maugham
    4. Passion in Shakespeare generally displays libertinism. Coleridge
    5. "... the Manacles / Of the all-building Law." Shakespeare
    6. As a dying woman, Alcestis aims to create a posthumous future.
    7. "... to distrust one's impulses is to be recreant to Pan." Stevenson
    8. A dozen of them here have ta'en the sacrament, ... Shakespeare
    9. It is challenging to plunge into the terrae incognitae of literature. H. Peyre
    10. Some people have understood by Levana the tutelary power that controls the education of the nursery. DeQuincy

V. Select from the following eight (8) linquistically related pairs of words. Show how the pairs are related. N.B.: four words do not apply.
    adventitious, artifact, belligerent, compel, compromise, conceive, conference, convenient, counterfeit, divide, festive, impulse, inception, insurrection, intermittent, jest, proviso, translation, venial, video.

VI. Give the doublets of cadence, feat, ligation, motif, pigment, regime, respect, virtuous.

VII. Complete the statements:
1. Document derives from L. _____, which means 'to _____.'
2. The agent noun denoting 'she who performs the action of making a will' is _____.
3. The reconstruction of a crime on the basis of guess-work would be an exercise in _____ futility. (Clue: prefix + L. jacere 'to throw.')
4. An abstract noun formed from the L. torquēre is _____ .
5. So far as etymology is concerned, fossils are found by _____.
6. A supposititious treaty is _____.
7. Nugatory commentaries are _____.
8. Money derives from L. _____ associated with Juno, as warner.
9. Sir John A. Macdonald was nicknamed "Old Tomorrow" for his _____ . (Clue: L. crās 'tomorrow')
10. Ration, reason and ratio are _____.
11. Figure and fictitious both derive from the same L. verb _____, which means 'to _____.'
12. There has been much controversy as to what the _____ ('law of nature') really is ... T.H. Green
13. A derivative from the frequentative verb versāre is _____.
14. One abrogates a law when one _____ it.
15. The force of the prefix in complement is _____.

VIII. Analyze the following; explain, where relevant, how prefixes affect meanings.
attenuate, detritus, explode, immure, ingratiate, interdict, obfuscate, obsess, occult, perquisites.

IX. Form Latin compound verbs having the following etymological meanings; form a derivative in each case.
'to bear (carry) down,' 'to save ahead,' 'to turn in secret (under),' 'to turn to the bad,' 'to see in front of (before),' 'to follow out,' 'to lead aside (apart),' 'to drive in,' 'to take between,' 'to build with.'

X. From the following make up 10 pairs; show the relationship:
coincide, collate, component, concise, conjoint, consult, content, contraction, convert, decompose, defer, deficit, demote, disappoint, effect, excide, excoriate, expunge, exquisite, exult, inoculate, insult, interfere, obverse, oculist, pertain, quarry, remove, souvenir, trait, vocation.

XI.   a)   Fill in the blanks in the following sentences.
      1)   The doublet of strait is _____.
      2)   de facto control means _____.
      3)   A derivative formed from solvere with the prefix
           meaning 'back' is _____.
      4)   From the verb meaning to play, lūdere, plus the
           prefix meaning 'with' we form the derivative _____
           _____. It means 'to conspire in a fraud.'
      5)   A loanword from the past ptc. of the verb meaning 'to
           witness' is _____.
      6)   A vāde mēcum is _____ _____ _____.

      b)   Answer the following questions.
      1)   Distinguish between: the retiree receives a pension
           and the tourist visits a pension in France.   Are
           these doublets?
      2)   Common Law Section has a periodical, Caveat.   Why
           this title?
      3)   Why are sumptuary laws so called?
      4)   In good literature there are no artistic pretens-
           ions. What are pretensions?

XII. Change the prefix to form the antonym of confident,
      ingress, obverse, progress (verb), retrospective.

XIII. Pair off the synonymous words in the lists.   List A:
      1) adscititious, 2) conciliatory, 3) justificatory,
      4) objurgatory, 5) perfunctory, 6) preclusive, 7)
      scabrous, 8) scrupulous, 9) transient, 10) ubiquitous.
      List B: a) improper, b) indifferent, c) omnipresent,
      d) pacific, e) preventive, f) punctilious, g) rebukeful,
      h) supplemental, i) temporal, j) vindictive.

XIV. 1)   Distinguish a) Monarchy in the West is obsolescent;
           from
                      b) "You are nothing but a set of obsolete
                         responses." Eliot
      2)   Quelle est l'origine du mot souligné dans:
           Nous sommes tous condamnés à mort avec des sursis
           indéfinis. Hugo
      3)   Comment on the connotation in: Magazines of a Porno
           nature are suggestive.

EXERCISE XXVII

These sentences, in relative order of difficulty, may be assigned
pari passu with the lessons. Students are asked to analyze the
underlined words, fill in the blanks, or answer the question
posed, as appropriate.

1.   Good/bad, strong/weak, divine/ridiculous Janus faces ...

2. Anything related to the planet Venus is called Venusian; why is anything related to the planet Jupiter called Jovian?
3. Centaurs are equine; Fauns, like Pan, are hircine.
4. What is the process whereby, like wench and knave, the word specious has lost its beauty and glitter?
5. The ideal type of Homo economicus is an anal character. N.O. Brown
6. The Crown Equerry allowed Judy Crawley to film the Queen on her ceremonial mount.
7. Latin students may not use interlinears.
8. Hence then, close Ambush and pernicious War,
Down to your pristin Seats of Night repair. M. Prior
9. Locke stated that a new-born's mind is a tabula rāsa.
10. ... having a sufficient fortune, I was careless of temporalities. Goldsmith
11. If I hadn't grown up on Latin and Greek I wouldn't be able to draw the line between a vernacular style and an illiterate ... style. R. Chandler
12. An oldster may socially withdraw through retirement, viduity or physical disability.
13. The fastidious taste will find offence in the occasional vulgarisms we call slang. Coleridge
14. The social amenities help us to internalize others' judgements at the expense of our own values.
15. In 1985 A.D., what does A.D. stand for?
16. An actuary, concerned with probabilities of death and survival, calculates insurance risks and _____.
17. Seldom are antiquarian and philosopher so happily blended. Gibbon
18. The Christmas wreath comes originally from the ivy crown worn by Romans in Bacchanalian festivals.
19. Caress and charity are not doublets. Show how each develops out of Latin carus.
20. The use of contranomers is fashionable in advertising.
21. ... the affected, wordy style that a schoolboy might use to a fancied, incorporeal sweetheart. E. Brontë
22. The meliorist believes that the world can be made better by wise human action.
23. A friend shares my sorrow and makes it but a moiety. J. Taylor
24. What does prō tem stand for? Write out the expression.
25. Linguistic chauvinism and purism is the systematic avoidance of foreign words for political reasons.
26. Pope's Iliad is a caput mortuum. (Clue: mortuum 'dead')
27. The columnella nāsi is the small column in the _____ between the 2 nostrils.
28. Homer was the fons perennis for all bards. A. Shewan
29. Look into Italy and Spain, whether those places be one scruple the better. Milton
30. In 1976 Ottawa celebrated its sesquicentennial.

31. Thoreau was a master solitudinist.
32. A triune being is composed of body, soul and spirit.
33. Medieval university students chose either the trivium or the quadrivium. What Latin word do these words partially conceal?
34. Give common abbreviations for the words acute, curiosity, engine, examination, omnibus, professor, property, taxicab, university.
35. What Latin number is concealed in carillon?
36. Does the etymology of cutlet have anything to do with cutting?
37. We associate (Antennas or antennae?) with crawling insects.
38. We associate (Antennas or antennae?) with pre-cable TV.
39. From Latin elements we form copious and verbose. Use a L. base and a suffix to form the word which might stand for 'loveful.'
40. The largest of the Canary Islands, Canaria, was so called by the Romans from the _____ found there.
41. Distinguish between biennial and biannual.
42. The Brooklyn Bridge celebrated its _____ in May, 1983, when it turned 100 years old.
43. What relationship prevails between dean and decurion?
44. LL. furetus, from L. fūr 'thief,' yields _____ through ME.
45. What L. noun is concealed in "plastics' virtual non-biodegradability?"
46. How are the Inquisitiones post Mortem, National Records in Britain, used?
47. Distinguish between matrix and nucleus.
48. Pluralize auditorium, corpus, formula, gladiolus, index, matrix, nucleus, opus and stamen.
49. Spenser's Una Vēra Fidēs is the true Una.
50. In vitro fertilization pregnancies may miscarry.
51. Children go from in vitro to in vīvō when they leave classroom for camp.
52. Zoölogists and botanists may object to the vōx barbara.
53. Based on the -īnus suffix, we have lacertīne, mustelīne, psittacine, sciurīne, struthionine, vervecine, vespine and vitulīne.
54. Which word is older, culture or civilization?
55. Which is older, the verb 'to civilize,' or the noun 'civilization?'
56. From donation by back-formation we have 'to donate,' and from escalator we have 'to escalate.' Comment on 'to curate,' 'to commentate,' and 'to coronate.'
57. Men may be united only because they live in a shapeless conurbation.
58. What English word derives from L. dēsultor? In Rome, he was an athlete who jumped from one horse to another while at full gallop.

59. When Trudeau coined fuddle-duddle (cf. expletive deleted) an opposition member quipped: "the PM wishes to be obscene and not heard."
60. The judge reviews the factums, then writes the decision.
61. What is the etymology of hoosegow?
62. What is the relationship between limn and illumine?
63. The oracles are dumb. Milton
64. San Francisco is a midway plaisance. L.H. Lapham
65. A member of the congregation was nettled by the minister's strictures.
66. The popular etymology carnem vale 'farewell to meat' is mistaken as the true origin of carnival. Determine the etymology.
67. English has not adopted F. planifier, but we do have amplify, exemplify, fortify, mortify, objectify, rectify, stratify, etc. Explain the -fy ending in these words.
68. You can sign default judgement by a praecipe order filed with the officer of the Court. D. Lang
69. Language is subject to the same disintegration and replacement as body tissues and social institutions.
70. Distinguish between a) Le Canada a 'évincé deux diplomates soviétiques' and b) His answers 'evinced both wisdom and integrity.'
71. L. foris 'out of doors, beyond' is the initial component of both forfeit and hors d'oeuvre. How does the current meaning of forfeit reflect this etymology?
72. Implicatur may be part of a theory 1) of how what we say tends to have the effects it does on others, 2) about the expectations which hearers have about, or which are aroused in them by what is said.
73. Now as for homecomings -- mirabile factu! -- New York's the only city to come back to. J. Hollander
74. The arctic tern is the champion migrator of the bird world.
75. Linnaeus applied a binary system of nomenclature to animals and plants, namely, of species and genera.
76. Witness the obduracy with which the popular world of colors, sounds, and smells holds its own... W. James
77. The scalpers charge extortionate prices.
78. Our books were not fabricated with an accommodation to prevailing usages. Paley
79. You will find in my speeches to juries no ... Latin phrases, no fieri facias. Hayne
80. His voice was like a strong soporific. Hugh Garner
81. It is a game in statu nascendi.
82. The cadets have a stringent code of honor.
83. In each of the following items form a word by combining the prefix, adjectival- or verbal-base, and noun- or adjectival-ending; change the prefix's spelling where necessary:

ad- firmat- -io, ad- null- -mentum, con- parat- -ivus,
con- lus- -ivus, ex- ros- -io, ex- fus- -ivus, in- rupt-
-io, ob- clus- -io, ob- press- -io, sub- cumb.

84. By changing the prefix form the antonym of appreciate,
consecrate, deflate, dissent, emigrate, excuse, post-
partum, pre-prandial, progress (verb), superhuman.
85. In heraldry, we see lions rampant and lions regardant,
crosses fitchee and eagles displayed. (N.B. the
adjectival position).
86. ... maleficium, that secret, malicious activity of
sorcerers ... Christina Hole
87. What is the key noun and the metaphor in the first element
of the expression: delirium tremens?
88. Some people even in conversation say i.e., or e.g.
89. The seeress Cassandra was tormented with prescience.
90. An abortifacient is the saline abortion technique.
91. When the patient reaches a point of egofication he
challenges the therapist.
92. Angelology, a kind of "microtheology," sees a continuity
in the salvific role of angels in both the OT and the NT.
93. It sounds futurific that future Homo sapiens will use a
GTE Viewdata to pay bills, buy plane tickets, and vote.
94. Determine whether the bases in irrefragable (argument) and
irrefrangible (light rays) are the same. N.B.: note the
use or non-use of the nasal infix; cf. tact and tangent,
from tangere 'to touch.'
95. Liking solitude, he became a true introvert.
96. Mangle a proverb as in the following: children should be
sane and not hurt; invention is a necessity of motherhood;
where there's a will there's a lawyer; do unto others
before they do unto you.
97. The Sioux Indians have punctilious national pride.
98. Differentiate the meanings of cadence and cadency. Do
they, by chance, have a triplet?
99. He felt a strange confluence of emotions in him when he
thought of her.
100. A broken and a contrite heart, O God, thou wilt not
despite. Ps. 51.17
101. Which of the following enjoins? 1) I promise you the room
will be painted, 2) Will the room be painted soon?, 3) The
room will soon be painted, 4) Have the room painted soon.
102. The expatriate mind of the twenties exiled many to France.
103. OL.: expectorāre 'to banish from the mind' ends up as 18c
E. 'to expectorate' = 'to get something off one's chest'
(cf. pectus, pectoris 'breast'). How do you suppose the
verb developed its modern meaning?
104. Montreal is at the junction of the St. Lawrence, Ottawa
and Richelieu rivers.
105. It is difficult to obviate the objections.
106. Orienteering originated in Sweden.

107. He walked around kicking at things <u>perfunctorily</u>. Alice Munro
108. Using prefixes and noun- or adjectival-endings of your choice, compose compounds with the following bases: jac- ject-; mitt- miss-; pati- pass-; pel(l)- puls-; pet- petit-; pugn- pugnat-; quir- quisit- (quest-); reg- (rig-) rect-; spec- (spic-) spect-; volv- volut-. The verbs' basic meanings are, respectively: to throw, send (let go), suffer, drive, seek, fight, seek an answer (ask), rule, look, roll.
109. My adventures were always <u>adventitious</u>.
110. Individual items on the <u>list of things</u> to be done are _____ (Agendums or agendas?) The plural of agenda <u>is</u> _____ (Agendums or agendas?)
111. The <u>R.C. Church</u> promulgates the dogma of the <u>Assumptio Mariae</u>.
112. <u>Politeness</u> demands that we be more often <u>deprecatory</u> than derogatory.
113. <u>What originally</u> took place in a <u>dispensary</u>?
114. What is the antonym of <u>feme covert</u> 'married woman' in legal terminology?
115. MacLennan portrays Canada through the <u>fractures</u>, dichotomies and divisions of its social structure.
116. Fundamentalists speak of the <u>inerrancy</u> of the text.
117. In feudal law a ceremonial <u>conveyance</u> of land was an <u>investiture</u>.
118. <u>Determine</u> the linguistic relationship prevailing among: major, majorette, major-domo, and mayor.
119. Something occurred which contravened the execution of the agreement and rendered it <u>nugatory</u>.
120. A logical fallacy in which <u>what is</u> to be proved is simply taken for granted is _____ _____ (i.e., begging of the question).
121. A radio <u>sextant</u> uses sensitive receiving equipment to locate the <u>sun</u>.
122. I was a well-meaning sutor who had ultra-crepidated with more zeal than wisdom. Coleridge What is an ultracrepidarian?
123. Analyze and segment antidisestablishmentarianism, antivivisectionist, counterrevolutionary, extraconstitutionality, incomprehensibility, interdenominational, rationalization, supernaturalistic, totalitarianism. (N.B.: <u>anti</u> 'against' is a Greek prefix.)
124. What are the antonyms of incommode, material, maternity, predictive?
125. His sermons want all that is called <u>unction</u>, and sometimes even earnestness. Hallam
126. Here Mr. Froude changes the <u>venue</u> and joins issue on the old battle ground. Spencer
127. One sees <u>votive</u> offerings at Lourdes and Fatima.

128. But my lazy little shadow, like an <u>arrant</u> sleepy-head,
Had stayed at home behind me and <u>was fast</u> asleep in bed.
Stevenson

129. The Whiskey-Jack ... is so much given to pilfering, that
no kind of provisions it can come at is safe from its
depredations. Hearne

130. <u>A dum casta</u> clause, whereby any right of a spouse is
dependent upon remaining _____, is void; it formerly
appeared in a domestic contract to take effect upon
separation. (Clue: dum 'so long as (she is)')

131. As penance duplicates penitence, voyage duplicates
viaticum, so repatriate duplicates _____, and Natal
duplicates _____. (N.B. Natal is a Brazilian
coastal city).

132. Barring the Bible, nothing is so <u>ubiquitous</u> as the English
dictionary.

133. Nash thanked his tutelary deity for leading him to the
word <u>velleity</u>.

134. The <u>doublet</u> of osprey is _____, the European
lammergeier.

135. The <u>placebo</u> effect is safe and inexpensive.

136. Cats are <u>digitigrade</u>, but man is <u>plantigrade</u>.

137. Show how cablegram, travelogue and participaction are
portmanteau words conveying multiple meanings.

138. Comment on R.J. Lifton's use of post- in "we speak of
ourselves as postmodern, postindustrial, posthistoric,
postidentity, posteconomic, postmaterialist, posttechno-
cratic."

139. How <u>precarious</u> is the hold of man on this planet. H.M.
Jones

140. A long, patched livery coat evidently belonged to some
corpulent <u>predecessor</u>. Dickens

141. The apple <u>orchard is proliferous</u>.

142. Frobert charged mass <u>ranacide</u> against the UN Environment
program from his <u>chair at</u> the Worldwide Fairplay For
_____ Committee.

143. <u>To what animal</u> is man compared when he is 'recalcitrant?'

144. Had I faith in astrology, I would have sworn some
<u>retrograde</u> planet was hanging over my house. Sterne

145. <u>Distinguish</u> between the meanings of the following pairs:
acceptance and acceptation, adverse and averse, affection
and affectation, continual and continuous, compulsive and
compulsory, discrete and discreet, immanent and imminent,
incredible and incredulous, obeisance and obedience,
obsolete and obsolescent, official and officious, perspic-
acious and perspicuous, presumptive and presumptuous,
reverend and reverent, tortuous and torturous, turbid and
turgid, vocation and avocation.

APPENDICES

LATIN PHRASES IN ENGLISH

Many Latin expressions or phrases have entered the English language and have become so familiar that they are scarcely considered to be foreign. It is not likely that we are even conscious of using a Latin expression, especially since our pronunciation of it is quite Anglicized. We speak, for instance, of ad hoc committees with their ex officio members, of an alter ego, a habeas corpus, a non sequitur, a post mortem. If we do not Anglicize such expressions, we may copy the pronunciations common to the ancient Romans from the Latin tradition in school or university. Many of us adopt the pronunciation of the Roman Catholic Church. There is, therefore, great flexibility in the handling of these words and expressions.

a fortiori
a mari usque ad mare (cf. Ps. 72.8)
a posteriori
ab ovo
ab ovo usque ad mala
ab uno disce omnes
ab urbe condita
acta diurna
acta est fabula
ad aperturam (libri)
ad hoc
ad hominem (sc. argumentum)
ad infinitum
ad libitum
ad nauseam
ad valorem
ad maiorem Dei gloriam
alea jacta est
Alma Mater
alter ego
amens amans
amici probantur rebus adversis
amicus curiae
anguis in herba
anima naturaliter Christiana
anno Domini
annuit coeptis
annus mirabilis
apparatus criticus
arbiter elegantiarum
arma virumque cano
ars est celare artem

ars longa, vita brevis
aurea mediocritas
aut Caesar aut nihil (nullus)
ave atque vale
Ave, maris stella
bacillus amatorius
beati pauperes spiritu (Matt. 5.3)
bis dat qui cito dat
bona fide
brutum fulmen
carpe diem
Carthago delenda est
cave canem
caveat emptor
caveat venditor
cedant arma togae
censor morum
cetera desunt
ceteris paribus
cogito, ergo sum
coram nobis
corona civica
corpus delicti
crescit eundo
crux medicorum
cui bono
cum grano salis
curriculum vitae
(pl. curricula vitarum)
cursus honorum
custos morum
de facto

de gustibus (non disputandum)
de jure
delenda est Carthago
dementia praecox
Deo gratias
Deo volente
de te fabula narratur
deus ex machina
dies irae
dis aliter visum
disiecta membra
divide et impera
do ut abeas
do ut des
dramatis personae
dum spiro, spero
dura lex, sed lex
ecce homo (Joh. 19.5)
errare humanum est
Et tu, Brute
est modus in rebus
ex abrupto
exempli gratia
ex officio
ex parte
ex post facto
fauna et flora
festina lente
Fiat lux (Gen. 1.3)
fides punica
(in) flagrante delicto
fons et origo
forsan et haec olim meminisse
  iuvabit
Gloria in excelsis
Graecum est, non legitur
grammatici certant
habeas corpus
(ad subjiciendum)
habenti dabitur
habitat
Herculeus labor
hinc illae lacrimae
homo homini lupus
homo sapiens
honoris causa
imprimatur
in camera
in cauda venenum
in extremis
in loco parentis

in medias res
in medio stat virtus
in propria persona
in saecula saeculorum
in situ
in vitro
infra dignitatem
inter alia
ipse dixit
ipsissima verba
ipso facto
ite, missa est
jus naturae
laborare est orare
lapsus calami (1. linguae)
litterae humaniores
locum tenens
locus amoenus
locus classicus
magister ludi
maxima debetur puero reverentia
me judice
memento mori
mens sana in corpore sano
miles gloriosus
mirabile dictu (visu)
modus vivendi
mons veneris
morituri te salutamus
mos maiorum
mutatis mutandis
ne plus ultra
ne quid nimis
nihil obstat
nil desperandum
nil medium est
nil nisi bonum (de mortuis)
nil novi sub sole
nolens volens
non compos mentis
non liquet
non obstante
non omnis moriar (Hor., Ode
  3.30.6)
non sequitur
nota bene
novus homo
obiter dicta
odi profanum vulgus (Hor.,
  3.1.1)
omnia vincit amor

onus probandi
ora et labora
orbis Romanus
o tempora, o mores!
otium cum dignitate (Cic., De
  Or., 1.1.1)
palma non sine pulvere
panis et circenses
pari passu
paternoster
paucis verbis
paulo maiora canamus
per fas et nefas
per se (cf. ampersand)
persona grata
petitio quaestionis
pollice verso
pons asinorum
post hoc, ergo propter hoc
post-mortem
prima facie
pro bono publico
pro domo sua
pro forma
prosit
proximo (contrast: ultimo)
  sc. mense
pulsus alternans
quis custodiet ipsos custodes?
  Juv., Sat. 6.347-8)
quod ad omnibus, quod ubique,
  quod semper
quod erat demonstrandum (QED)
quorum pars magna fui
rara avis
res gestae
res ipsa loquitur
rigor mortis
salus omnium, suprema lex
salve!
sanctum sanctorum
scilicet
scriptio continua
sermo plebeius
sesquipedalia verba
si parva licet componere magnis
sic itur ad astra
sic semper tyrannis
sic transit gloria mundi
silent leges inter arma
similia similibus curantur

sine die
sine ira et studio
(conditio) sine qua non
sit tibi terra levis
splendide mendax
(in) statu quo ante
status quaestionis
status quo
suave mari magno
sub judice
sub rosa
sub specie aeternitatis
sui generis
sunt lacrimae rerum
sursum corda
tabula rasa
taedium vitae
tempus fugit
tepidarium (frigidarium)
terminus a quo (et ad quem)
tertium quid
tu quoque
ultima ratio (regum)
ultima Thule
ultra vires
Urbi et Orbi
vade mecum
vae victis
vale
varium et mutabile (Aen. 4.569)
veni, vidi, vici
verba volant, scripta manent
verbatim ac literatim
veritas odium parit
vetere in vino salus, iuventus,
  laetitia
vice versa
vir bonus dicendi peritus
virtus Catonis
vis comica
vitia capitalia
vive valeque (Hor., Sat.
  2.5.10)
vivida vis animi
vox populi, vox Dei

absence	sans (arch.)	
adept	adapt	
ague	acute	cute
alb	album	
alt	alto	
amend	emend	
ampule	ampulla	
antique	antic	
appraise	apprize	
arc	arch	
army	armada	
arrant	errant	
attitude	aptitude	
Augustus	august	August
auricle	auricula	
auscultate	scout	
avouch	avow	
Bella	belle	
belladonna	beldam	
benediction	benison	
biennial	biannual	
bonus	boon (adj.)	
bottler	butler	
brute	brut	
bull	bill	bulla
bus	omnibus (adj.)	
cadence	chance	cadenza
cadet	cad	caddie capitellum
Caesar	Czar	Kaiser
cage	cavie (cavy) Sc.	cave
calx	chalk	
camera	chamber	
campaign	Champagne	Campania
campus	camp	
canal	channel	kennel
		(< ONF. canel = gutter)
cancer	chancre	canker
candelabrum	chandelier	
canna	cane	
cant	chant	
cantor	chanter	
cape	cap	
capitulum	chapter	
captain	chieftain	
captive	caitiff	
carillon	quaternion	
carnal	charnel	
case	cash	

castle	chateau		
catch	chase		
catena	chain		
cattle	chattel	capital	
cause	chose (n.)		
cavalier	chevalier	caballero	
cavalry	chevalry (obs.)	chivalry	
chalumeau	calumet	caramel (?)	
chaplain	capelin		
charter	cartel		
chaste	caste		
chief	chef	capo	cape (headland)
Christian	cretin		
Cicero	cicerone		
clamant	claimant		
clauster	cloister		
cleric	clerk		
coda	queue		
codex	code		
cognate	connate		
cohort	court		
colloquy	colloquium		
cologne	colony	Cologne	
complaisance	complacency		
compute	count		
concept	conceit		
conduct	conduit		
confect	comfit		
confidant	confident		
Constance	constancy		
convey	convoy (v.)		
coronary	coroner	crowner	
corpus	corps	corpse	
costive	constipate		
countenance	continence		
covenant	convenient		
Covent	convent		
crass	grease	(foie) gras	
crate	grate	hurdle	
credence	credenza		
crescent	croissant		
cross	crux		
curricle	curriculum		
curtesy	curtsy	courtesy	
curve	curb		
custom	costume		
dame	duenna	Donna	(prima) donna
damsel	demoiselle		
dean	doyen		
defer (=postpone)	differ		

191

deploy	display			
depot	deposit			
desperate	desperado			
Detroit	district			
devout	devote			
dictate	ditty			
dictum	ditto			
die	dado			
digital	digitalis			
dignity	dainty			
discreet	discrete			
diurnal	journal			
doge	duce	duke		
Dominic	demesne	domain		
dominion	danger			
domino	Dom	don	Don (Juan)	dominie
dulcet	dowcet			
employ	imply			
engine	gin			
ennui	annoy			
escalate	escalade			
esteem	aim			
example	exemplum	sample		
excerpt	scarce			
expand	spawn			
explicit	exploit (n.)			
express	espresso			
extravagance	extravaganza			
fabric	forge			
factitious	fetish			
fact	feat	factum	fait (accompli)	
facture	feature			
faerie	fairy			
faint	feint			
farce	force (meat)			
farm	firm			
fashion	faction			
fate	fado (P.)			
febrifuge	feverfew			
fête	-fest (comb. form)			
fidelity	fealty			
file	filum			
final	finale			
finis	fine (n.)			
flagellum	flail			
foible	feeble			
foil	folium			
font	fount			

force	fort	forte	
fragile	frail		
friar	Fray (cognates: pal	br'er)	
fusion	foison (arch.)		
gaud	joy		
gem	gemma		
genius	genie		
gentile	gentle	genteel	jaunty
genus	gender	genre	
germane	(cousin) -german		
granary	garner		
grave	grief		
herbarium	arbor		
honorary	honorarium		
horrid	ordure		
hospital	hostel	hotel	
host	(table d') hôte		
(h)ostler	hôtelier		
human	humane		
hussar	corsair		
inequity	iniquity		
influence	influenza		
insulate	isolate		
integer	entire		
invidious	envious		
jactation	jettison		
jet	jut		
juggler	jongleur		
Julius	July		
lace	lasso		
lacuna	lagoon		
legal	loyal		
lenticule	lentil		
lesson	lection		
lien	ligament		
limb	limbo	limbus	
limn	illumine		
liquor	liqueur		
livre	lira	£	
Madame	Madonna	madam	
maison (de santé)	mansion		
mantel	mantle		
manure	manoeuvre		
master	Mister	maestro	maître (d')
masticate	(papier-) mâché		
material	materiel		
maximum	maxim		
median	mean		
memoir	memory		
ministry	métier		

193

minstrel	ministerial		
mint	money		
minute (n.)	menu	minuet	minute (adj.)
mistral	magistral		
model	module	mold	
moment	momentum		
moral	morale		
motif	motive		
musket	mosquito		
natal	Noël	Natal (Brazilian & African cities)	Noel (proper name)

native	naive
nausea	noise
neat	nitid
ninny	innocent
node	nodus
none	noon
norm	Norma
novel (n.)	novella
noyau	newel
obeissance	obedience
oboe	hautboy
ointment	unguent
oleo	oil
olla	olio
oration	orison
oratory	oratorio
ossifrage	osprey
ounce	inch
overture	aperture
pace	passus
paint	pinto
palatine	Palatine
Palatium	palace
pale	pallid
pall (n.)	pallium
par	peer (n.)
parfait	perfect
parlous	perilous
pasta	paste
pater (Brit.)	padre
patina	paten
pattern	patron (obs. variant)
paynim	paganism
penance	penitence
pension	pension (board- inghouse)
pensum	poise

palatine   Palatine   paladin

194

peregrine	pilgrim		
person	parson	persona	
personal	personnel		
pert	expert		
pestle	pistil		
piety	pity		
pigment	pimento		
plain	piano	plan	
plaintiff	plaintive		
podium	pew		
poignant	pungent		
poor	pauper		
port	Oporto		
pose	pause		
potion	poison		
precise	précis		
prehension	prison		
premier	primary	primer	primer (paint)
prime	prim	primo	primus (inter pares)
principium	principle		
private	privy		
prize	price	praise	
probable	provable		
procuracy	proxy		
procurator	proctor		
prompt	pronto		
propose	purpose		
proprietor	proprietary		
propriety	property		
prospect	prospectus		
prove	probe (v.)		
provender	prebend		
provident	prudent		
pueblo	people		
puny	puisne		
purvey	provide		
quiet	coy	quite	
rabies	rage		
raceme	raisin		
radius	ray		
radix	radish		
ranch	rank		
ratio	reason	ration	raison (d'être)
rational	rationale		
ravine	rapine		
redemption	ransom		
regal	royal	real (Sp.)	
regimen	régime		
relax	release		
renegade	runagate		
repatriate	repair		

reticle	reticule	reticulum
respect	respite	
reticle	reticule	
revel	rebel	
Rex	Roy	
rotund	rondo	round
route	rut	rout
sacristan	sexton	
salon	saloon	
sanctuary	sentry	
sauce	salsa	
savior	Salvatore	(San) Salvador
	(proper name)	
saxifrage	sassafras	
scintilla	tinsel	stencil
secret	secrete	
secure	sure	
seminary	seminar	
senior	seignior	Sir Sire
sericeous	Seric	
servant	sergeant	
sinus	sine	
skirt	shirt (< VL tunica excurta < ex-curtus)	
soil	sully	
solitary	solitaire	
sovereign	soprano	
special	especial	
spend	expend	
spice	species	
spirit	sprite	esprit
squire	esquire	
stabile	stable (adj.)	
stance	stanza	
state	estate	status
stationary	stationery	
stilus	style	
strict	strait	
stubble	stipule	
study	étude	studio (via It.)
suffix	soffit	
superficies	surface	
supervisor	surveyor	
suspicion	soupçon	
tegula	tuile	tile
terebinth	turpentine	
terminus	term	
terrene	terrane	terrain
testa	(tête-à) -tête	
tone	tonus (e.g. muscular)	
tophus	tuff	

tractate	treaty	
tradition	treason	
trait	tract	tret
traitor	traditor	
transverse	traverse	
travail	travel	
trellis	drill (n.)	
tremolo	tremulous	
triumph	trump	
union	onion	
urban	urbane	
usher	ostiary	
vague	vagus	
vair	various	
value	valuta	
vaquero	buckaroo	
vault	volute	
venin	venom	
vermeil	vermillion	vermicule
vestiary (adj.)	vestry	
viaticum	voyage	
victory	Victoria	
villous	velure	
virtue	virtū	
virtuous	virtuoso	
volunteer	voluntary	
vocal	vowel	
vote	vow	
Vulcan	volcano	

DOUBLETS D'ORIGINE LATINE

aigue (-marine)		eau
aire		are
alter (ego)		autre
août	auguste	Auguste
armée		armada (hispanisme)
attitude		aptitude
auriculaire		oreille
avoué		avocat
bayer		béer
benêt	benoît	béni	bénit
biche		bête
bill		bulle
(anglicisme)		
cadran		quadrant
cailler		coaguler
Canicule		chenille
cannabis		chanvre	canevas
capitaine		capitan
caporal		corporel

chambre		caméra	
champ	campus	campos (?)	camp
Champagne	campagne	Campanie	
chance		cadence	
chancre	cancer	Cancer	
chapître		capitule	
charbon		carbon	
charbonnée		carbonnade	
charte		carte	
chaste		caste	
chenal		canal	
cheptel		capital	
cherté		charité	
chétif		captif	
cheval		joual	
chevalerie		cavalerie	
chevauchée		cavalcade	
cheville		clavicule	
chevreuil		cabriole	
chose		cause	
Cologne		colonie	
combler		cumuler	
compter		computer	
contenance		continence	
copain		compagnon	
corps		corpus	
coucher		colloquer	
cour		cohorte	
coûtume		costume	
crétin		chrétien	
croyance		créance	
cueillette		collecte	
daintier		dignité	
dame		duègne	
déchéance		décadence	
décor		décorum	
devin		divin	
dîme		décime	
dîner		déjeuner	
dom		domino	
donzelle		demoiselle	
droit		direct	
duce		duc	
duché		ducat	
écolier		scolaire	
écouter		ausculter	
employer		impliquer	
entier		intègre	
épaule		spatule	
épice		espèce	
espresso		exprès	

essaim		examen
étinceler		scintiller
étroit		strict
facende		hacienda
faute		faillite
for		forum
forge		fabrique
frêle		fragile
froid		frigide
gaine		vagin
graisse		crasse
grêle		gracile
grief		grave
hautesse		altesse
hôtel		hôpital
humeur		humour
inclinaison		inclination
journal		diurnal
labre		lèvre
lagune		lacune
laquis		lacs
larme		lacrima (-christi)
libérer		livrer
linge		ligne
liure		ligature
livrer		libérer
loyal		légal
mâcher		mastiquer
maire	major	majeur
maison		mansion
maître		maestro (italisme)
mantille		manteau
métier		ministère
meuble		mobile
moule		muscle
moutier (Vx)		monastère
mouvement		moment
muer		muter
mûr		mature
nager		naviguer
naïf		natif
Noël		natal
noir		nègre
noise		nausée
nombre		numéro
oignon		union
on		homme
ouverture		aperture
païen		paysan
parcelle		particule
pâtre		pasteur

paume		palme	
pavillon		papillon	
peser		penser	
pitié		piété	
plaisir		plaire	
ployer		plier	
poêle		patelle	
poison		potion	
pommée		pommada	
port		Oporto	
prêcheur		prédicateur	
préhension		prison	
préséance		présidence	
prévost		préposé	
primaire		premier	
quart		(in-) quarto	
queue		coda (de l'italien)	
raide	roide	rigide	
raison		ration	
rançon		rédemption	
ravine		rapine	
rayon		radium	
régal		royal	
reille (Vx)		règle	
rouleau		rôle	
sans		absence	
santé		sanité	
saut		saute	
sembler		simuler	
serment		sacrement	
sevrer		séparer	
sinistre		senestre	
sire	sieur	seigneur	sénieur (Vx)
songer		soigner	
soucier		solliciter	
soudard		soldat	
souverain		soprano	
terme		terminus	
terroir		territoire	
trahison		tradition	
tsar		César	
tunnel		tonnelle	
veille		vigile	
verre		vitre	
vipère		vieuvre	
voeu		vote	
volcan		Vulcain	
voyage		viatique	
voyelle		vocal	
voyer		vicaire	

FAMILIAR NAMES AND EXPRESSIONS DERIVED
FROM LATIN LITERATURE, HISTORY, ETC.

Faithful Achates, loyal friend and companion of Aeneas, hence, loyal friend.

Pius Aeneas was pater Aeneas, son of Venus and Anchises, hero of the Aeneid.

Augustan Age, literary period during Augustus Caesar's reign, ca. 27 B.C. - 14 A.D.

Augustus Caesar, after whom our eighth month is named.

Aurora Borealis, i.e., dawn of the north; the aurora glory is its corona; Aurora was the goddess of the dawn, counterpart of the Greek goddess Eos.

Bacchanalian orgy; Bacchus taught the cultivation of the grape.

Bavius & Mevius, poets satirized by Vergil.

Bellona (a woman of commanding presence) was, in Roman mythology, the goddess of war and sister of Mars.

St. Benedict, founder of monasticism; cf. a "benedick," a bachelor finally caught in the bond of matrimony.

Caesarian birth, supposedly because Julius Caesar was born in this manner.

Stern Cato, champion of ancient Roman ideals.

A Cerberus of the stage door is a rough, vigilant guardian, from the 3-headed dog guarding Hades' entrance; (cf. Cdn F. le cerbère, "the goalie" in hockey matches).

A cicerone is a guide who points out places of interest on a tour and shines for his loquacity, after the famous Roman orator, Cicero.

A Cincinnatus is a retired man who is recalled in a crisis.

"If he were a cloaca, he would want to be the Cloaca Maxima." Cicero (of a braggart)

"If they will not eat, then let them drink." a Roman Admiral (of sacred chickens)

Graceful Diana, goddess of the chase, chastity, and the moon.

Poor Dido (infelix) fell in love with Aeneas when shot by Cupid's arrow. In the Aeneid she is a deserta femina.

Dives, the rich, insensitive man (cf. Luke 16.19.31)

'Domi mansit, lanam fecit' is a frequent tombstone inscription.

The Genius, or attendant spirit of Roman men, was a tutelar deity.

"How can one haruspex (diviner) pass another without laughing in his face?" Cicero

A Hercules choice; a Herculean labor, from the 12 nearly impossible tasks set the ancient Greek hero, Heracles.

Humanitas, coined by Cicero to mean virtues, especially intelligence and kindliness.

Two-headed Janus, guardian of portals, patron of beginnings; he gives us our first month's name.

Stately Juno, goddess of marriage, wife of Jupiter.

Chaste Lucretia, when dishonored by Sextus Tarquinius, killed herself, bringing about the expulsion of the Etruscan kings from Rome.

Lucullan feast, after Lucullus, who gave luxurious banquets in the 1c B.C. "Lucullus will sup with Lucullus," i.e., a banqueter will dine alone.

A Maecenas is a patron of letters, the arts, theatre, etc.

Magna cum laude, a phrase signifying highest academic honors obtained at graduation from a college or university; in literature, we often find maxima cum laude.

Mercury is often a newspaper title, since M. was the messenger of the gods and god of commerce. He is identified with the Greek Hermes as one who protects tradesmen (cf. merx 'merchandise').

Morituri te salutamus (we who are about to die salute you) was the gladiators' last declaration.

Neptune's ocean, after the Roman sea-god who bore a trident; the 3rd largest planet is named after him.

Cynical Nero, a cruel, depraved, despotic emperor who ordered his mother's death; he had ordered Seneca, his tutor, to commit suicide. He is said to have fiddled while Rome burned.

Omne ignotum pro magnifico: 'whatever is unknown is held to be magnificent.'

Roscian, an adjective implying perfection in action, from Roscius, a comic actor of the 1st c. B.C.

To cross the Rubicon, i.e., take an irretrievable step; Julius Caesar crossed this river to invade the Republic in 49 B.C.

Born under the planet Saturn refers to an unforgiving enemy. This is because Saturn "never helps people out of scrapes."

Between Scylla & Charybdis: monstrous perils to pass between, of which it is hard to avoid one without running into the other; these are creatures in Homeric literature and in Vergil's Aeneid.

A Sibyl was a female fortune teller. She was originally the mouthpiece of the god Apollo. The most celebrated is the Cumaean Sibyl.

'Una est quae reparet seque ipsa reseminet ales." The phoenix is the only bird which renews itself and reproduces its wings; cf. Ovid, Metamorphoses 15.392.

Nouns, Adjectives, Adverbs

acer sharp (cf. acutus)
acerbus harsh, bitter
aedēs, aedis building, house
aequus equal, level
aestus heat, tide
aetas age
aevum age
ager, agrī field, land, farm
albus white
aliās at another time, elsewhere
alibī elsewhere, at another place
almus food-giving, nurturing, fostering
altus high, deep
alumna foster daughter, pupil
alvus belly
amātor lover
amīcus friend
amita aunt
amoenus pleasant, charming
amplus spacious, large, great
ancilla servant girl
angulus angle, corner
anima air, breath, life, soul
annus year
antenna sailyard
antīquus ancient, old, former
anus old woman
apex, apicis point, top
apis bee
aptus fit, suitable
aqua water (adj., aqueus watery)
aquila eagle
arbiter, arbitrī judge
arbor, arboris tree
arcus bow, arch
ārea vacant plot of land in town
arēna sand, arena
arma arms, weapons
ars, artis skill
artus joint
asinus ass

ater, atrī black
augustus reverend, majestic
aureus golden, of gold
aurum gold
avārus grasping, greedy
avis bird
avunculus mother's brother
bacca berry
barba beard
barbarus savage, rude
beatus happy
bellum war
bellus pretty
bene well, rightly
bīlis bile, anger
bipēs two-footed animal
bis twice, a second time
bonus good, kind
bōs, bovis ox, bull, cow; pl. cattle
brutus dull, irrational
bulla water-bubble, amulet
caecus blind
caelebs bachelor
caelum sky
calumnia false accusation
calx, calcis limestone, pebble
camera vault, chamber
campus plain, field
cancer, cancrī crab
canis dog, hound
cantus song, incantation, music
caper, caprī he-goat
capillus hair
capsa box
caput, capitis head
carbō, carbōnis coal
cardo, cardinis hinge
carō, carnis flesh
carpentum carriage
cārus dear, precious
castor beaver
castus pure
cauda (or cōda) tail
causa motive

204

cavilla mockery
cavus hollow
celeber frequent, thronged
cella cell, strore-room
centum hundred
cerebrum brain
Cerēs Ceres
certus definite, fixed, sure
cilium eyelid
cinis, cineris ashes
circā about, around
circus ring
citrus citrus-tree, citron-tree
cīvis citizen, fellow citizen
clamor shout
clandestinus secret
clārus clear, bright, famous
clavis key
cliēns, clientis dependant,
  follower
clīvus slope, hill
cloaca sewer
cōdex, cōdicis ancient form
  of book
cohors cohort, yard
colonus settler, husbandman
comes, comitis companion
cōmis courteous
commūnis common
congeriēs heap, mass
contrā against
contumelia insult, abuse
cōnus cone
cor, cordis heart
corium skin, hide
corōna garland, crown
cornū horn
corpus, corporis body
costa rib, side
crās tomorrow
crassus thick, gross
crimen crime
crūdus raw
crux, crucis cross
cubitum elbow
culīna kitchen
culpa fault, blame
cuneus wedge
cūpa cask, barrel
cūra care, trouble, attention

curvus bent, curved
cutis skin (cf. cutīcula)
damnum loss, harm
decor, decōris comeliness
decōrus becoming, seemly
dēlictum crime
deni by tens
dēns, dentis tooth
deus (or dīvus) god
dexter, dexterī (or dextrī)
  right
diēs day, interval
digitus finger, toe
dīgnus worthy, fit
dominus lord, master
dorsum back
dōs, dōtis dowry, marriage
  gift
dūrus hard
dux, ducis leader
ecce lo! see! behold!
ego I
equus horse
exemplum sample, precedent
exterus outside (cf. adv.,
  extrā)
fabula story, tale
faciēs appearance, surface,
  shape, face
falx, falcis sickle, pruning-
  hook
fāma report, rumor
fānum shrine, temple
fascis bundle, bundle of
  faggots
fatuus silly
faustus favoring, lucky
febris fever
fecundus fertile
fēlīx, fēlīcis fortunate,
  fruitful
fēmina woman
femur femoris thigh
ferrum iron, sword
fēstus joyful
fibula brooch
fidēs trust, faith, loyalty
fīlum thread
finis limit, boundary, end
fīrmus steadfast, powerful

205

fiscus basket, money-basket, purse
flos, floris flower, blossom
focus hearth
folium leaf
forma shape
fortior comparative of fortis
fortis strong, brave
fortissimus superlative of fortis
fortuna fate, fortune; pl. possessions
frater, fratris brother
frigus, frigoris coldness
frons, frontis forehead
fulmen, fulminis lightning, thunderbolt
fumus smoke, steam
funus, funeris funeral, death
gelidus icy, extremely cold
genius guardian deity
gens, gentis tribe, race
genus, generis race, kind, sort
germen, germinis seed
glacies ice
gladius sword
globus ball, sphere
gloria renown
gradus step, degree, rank
grandis great, lofty
granum grain, seed
gratus pleasing, agreeable, grateful
gravis heavy, important
grex, gregis flock, herd
herba blade of grass, herb
hiatus gap, yawn
histrio, histrionis actor
hoc this
homo, hominis man
hospes, hospitis host, guest
hostis enemy
humor liquid, fluid
humus earth, ground
ignis fire, signal fire
imperium sovereign power, control
inanis empty
index, indicis forefinger
industria diligence
inferus down, low; pl. the dead

insula island
integer, integri untouched, fresh, whole
interim meanwhile, in the meantime
interior inner
ipse self, own; pl. ipsi themselves
ira anger, rage
iter, itineris journey
iterum again
Janus god of openings
jejunus hungry, scanty, barren insignificant
jocus jest
judex, judicis judge, juror
Juppiter, Jovis Jupiter, Jove
jus, juris law, right
justus upright, righteous
juvenis adj., young; young man
labium lip
labor, laboris work
lac, lactis milk
lacrima tear
lacuna gap, ditch
lapis, lapidis stone
Lares Lares
lassus languid, weary
latus wide
latus, lateris side
laus, laudis praise
leo, leonis lion
levis light, light-minded
lex, legis law
liber, liberi free, unrestrained
liber, libri book
lignum wood
limbus border, edge
limen, liminis threshold, border
linea line
lingua tongue, language
lira furrow
littera letter
lividus blue, black and blue
locus place
longaevus of great age, ancient
longus extended
lucrum gain, profit

206

lūdus game, school
lumbus loin
lūmen, luminis light, torch
lupus wolf
lūridus pale yellow, wan,
  ghastly
lūx, lūcis light, daylight
magister, magistrī master,
  teacher
magnus great
mājōres, -um ancestors
malus bad
manēs shades of the dead,
  ghosts
manus hand
mare, maris sea
margō, marginis border, edge
marītus husband
māter, mātris mother
māteria matter, wood
mātrōna married woman
mātūrus ripe, early
medicus doctor; adj., medical
medius middle
memor, memoris mindful,
  relentless
mendicus beggar
mēns, mentis mind,
  understanding, purpose
Mercurius Mercury
merx, mercis wares, merchandise
meus adj., mine; meum my thing
mīles, mīlitis soldier
minera mine, ore
minister, ministrī servant
minium red lead
minūtiae details, trifles
miser, miserī wretched
missa mass (Ite, missa est)
mītis mild, soft
modus measure, method, fashion
mollis soft
mōns, montis mountain
mōnstrum wonder, miracle,
  monster
morbus disease
mors, mortis death
mōs, mōris custom
multus much, many
mundus world, earth

mūnus, mūneris duty, gift,
  reward
murus wall
mūs, mūris mouse
musca fly
nāsus nose
nē not (as in nē plūs ultrā)
nebula mist, vapour, fog
nēmo nobody
nepōs, nepotis grandson,
  nephew
nervus sinew
niger, nigrī black
nihil nothing
nimbus thick shower, cloud
nōdus knot, node
nōmen, nōminis name,
  reputation
norma measure, standard,
  pattern
noster, nostrī our
nota mark
novus new, strange
nox, noctis night
noxa harm
noxius harmful
nūgae jests, trifles
nullus not any, none
numerus number, quantity
nunc now, at present
nuntius messenger, courier
nux, nucis nut
oculus eye
odium hatred, ill will
officium service, duty
oleum oil
ōmen, ōminis foreboding, sign
omnis all
onus, oneris burden,
  responsibility
opera work, attention, help
ops, opis aid; pl. influence,
  wealth
opus, operis work, labor
orbis circle
ordō, ordinis order, regular
  succession
orīgō, orīginis beginning,
  source, descent
ōs, ōris mouth

os, ossis bone
ostiarius doorkeeper
ostium door, mouth, entrance
otium leisure, idleness, peace
ovis sheep
ovum egg
paene nearly, almost
Palatium Palatine Hill
palus stake
panis bread
par, paris equal
pars, partis portion
parvus small
passus pace, step
pater, patris father; pl.
  senators
paucus few
paulus little
pax, pacis peace
pectus, pectoris breast
pecunia money
pecus flock
Penates Penates
penna feather
penuria want, destitution
peregrinus wanderer
persona mask, role, character,
  person
pes, pedis foot
pestis disease, plague
pica magpie
pila ball
pilus a hair
piscis fish
pius dutiful, loyal, pious
planus level, flat
plebs, plebis common people
plenus full
plumbum lead
plus, pluris more
poena penalty, punishment
populus people, nation
porcus hog, pig, swine
portus port, harbor
posterus following, next
praeda booty, prey, plunder
pretium value, worth
prex, precis prayer
primus first
prior former, preceding,
  earlier, first

pristinus early, original,
  former
privus one's own, private
probrum infamy, reproach
probus good
proles, prolis offspring
pronus bent over, leaning
proprius one's own, special,
  characteristic
puer boy, child
pugna fight, battle
pulmo, pulmonis lung
pulpitum scaffold
pupa girl
pupus boy
purus pure, unstained
pusillus very little, petty
quadraginta forty
qualis of what sort? such as
quantus of what size? how
  much? how great?
quartus fourth
quid what?
quondam formerly, once
quot how many? as many as
rabies madness
racemus bunch, cluster
radius staff, rod, spoke of a
  wheel
radix, radicis root
ramus branch, bough
rana frog
rarus rare
rectus direct, straight,
  upright
regina queen
regnum kingdom, rule,
  sovereignty
regula ruler, rule
renes kidneys
res thing, matter, possession
rete, retis net
rex, regis king
ripa bank of a river
ritus form of religious
  observance, ceremony
robur, roboris oak, strength
robustus of oak wood, firm
rota wheel
rotundus rolling, circular
ruber, rubri red

rūga wrinkle
sacer, sacrī sacred, holy
saeculum generation, life-time, the world
sagāx, sagācis keen-scented
sal, salis salt
salūs, salūtis health, safety
salvus safe
sānctus holy, sacred
sanguis, sanguinis blood, race
sānus healthy, rational
satis enough, sufficient
scintilla spark
scutārius shield-bearer
sēmen, sēminis seed
semper always
senex, senis old man
septuāgintā seventy
seriatim in order
seriēs row, succession, series
sermō, sermōnis talk, conversation
servus slave
sexus sex
sic so
sīgnum mark, token
silva forest
similis like, similar
sinister on the left hand
sinus curve, bosom
sōbrius sober, moderate
soccus light shoe, slipper
socius associate, ally
sōl, sōlis sun
solidus firm compact
sōlus alone, single, only
somnus sleep
sonus sound, noise
sopor, sopōris deep sleep
soror sister
sors, sortis lot, fate
spatium space, distance, time interval
speciēs appearance
specula watch-tower
spīna thorn, spine, barrier
spīritus breath
stella star
stimulus prick, goad, spur
stirps, stirpis stem, root
strenuus vigorous

subter beneath
succus juice, sap, taste
summus highest
superbus haughty, proud
supercilium eyebrow
superus upper; pl. gods
supīnus lying on the back
suus its own
taberna rude dwelling, hut
tabula plank, tablet
taedium weariness, disgust
taurus bull
tempus, temporis time, season
tenuis slender
tepidus lukewarm
tergum back
terminus boundary stone, boundary
tertium quid some third thing
tessera cube, square piece, die
testis witness
tibia shin-bone
tōtus whole, the whole
trux, trucis savage, wild
tūber, tūberis bump, swelling, truffle
tumor swelling
turba turmoil, confusion
turpis shameful
tūtela a watching, safeguard, protection
tuus adj., your; tuum your thing, yours
ubi where
ultrā beyond, farther, in addition
umbra shadow, shade
uncia ounce
unda wave
urbs, urbis city
ursus a bear
ūsūra a using, a loan, payment for use of money
ūtilis useful
vacca cow
valētudinārius invalid
vānus empty, vain
vapidus flat, stale
varius varied
vēlōx, vēlōcis swift

209

vēna blood-vessel, vein
venia pardon
venter, ventris belly
vēnum sale
verbātim word for word
verber, verberis lash, whip
verbi gratiā for instance
verbum word, saying
vērē truly, rightly
vermis worm
vertebra joint
vertex, verticis peak, tip
vērus true
vestibulum entrance-court
vestīgium footstep, track
vestis garment, clothing
vetus, veteris old
via way, road, street
vicis change, alternation
vīllānus farm-laborer
vinum wine
vir, virī man, husband
virāgō, virāginis man-like
  woman
virgō, virginis maiden
viridis green
vīrus venom, potent juice
vīs force, energy, strength
vīta life
vītis vine
vitium defect, flaw
vitulus calf
vīvus alive, living
voluntās free will, choice
vortex, vorticis whirl, eddy,
  whirlpool
vōtum promise
vōx, vōcis voice
vulgus the public, the common
  people
vulpēs, vulpis fox
vultus face, expression

accēdere, accessum to come near, approach

adolescere, adultus to grow up (see olēre)

affīdāre to take oath, pledge (see fidēs)

agere, actus (-igere, -actus) to do, act, drive

amāre to love

ambulāre to walk

arāre to plow

arbitrārī, arbitrātus to think, judge (see arbiter)

audēre, ausus to dare

audīre, audītus to hear

augēre, auctus to increase

beāre to make happy, bless

bibere to drink

bullīre, bullītus to bubble, boil

cadere, cāsus (-cidere, -cāsus) to fall

candēre to be a glowing white

canere, cantus to sing

capere, captus (-cipere, -ceptus) to take, hold, grasp

carēre to lack

carpere, carptus (-cerpere, -cerptus) to pick, pluck

cavēre, cautus to take care, beware, guard against

cēdere, cessum to go, yield (see accēdere)

-cendere, -census to burn (see incendere)

cēnsēre, cēnsus to rate, assess

cernere, crētus to sift, distinguish

citāre to rouse, mention

clāmāre to cry out

clangere to ring, clang

claudere, clausus (-clūdere, -clūsus) to shut

clīnāre to lean

cogere, coāctum to drive together, compel

colere, cultus to till, cultivate

comminīscī, commentus to invent, reflect upon

condere, conditus to establish, lay up, store

confūtāre to check

consīderāre to examine, reflect

consulere, consultus to have regard for

coquere, coctus to cook

creāre to create

crēdere, crēditus to believe, trust

crēscere, crētus to grow

crūdēscere to become raw, worsen (see crudus)

-culere, cultus to hide (see occulere)

-cumbere, -cubitus to lie (see incumbere)

cupere (-iō), cupītus to long for, desire

currere, cursus to run

dare, datus (-dere, -ditus) to give

dēficere (-iō), dēfectus to make absent or lacking, fail, be wanting

dēlēre, dēlētus to destroy

dēsīderāre to desire, long for

dīcere, dictus to say, tell

dīvidere, dīvīsus to divide

docēre, doctus to teach

dormīre, dormītus to sleep

dūcere, ductus to lead, regard, prolong

emere, emptus (-imere, -emptus) to buy, take

errāre to wander, be mistaken

exīre, exitus to go out

facere (-iō), factus (-ficere, -fectus) to make, do

fallere, falsus to deceive

fārī, fatus to speak

ferīre to strike

ferre (base fer-), lātus to bring, bear

fervēre to seethe

festināre to hurry
fīdere, fīsus to trust, rely on
fierī, factus to be made, be done, become
fīgere, fīxus to fix, fasten
findere, fissus to split
flāre to blow
flectere, flexus to bend
flōrēre to bloom, flourish (see flos)
fluere, fluxus to flow
fodere (-iō), fossus to dig
frangere, frāctus (-fringere, -frāctus) to break
fugere (-iō), fugitus to flee, avoid, shun
fulgēre to flash
fundere, fūsus to pour
fungī, fūnctus to do, perform
furere to rage, be mad
-fūtāre (see confūtāre, refūtāre)
garrīre to chatter
gerere, gestus to bear, carry on, conduct
gignere, genitus to beget, bring forth
gradī, gressus (-gredī, -gressus) to step
gubernāre to steer
habēre, habitus (-hibēre, -hibitus) to have, hold, consider
habitāre to have possession of, dwell, reside (see habēre)
haerēre, haesus to stick
haurīre, haustus to draw out
hiāre to stand open, gape (see hiatus)
horrēre to shrink, shudder
humēre to be moist (see humus)
ignorāre to be ignorant, not know
incendere, incēnsus to set fire to, burn
incumbere, incubitus to lie on, pay attention to
interesse to be important
īre, itum to go
jacēre to lie (dead)

jacere (-iō), jactus (-jicere, -jectus) to throw, hurl
judicāre, judicātus to judge
jungere, junctus to join
jūrāre to swear
juvāre, jutum help, assist
lābī, lapsus to fall, slip
laedere, laesus (-līdere, -līsus) to strike
lambere to lick
languēre to faint
latēre to lie hid
laudāre to praise (see laus)
lavāre, lavātus or lōtus to wash
legere, lēctus (-ligere, -lēctus) to gather, read, choose
licēre, licitum to be allowable, permitted
ligāre to bind
linere, litus to smear, anoint
linquere (-lictus) to leave
liquēre, lixus to be liquid
loquī, locūtus to speak
lūcēre to be light, shine (see lūx)
luctārī to struggle
lūdere, lusus to play
luere (-lūtum) to wash, loosen, at one for
manēre, mānsus to remain
mederī to heal
merēre, meritus to earn
mergere, mersus to dip, plunge
metīrī, mēnsus to measure
mīlitāre to be a soldier, fight (see mīles)
-minēre to project, threaten
-miniscī, -mentus (see comminiscī)
mīrarī to marvel at, admire
miscēre, mīxtus to mingle
mittere, missus to let go, send
monēre, monitus to warn, remind, advise
mordēre, morsus to bite
movēre, mōtus to move
mulctāre to fine, penalise

212

mutāre to change, alter
nasci, natus born
necāre to kill
nectere, nexus to bind
nocēre to harm
nōscere, nōtus to know
oboedīre to obey
obsolēscere, obsolētus to wear
  out, fall into disuse (see
  olēre and -olēscere)
occulere, occultus to cover up,
  hide
olēre to smell
olēre to increase
-olēscere (see adolēscere,
  obsolēscere and olēre - to
  increase)
opīnārī to suppose, think
ōrāre to pray, speak
ōrdinare to arrange (see ōrdō,
  ōrdinis)
ōrdīrī, orsus to arise
orīrī, ortus to arise
ōrnāre to equip, adorn
ōscillāre to swing
ostendere, ostentus to show
pacīscī, pactus to make an
  agreement
paenitēre to repent
pallēre to be pale
palpāre to stroke, feel
pangere, pactus (-pingere,
  -pāctus) to strike, fasten
parāre to prepare
parere (-iō), partus to give
  birth
partīrī, partītus to share (see
  pars)
pāscere, pāstus to feed, graze
patēre to stand open
pati (-iōr), passus to suffer,
  bear
pausāre to cease
pellere, pulsus to drive
pendēre (-pēnsus) to hang
pendere, pēnsus to weigh, pay
penetrāre to pierce
perquirere to purchase, acquire
petere, petītus to seek
pingere, pictus to paint

placēre, placitus to please
plangere, planctus to strike,
  lament
plaudere, plausus (or plōdere,
  plōsus) to clap
-plēre, -plētus to fill
plicāre, plicātus or plicitus
  to fold
polīre, polītus to polish,
  smooth
ponere, positus to place, put
portāre to carry
posse (pot-) to be powerful,
  be able
postulāre, postulātus to ask,
  demand
precārī to beg, pray (see
  prex)
prehendere, prehensus to grasp
premere, pressus (-primere,
  -pressus) to press
privāre to deprive (see
  prīvus)
propāgāre to multiply, to
  spread
prurīre to itch
pūgnāre to fight (see pugna)
pungere, punctus to prick
pūrgāre to make clean, or
  pure, cleanse
putāre, putātus to reckon, to
  think
quaerere, quaesītus (-quīrere,
  -quīsītus) to seek
quatere (-iō), quassus
  (-cutere, -cussus) to shake
querī, questus to complain
quiēscere, quiētus to be quiet
rādere, rāsus to scrape
rapere (-iō), raptus (ripere,
  -reptus) to seize and carry
  off, rob
recipere (-iō), receptus to
  take back, get back, take
  (see capere)
redimere, redemptus to ransom
refūtāre to check, disprove
regere, rēctus (-rigere,
  -rectus) to straighten, rule
rēpere, rēptus to creep, crawl

requiescere, requietus to rest
rērī, ratus to think, reckon
rigēre to be stiff
rogāre to ask, propose a law
ruere, rutus to tumble down
rūgāre to wrinkle (see rūga)
rumpere, ruptus to break
saepīre, saeptus to enclose
sagīre to discern acutely
salīre, saltus (-silīre,
  -sultus) to leap
salvēre to be well (see salūs)
sānāre to heal (see sānus)
sancīre, sānctus to make holy
scandere, scānsum (-scendere,
  -scēnsum) to rise, climb
scindere, scissus to cut, split
scīre, scītus to know
scribere, scriptus to write
secāre, sectus to cut
sedāre to calm
sedēre, sessus (-sidēre,
  -sessus) to sit
sentīre, sensus to feel
sequī, secūtus to follow
serere, satus to sow
serere, sertus to bind, join,
  connect
servāre to save
servīre, servītus to serve (see
  servus)
-sīderāre (see cōnsīderāre,
  dēsīderāre)
sistere, status (-sistere,
  -stitus) to cause to stand,
  stand
sōlārī to comfort
solvere, solūtus to loose, free
sonāre to sound (see sonus)
sortīrī, sortītus to cast lots
  (see sors)
spargere, sparsus (-spergere,
  -spersus) to scatter
specere (-iō), spectus
(-spicere, -spectus) to look
speculārī to spy out, observe
  (see specula)
spīrāre to breathe
spondēre, sponsus to promise
squālēre to be foul

stāre to stand
statuere, statūtus (-stituere,
  -stitūtus) to set up
sternere, strātus to spread
-stinguere, -stinctus to
  prick, quench
stringere, strictus to draw
  tight
struere, structus to build
studēre to be eager
stupēre to be struck senseless
-sulere, sultus (see cōnsulere)
sūmere, sūmptus to take
tacēre, tacitus (-ticēre) to
  be silent
tangere, tāctus (tingere,
  -tāctus) to touch
tegere, tēctus to cover
tendere, tentus or tēnsus to
  stretch, hold a course
tenēre, tentus (-tinēre,
  -tentus) to hold
terere, trītus to rub, wear
terrēre, territus to frighten
texere, textus to weave
tingere, tinctus to dip, dye,
  wet
torpēre to be stiff, be numb
torquēre, tortus to twist
trahere, tractus to draw, drag
tremere to tremble
tribuere, tribūtus to assign,
  allot
trūdere, trūsus to push
tuērī, tūtus to protect
tumēre to swell (see tumor)
unguere, ūnctus to smear,
  anoint
urgēre to press
ūtī, ūsus to employ, use
vacillāre to waver, totter
vādere to go, walk
vagārī to wander
valēre to be strong, be worth
vehere, vectus to carry
velle (vol-) to wish
vellere (-vulsus) to pluck
venīre, ventum to come
verērī, veritus to fear, feel
  awe for

vergere to bend, to turn, to
  incline
vertere, versus to turn
vetāre, vetitus to oppose,
  forbid, prohibit
vidēre, visus to see
vigēre to thrive
vincere, victus to conquer
vīvere, vīctum to live
volāre to fly
volvere, volūtus to roll
vorāre to devour
vovēre, vōtus to vow
vulgāre to make general, spread
  abroad

A SELECTIVE LIST OF DERIVATIVES FROM LATIN

abject, 107
ablation, 170
ablutions, 98
abominate, 165
aborad, 28
abortifacient, 184
ab ovo, 155
abstract, 139
accretion, 146
acerbity, 37
acumen, 145
addendum, 91
adhesive, 162
adjudicator, 115
ad libitum, 158
adscititious, 180
adventitious, 174, 178, 185
affinities, 113
aggregate, 163
albescent, 169
allocation, 123
allusion, 154
Amanda, 91, 133
ambience, 147
ambivalence, 138
amenity, 87, 181
amicus curiae, 36
anile, 72
anima, 9
animalcule, 45
animus, 8, 9, 10
annals, 45
anticipatory, 174
antiquary, 49, 181
antivivisectionist, 171
aperture, 99
apicad, 28
aqueous, 28, 35
arbor vitae, 10
arboricolous, 173
arcana, 10
armipotent, 137, 186
arrant, 137, 186
artifice, 97
aspersion, 156
assiduous, 174
atrabilious, 74, 151
augury, 55, 97
august, 190

auriferous, 169, 174
bacciferous, 170
beatific, 174
beldam, 18, 88
bellum justum, 21
beneficent, 89
bibulous, 101, 117, 153
biped, 74
brachiate, 163
candor, 97
canescent, 169
canticle, 46, 79
caudad, 28
cavalier, 32, 60
censor morum, 165, 187
chancellor, 33, 47
charnel-house, 57
clamant, 129
codex, 9, 46
codicil, 55
coeval, 52
colloquy, 123, 169
condign, 74
contingent, 139
contumacious, 117, 174
co-vivant, 155
crass, 15, 25
credenza, 150
crescendo, 169
curate, 146
curtsy, 47
decelerate, 162
deciduous, 102, 107, 111
deity, 42, 56
deletion, 141
deodand, 139, 140
depredation, 186
destitution, 109
desultory, 170, 182
diffidence, 138, 140, cf. 146
diffuse, 139, 157
digitalis, 51
disanimate, 114
dissent, 141, 162
dissident, 151
docent, 98
duenna, 25
edentulous, 35
effusive, 162

superannuated, 166
supposititious, 179
svelte, 153
tabula rasa, 123, 181
tangential, 139
tenacious, 101, 164
tendentious, 139
tenet, 91, 92
tercentenary, 57
tergiversation, 164
terra alba, 25, 26
terra firma, 21, 26
terra incognita, 178
terra sigillata, 147
terraqueous, 74
tessellate, 162
testator, 85, 115
torpid, 103
torsion, 179
traduce, 107
transcendental, 141
transmute, 141
transubstantiation, 99
triune, 182
trivium, 78, 179
truculent, 49, 56, 58
tumescent, 171
tutelary, 58, 178
ubiquitous, 186
ultramundane, 138
ultrastellar, 65
unctuous, 171
ursine, 74, 75
vacillate, 163
vacuity, 103
valedictorian, 139
variegated, 170
velleity, 186
venial, 51, 178
ventricle, 162
ventriloquial, 147
verificatory, 174
vernal, 57
vestigial, 55, 57
vicarious, 35
viduity, 181
virilocal, 115
virulent, 45
visceral, 57
vitiator, 85
vitrification, 99

vituline, 74, 182
viva voce, 123
viviparous, 175
votive, 185
vox barbara, 182
vox populi, 123, 189
vulpine, 72

AGARD, Walter H. & HOWE, H., Medical Greek and Latin, (New York, 1955, HERBER).

ALGEO, John, 'The voguish uses of non,' (Amer. Speech 46, 1971, 87-105).

AMBROSE, Z.P., B.B. GILLELAND & R. SCHLUNK, English Etymology, 4th ed., (Burlington, VT, 1985).

ANDERSON, D. & BUXTON, R., A Pocket Etymology..., (Bristol, 1981).

AYERS, Donald, Bioscientific Terminology, (Tucson, 1972).

AYERS, Donald M., English Words from Latin & Greek Elements, (Arizona, 1965; revised ed., 1986, by T. Worthen).

BARFIELD, Owen, History in English Words, new ed. (London, 1954, Faber and Faber).

BAUGH, A.C. & CABLE, T., History of the English Language, 3rd ed., (Englewood Cliffs, 1978, Prentice-Hall).

BIRMINGHAM, J.J., Medical Terminology, (New York, 1981, McGraw-Hill).

BROWN, Charles B., The Contribution of Greek to English, (Nashville, 1942, Vanderbilt University Press).
          The Contribution of Latin to English, (Nashville, 1946, Vanderbilt University Press).

BRUNNER, T. & BERKOWITZ, Luci, Elements of Scientific... Terminology, (Minneapolis, 1967).

BURRISS, Eli E. & CASSON, Lionel, Latin and Greek in Current Use, 2nd ed. (New Jersey, 1949, Prentice-Hall).

CHABNER, Davi-Ellen, The Language of Medicine, (Tor., 1976, Saunders).

DAUZAT, A. et al., Nouveau Dictionnaire Étymologique et Historique, (Paris, 1971, Larousse).

DETTMER, Helena & LINDGREN, M.H., Workbook... D.M. Ayers' English Words, (Tucson, 1986).

DEWITT, N.W., 'On Making New Words,' (CW, 15, 1922, 89-91).

DUNMORE, Charles & FLEISCHER, R., Med. Terminology, 2nd ed., 1985, (Phila, 1977, Davis).

ERICKSON, Gerald, Computer-aided Instruction Software..., (Minneapolis, 1982, University of Minnesota). Material for 4 etymology courses.

FUNK, Charles E., Thereby Hangs a Tale, (New York, 1950, Harper and Brothers).
          A Hog on Ice, (and Other Curious Expressions), (New York, 1948, Harper and Brothers).

FUNK, Wilfred, Word Origins and Their Romantic Stories, (New York, 1950, Wilfred Funk).

GENOVESE, E.N., English from Latin & Greek, SDSU Syllabus, (San Diego, CA, 1984).

GIANGRANDE, L., Greek in English, (North York, 1987, Captus).

GREEN, Tamara M., The Greek and Latin Roots of English, (New York, Hunter College, xerox).

GREENOUGH, James B. and KITTREDGE, George L., Words and Their Ways in English Speech, (New York, 1901, Macmillan; paperback edition, 1961).

GRESSETH, G.K., English Vocabulary, (University of Utah).

GROOM, Bernard, A Short History of English Words, (London, 1949, Macmillan).

GRUMMEL, W.C., English Word Building from Latin and Greek, (Palo Alto, Calif., 1961, Pacific Books).

HETTICH, E.L., 'The Jargonnaut among the Educasters,' (CW, Dec. 6, 1937, 53-55).

HOUGH, John N., Scientific Terminology, (New York, 1953, Rinehart).

HUMEZ, Alexander & N., From Alpha to Omega, (Godine).

JENNINGS, Charles, KING, Nancy and STEVENSON, Marjorie, Weigh the Word, (New York, 1957, Harper and Brothers).

JOHNSON, Edwin L., Latin Words and Common English, (Boston, 1931, D.C. Heath).

KENT, Roland, Language and Philology, (New York, 1963, Cooper Sq.)

LAFLEUR, M.W. & STARR, W.K., Exploring Medical Language.

LANE, Robert E., Etymology -- Analysis of Meaning, (Phillips Academy Secondary School, 1986, xerox).

LEE, Latin Elements in English Words, (New York, 1980, Exposition).

LEVITT, John and Joan, The Spell of Words, (New York, 1969, Greenwood).

LEWIS, C.S., Studies in Words, (1960, Cambridge University Press).

LOGOPHILE PRESS, Logophile, (47 Caledonian Rd., London NI 9BU, England), a journal.

LUSCHNIG, C., Etyma, (Wash. D.C., 1982, Univ. Press of America.)

MASCIANTONIO, R. et al., Word Power through Latin, (Philadelphia, 1974).

MAY, Margaret L., Medical Terminology.

McCULLOCH, J.A., Medical Latin & Greek Workbook, (Springfield, 1962, Thomas).

McKNIGHT, George H., English Words and Their Background, (New York, 1923, Appleton).

NURNBERG, M. & ROSEMBLUM, M., All About Words, (1968, New American Library).

NYBAKKEN, Oscar E., Greek and Latin in Scientific Terminology, (Ames, Iowa, 1959, Iowa State College Press).

PARTRIDGE, Eric, Name into Word, (New York, 1950, Macmillan).
          Origins: A Short Etymological Dictionary of Modern English, (London, 1958, Routledge and Paul).
          The World of Words, 3rd ed., (London, 1948, Hamis Hamilton).
          Adventuring Among Words, (London, 1961, A. Deutsch).

PEARCY, L.T., 'Computer-Assisted Instruction...,' (CJ, 74, 1978, 53-59).

PEI, Mario, The Families of Words, (New York, 1962, Harper).

PEI, Mario, The Story of Language, (New York, 1965).
PHILLIPS, J.H., 'The Medical Terminology Course,' (CO, March, 1981), 65-66.
PRENDERGAST, Alice, Medical Terminology, (Indianapolis, Addison-Wesley, 1977).
REEDY, Jeremiah, 'It's a Factoid...' (CJ, 76.3, 1981, 259-265).
RIVARD, A. & GEOFFRION, L.-P., Glossaire du Parler Français au Canada, (Québec, 1930, Action Sociale).
SADLER, J.D., 'Latin Word Building,' (CB, Nov., 1972, 3-7).
          'Etymology and Latin Teaching,' (CW, Dec., 1970, 117-120).
          'Idiosyncrasies of Suffixes,' (CB, Nov., 1969, 8-11, 16).
          'Classical Trade Names,' (CO, Jan., 1970, 52-54; Sept., 1972, 8-9).
          'Participles are where you find them,' (CO, Oct., 1970, 17-18).
SAVORY, T.H., The Language of Science, (London, 1953, Andre Deutsch).
SCANLAN, Richard T., Power in Words, (Minneapolis, 1986, A. Burgess); Word Power, (Minneapolis, 1986, Control Data).
SERJEANTSON, Mary S., A History of Foreign Words in English, (New York, 1936; Dutton; New York, 1961, Barnes and Noble).
SHAW, Michael, Word Power, (Lawrence, KS, 1984).
SHEARD, J.A., The Words We Use, (London, 1954, André Deutsch).
SKEAT, Walter W., An Etymological Dictionary of the English Language, rev. ed. (4th), (Oxford, 1946, Clarendon).
SLOAT, Clarence & TAYLOR, S., Structure of English Words, (Eugene, Or.: Pacific, 1983; 3rd ed., Dubuque, 1985, Kendall-Hunt).
SMITH, G.K. & DAVIS, P.E., Medical Terminology, (New York, 1981).
SMITH, Logan P., Words and Idioms, (Mich., 1971, Gryphon).
SPILMAN, Mignonette, Medical Latin and Greek, (Salt Lake City, 1957; Edwards Bros., Ann Arbor).
STEWART, George R., Names on the Land, (New York, 1945, Random House).
STURTEVANT, Edgar H., Linguistic Change, (Chicago, 1971, University of Chicago Press; paperback edition, 1961, Phoenix Press).
SWEET, W. & KNUDSVIG, G., A Course on Words, (Atlanta, 1982, HBJ).
TAYLOR, B.C., The Greeks Had a Word for It, (Toronto, 1973).
          Latin is Alive and Well, (Toronto, 1973).
TAYLOR, Isaac, Words and Places, abridged and ed. by Beatrice S. Snell, (London, 1925, Thomas Nelson).
TEBBEN, J.R., A Course in Medical & Technical Terminology, (Columbus, 1978, Collegiate).
TYRRELL, W.B., Medical Terminology, (Springfield, 1979, Thomas).
URDANG, L., ed., Verbatim, (Old Lyme, CT 06371), a journal.
VALLINS, George H., The Making and Meaning of Words, (London, 1949, A. and C. Black).

WALKER, Thomas E., Word Resources, (Indianapolis, 1979, Bobbs-Merrill).

WATKINS, Calvert, American Heritage Dictionary of Indo-European Roots.

Webster's Ninth New Collegiate Dictionary, (Springfield, Mass., 1983, Merriam-Webster).

WEEKLEY, Ernest, Etymological Dictionary of Modern English, (London, 1921, John Murray).

_____ More Words Ancient and Modern, (London, 1927, John Murray).

_____ The Romance of Names, (London, 1914, John Murray).

_____ The Romance of Words, (London, 1912, John Murray; New York, 1961, Dover).

_____ Surnames, (London, 1917, John Murray).

_____ Words Ancient and Modern, (London, 1926, John Murray).

_____ Words and Names, (New York, 1933, Dutton).

ZETTLER, H.G., -Ologies and Isms, (Detroit, 1978, Gale).

A Concise Dictionary of Canadianisms, (Toronto, 1973, W.J. Gage).